The Golden Path to Successful Personal Soul Winning

By

JOHN R. RICE

SWORD of the LORD
PUBLISHERS
P.O. BOX 1099, MURFREESBORO, TN 37133

ISBN 0-87398-306-8

Printed in the U.S.A.

Table of Contents

Foreword

Probably no man of our generation has done as much for New Testament evangelism as Dr. John R. Rice. Hence, it is fitting and proper that Dr. Rice share with thousands of others his burden for soul winning and his wisdom and knowledge concerning this vital subject. It is my belief that this book will be among the best received of the many that Dr. Rice has written.

Soul winning is the purpose of Calvary; the heart of the Great Commission; the main ministry of the Holy Spirit; the joy of Heaven; and the heartbeat of John Rice. This book will give the subject the much-needed emphasis it deserves in our day.

I have had the joy of knowing Dr. Rice intimately for a number of years. I have seen him pray. I have heard him preach. I have fellowshipped across the table with him. I have found him to be a pastor to pastors; a friend to the evangelist; a father to the young preachers; and an intercessor for those who hold forth the truth. God has given him a ministry concerning the "care of all the churches."

It was through the influence of THE SWORD OF THE LORD that my own ministry was blessed and changed. I predict that God will use this book to do the same for thousands of others.

I pray that God will use this book to set afire cold hearts; resurrect dead churches; revive sleeping Christians; and lead thousands of us to rededicate our lives to the biggest business in all the world.

Jack Hyles, D.D.
Pastor, First Baptist Church
Hammond, Indiana

September 20, 1961

Author's Introduction

More than twenty years ago Moody Press published my little book, *The Soul-Winner's Fire,* and tens of thousands of copies have been blessed to the hearts of many. That is eight sermons on soul winning. However, for years the dear Lord seemed to press on my heart that there ought to be a thorough exposition of what the Bible teaches about soul winning, the duty and doctrine and methods as revealed in the Word of God. Ten years ago the first chapters were written. Now, by God's mercy, they are completed.

These chapters are written in such stress of duties that they are not as beautifully finished and polished as I could wish. But between speaking two or three times a day in revival services, editing THE SWORD OF THE LORD, and much travel, I have tried to put on paper what I found in the Bible, along with the burning in my own heart.

Two things may be said for this teaching in these chapters. First, as I have taught these truths and preached them in great conferences on revival and soul winning, or in the pastorate, or in revival campaigns, God has used them to make soul winners out of many hundreds of people who had never won a soul. And second, God in mercy has seen fit to help me personally win literally thousands of souls, one at a time, in the midst of other tremendous burdens and constant preaching.

Two features, we hope, will make the book valuable and interesting. Many, many Scriptures are used and plainly expounded; and the author has used many, many personal experiences to illustrate the truths taught.

Since it is hoped this book will be used in Bible institutes, Bible colleges and seminaries, and classes on soul winning, the chapters are carefully outlined with subheads and there are indices of Scriptures used of names and incidents, for easy reference.

There are many to whom we owe grateful thanks, including men and books quoted, the faithful workers who have helped me in preparation on the manuscript, and perhaps most of all, the kindly readers who will overlook the faults of the book because of its sincere earnestness and its scriptural message on the most important theme in the world for Christians.

John R. Rice

August, 1961

1. Soul Winning: Its Meaning and Requirements

"And he said unto them, Go ye into all the world, and preach the gospel to every creature."—Mark 16:15.

"The fruit of the righteous is a tree of life; and he that winneth souls is wise."—Prov. 11:30.

". . . I am made all things to all men, that I might by all means save some."—I Cor. 9:22.

WE ARE ABOUT to discuss the most important business in the world. To make people good and make them happy and blessed through eternity, to keep people out of the fires and torment of Hell forever—that is the most important business in the world. And, of course, he who would succeed in such a tremendously important work for God needs to clearly understand what he is trying to do, and needs to develop the character and prerequisites necessary for this blessed work.

What does it mean to win souls? What must be the soul winner's convictions? How much knowledge of the Bible must he have? What about the soul winner's moral character, his devotion to Christ, his prayer habits? One who would be a soul winner should know exactly what is involved and what is required.

I. What We Mean by Soul Winning

When we speak of winning souls we use Bible language. Proverbs 11:30 says, "He that winneth souls is wise." Paul was inspired to write, ". . . I am made all things to all men, that I might by all means save some." David pleaded that the Spirit of God should not leave him, but that God would renew a right spirit within him and cleanse him of his sins; and David promised, "Then will I teach transgressors thy ways; and sinners shall be converted unto thee."

In the Great Commission we are plainly commanded, "Go ye therefore, and teach all nations . . . ," but the word *teach* here in the original language actually means "to make disciples." We are to go into all the world and make disciples, that is, to win souls. In Mark 16:15 we are commanded, "Go ye into all the world, and preach the gospel to every creature," and those who believe will be saved and those who do not believe will be lost. In the last invitation of the Bible the Lord Jesus commanded the Apostle John to write, "And the Spirit and the bride say, Come. And let him that heareth say, Come . . ." (Rev. 22:17). Every Christian should be a winner of souls. He should get people saved. He should take the Gospel to every creature. He should make disciples. These are different ways of saying that it is the duty of Christians to go out and show people how to be saved and get them to trust in Jesus Christ and be born again.

Let it clearly be understood there are certain things we do *not* mean when we speak of winning souls. We are not speaking of getting members for a church. Now it is right for people who are already Christians to join a church. It is not right for anyone who has not been born again, who has not already become a child of God, to join a church. Soul winning is not getting church members.

Winning souls is not the same as getting people baptized. We ought to get young Christians baptized. And everyone who believes in Christ and takes Him as Saviour then should obey Him, but the baptism is not a part of salvation. It is to follow salvation. Getting people baptized is not the same as winning souls.

Getting people to live a better life, to quit drinking or cursing, to start attending church—these are not soul winning. It is true that after one has trusted in Christ as Saviour, he ought to set out to make his habits fit his profession; he ought to attend the house of God; he ought to seek Christian companionship; he ought to read his Bible. But getting people to do these things is not soul winning. If one should get a wicked sinner to quit his cursing and join a church and be baptized and read his Bible every day, that would still not make him a Christian. Winning souls is not the same as making church members, or getting people to reform, or to go through some church rites, or to live a good life.

Winning souls means to get a sinner changed into a child of God. It means that he has a supernatural change of heart. He is to be "born again." He is to become a "partaker of the divine nature" (II Pet. 1:4).

In order to win a soul, then, we must teach people to turn their hearts from their sins in repentance and turn to Jesus Christ and trust Him for forgiveness and salvation. God must work the miracle and must change the heart. But God gives us Christians the responsibility of carrying the message, the Gospel, and explaining it and pleading and helping people to the honest heart decisions.

Winning souls means that we can take the Bible and show people that they are sinners, show people that according to the Scriptures God loves them, that Christ has died on the cross to pay for their sins, and that now all who honestly turn in their hearts to Christ for mercy and forgiveness may have everlasting life. And we can encourage them to make that heart decision that they turn from sin and trust Christ to save them. So winning souls means getting the Gospel to people in such power of the Holy Spirit that they will be led to turn to Christ and be born again, be made children of God by the renewing of the Holy Ghost.

II. The Soul Winner Must Be Saved

It goes without saying that to be a soul winner, one must be saved himself. The liberal preacher who does not believe the Bible is the Word of God, who does not believe that Jesus Christ is deity, who does not believe in His virgin birth, His blood atonement, His bodily resurrection, cannot win souls. There would be a fundamental insincerity in his telling others to trust in Christ when he had not personally trusted Christ. So the evangelism of the liberals generally means the so-called "social gospel" and such people, instead of promoting scriptural evangelism, spend their time on racial issues, labor unions, social problems. Since they do not have Jesus Christ's own answer to man's problem, regeneration, they usually tend to take Karl Marx's answer. Since they do not have the true Gospel to preach, they bring the curse of Galatians 1:8 and 9 on themselves by preaching another gospel, a perverted gospel.

Oh, reader, if you would do any service acceptable to Christ, first of all, you must love Him, must turn to Him for mercy and forgiveness and receive a new heart. It is foolish to talk about living the Jesus way until one has a Jesus heart. It is foolish to talk about building the house of Christian service until one has the foundation, Christ Himself.

Salvation comes before soul winning. One must be a Christian, a born-again child of God, before he can be a soul winner.

If this seems very trite to you, an unnecessary warning, then I remind you that John Wesley was one of the most earnest preachers and came as a missionary from England to the Indians of North America before he ever consciously trusted Christ as his own Saviour or knew how to be saved. He grew up in a parsonage, his father was a preacher, his mother a most devout and spiritual woman. And John Wesley himself was as regular in his prayers, as fervent in his self-denial, as busy and conscientious in his religious life as any Pharisee of the time of Christ, or any monk of the Middle Ages. But he could not win souls. He had never knowingly trusted in Christ as his own Saviour and did not know how to win anybody else.

Martin Luther was a conscientious and religious man who had given up the world for the poverty and religious activity of the priesthood, but he did not know peace of heart, did not know Christ as his Saviour until years later. Let no one think, then, that to have been raised in a Christian home, to be a member of a church, to be moral and religious in outward life, fits one to be a soul winner. First, the soul winner himself must have been born again.

In the first place, one who has not personally come to know Christ as his own Saviour will not have the spiritual perception which is absolutely necessary to please God and serve God. "But the natural man receiveth not the things of the Spirit of God: for they are foolishness unto him: neither can he know them, because they are spiritually discerned" (I Cor. 2:14). So says the Word of God.

In the second place, an unconverted lost sinner cannot have the power of God upon him to serve God acceptably. "Without faith it is impossible to please him," says Hebrews 11:6. And one without saving faith in Christ is an enemy, an alien from God, an unreconciled sinner. Nothing such a one could do would please God until he is willing to personally thrust himself on Christ's mercy for salvation and depend upon the Saviour for the forgiveness He has promised those who trust Him.

In the third place, lost sinners themselves would have no confidence in the teachings and instructions of a man who could not tell what it means to be saved, illustrated by his own testimony. A doctor who will not take his own medicine, a cook who will not eat her own cooking, a Christian

worker who does not practice what he preaches, would win
scant confidence among people.

Therefore, let everyone who would do any service for
Christ first definitely confess his own sinful state, repent
in his heart, and turn to Christ in penitent faith for salvation. After one has trusted Christ as his own Saviour and
has been born into the family of God, he may well seek to become a soul winner, but not before.

III. The Soul Winner Must Have Full Assurance of His Own Salvation

Evangelist D. L. Moody said that he had never known a
good soul winner who was not sure of his own salvation.
With a little thought, one can understand why. On your own
part, how could you have any boldness in speaking to sinners
about salvation if you were uncertain of your own salvation?
You would feel, "Here I am trying to get others to trust in
Christ when I don't know whether I have trusted Him myself!" You might well feel like John Wesley, defeated, who
returned from the American colonies to England, having
written in his diary, "I came to America to convert the
heathen, but oh, who shall convert me!"

And why should sinners have confidence in the exhortation of one who does not know for sure whether he himself
is saved? He could not speak with glad joy and assurance.
And the most ignorant sinner would feel the insincerity and
the unsteadiness of the one who was trying to get him to
turn from his sins and trust in Christ if the would-be soul
winner had no certainty that his own sins were washed
away, that he himself was a child of God, that Heaven would
be his blessed home hereafter.

You remember that Jesus told the former maniac of
Gadara, after he had been wonderfully healed and saved,
"Go home to thy friends, and tell them how great things the
Lord hath done for thee, and hath had compassion on thee"
(Mark 5:19). Then the Scripture continues, "And he de-

parted, and began to publish in Decapolis how great things
Jesus had done for him: and all men did marvel" (Mark 5:
20). That element of personal testimony is vital to soul
winning. Paul used it continually. Go visit the rescue mission where, continually, drunkards and harlots and criminals and bums find Christ, and you will see that God has
chosen to wonderfully honor the straightforward testimony
of a man who knows that his sins are forgiven, who can
tell when it happened and where, the very date and place.
One example is worth a thousand arguments, we are told;
and if you do not know of your salvation well enough to give
your own testimony, you are not ready to win souls.

Another fundamental reason makes the Christian who
has no assurance of salvation unfitted for soul-winning work.
We are to use the Word of God in soul winning. One must
be able to tell the sinner how to find Christ, how to get his
sins forgiven. And one who does not have assurance of his
salvation does not clearly understand the plan of salvation.
For when one knows clearly the blessed Word of God and
does not depend on any sense of his own merit, nor his righteousness, nor upon church membership, nor any religious
rites, but only on the blood shed on Calvary and the promises
of the Lord Jesus, he can know for sure about his own salvation. Any poor sinner who wants salvation may have it,
may have it instantly. But the assurance of salvation is
based upon the plain statements of the Word of God. And
when you are not sure of your own salvation, then obviously
you are probably not clear on how God saves men in answer
to simple, penitent faith. How can one tell others what he
does not know?

And I ought to say that often our doubtings and fears
come from sin. One who does not live right is likely not to
feel right! Sin in the life, unconfessed and unlamented, takes
away our sense of acceptance with God. It may be that you
have truly been converted, born again, and it may be that
you know when you trusted Christ. But your sins may have

so grieved the blessed Holy Spirit that you have lost the witness within which once was very clear. It may be that now you feel that God is displeased with you, and you do not find His smile upon you as it once was. So your joy may have fled, and with it part of your assurance of salvation. But the sin which hinders your joy will hinder your soul winning, too. So whatever be the reason for your lack of assurance, you need to get it settled if you are going to be successful as a soul winner.

If you have trusted Christ in your heart, then find some clear promises in the Word like John 3:16 or John 5:24 or John 6:37 or Acts 16:31, and accept God's gracious promise as your own and claim the salvation He offers freely. Base your claim to salvation on the plain Word of God. Do not heed your feelings, but rely on the plain Word of God and have the assurance which God promises. If you came to Jesus Christ, and you know that He said, ". . . him that cometh to me I will in no wise cast out" (John 6:37), then you ought to accept on His word of honor that He has received you and did not reject you and never will! If you have called upon Christ for salvation in your heart, and you find that the Scripture says, "For whosoever shall call upon the name of the Lord shall be saved" (Rom. 10:13), then you ought to believe what God has promised, that is, that He saves all who honestly, in the heart, call upon Him for salvation.

If you suffer for lack of assurance of salvation, I suggest that you get my pamphlet *The Seven Secrets of a Happy, Prosperous Christian Life* (Sword of the Lord Publishers) and read it prayerfully until the matter is thoroughly clear in your mind. Or if sin has grieved the blessed Spirit of God who dwells within you until you do not feel assured of God's favor, then confess that sin today and forsake it and wait before the Lord penitently until you are assured that no unconfessed sin stands between you and the smile of your Heavenly Father, the sweet fellowship that the Father wants to have with His child. Every Christian can know beyond any doubt that his sins are forgiven. And only such Christians who do know that they are saved are successful soul winners.

IV. The Soul Winner Needs to Know Clearly the Saving Gospel of Christ

A distressed wife said to her husband, "Bill, why don't you join the church with me and be a Christian? You don't have much to give up. You are already a good man." But that kind of counsel did not get him saved. That is not soul winning.

A mother said to her grown son, "Son, you are breaking my heart with your drinking. Why don't you quit your wicked way and live right?" That was an earnest entreaty, but it takes more than that to win a soul to Christ.

Jesus said to the disciples and then to us, "Go ye into all the world, and preach the gospel to every creature. He that believeth and is baptized shall be saved; but he that believeth not shall be damned" (Mark 16:15, 16). Note that the Gospel must be preached to every creature. One who believes on Christ according to the Gospel is saved, and his baptism is his open profession of that fact. The one who does not trust Christ for salvation shall be damned, we are plainly told. So there is no way for anybody to be saved without the Gospel. And the Lord here speaks of the preaching of an individual who takes the Gospel to individuals, as well as of the preacher who speaks to a congregation.

All soul-winning effort is really preaching the Gospel. We may add our personal testimony and our earnest entreaty, but without the preaching of the Gospel no one is ever saved. "For after that in the wisdom of God the world by wisdom knew not God, it pleased God by the foolishness of preaching to save them that believe" (I Cor. 1:21).

You see, one's personal testimony and the fervent pleading of a loved one may make a sinner want to be saved, but these alone do not show him how to be saved. People are not saved without the Gospel.

And what is the Gospel? What is this saving Gospel without which a sinner will never be changed from a child of Satan into a child of God? Paul defines the Gospel, in inspired language, in I Corinthians 15:1-4 as follows:

"Moreover, brethren, I declare unto you the gospel which I preached unto you, which also ye have received, and wherein ye stand; By which also ye are saved, if ye keep in memory what I preached unto you, unless ye have believed in vain. For I delivered unto you first of all that which I also received, how that Christ died for our sins according to the scriptures; And that he was buried, and that he rose again the third day according to the scriptures."

This saving Gospel which Paul preached and whereby the Christians at Corinth had been saved is "that Christ died for our sins according to the scriptures; And that he was buried, and that he rose again the third day according to the scriptures." The atoning death of Christ on the cross, His miraculous resurrection from the dead, all according to the Scriptures, is the blessed Gospel we must take if we would win people to Christ and get them saved.

Let us analyze, then, the Gospel truths which a soul winner must clearly understand.

1. He Must Realize That All Men, Women, and Children Everywhere Are Sinners, Depraved by Nature, Who Need Regeneration, That Is, the New Birth.

The Pharisee may be better than the publican to outward appearance, but both alike are sinners. The chaste wife and mother may appear better than the harlot, the tender child may appear better than the aged reprobate, the moral, responsible and decent man may appear better than the drunken wretch and the criminal, but in the heart where God looks, all alike are guilty sinners. So Paul concludes by divine inspiration, ". . . for there is no difference: For all have sinned, and come short of the glory of God" (Rom. 3:22, 23). If the soul winner does not know that sinners are sick unto death, he will not know how to get them to turn to the Great Physician. If he is not able to show people that they are wicked sinners, he will not lead them to repent.

2. The Soul Winner Must Understand That the New Birth Is a Miraculous Work of God in the Heart of a Sinner, Making Him a Child of God.

If the would-be soul winner thinks that joining a church or turning over a new leaf or living a better life will make a lost sinner into a child of God, he certainly is not a soul winner. One is dealing in miracles when he makes a child of Hell into a child of God by the supernatural power of the Holy Spirit. Jesus said to Nicodemus, "Except a man be born again, he cannot see the kingdom of God." And again, "Except a man be born of water and of the Spirit," (I believe He means by the cleansing Word of God and the life-giving Holy Spirit) "he cannot enter into the kingdom of God." He said, "Marvel not that I said unto thee, Ye must be born again." So Jesus was insistent, and every soul winner must be insistent, that even a good, moral, religious Pharisee, like Nicodemus, must be born again.

3. The Soul Winner Must Know That the Way a Sinner Gets the New Birth Is By Simple Dependence on Christ as Saviour.

Many Scriptures plainly say so. John 1:12, John 3:16, John 3:18, John 3:36, John 5:24, Acts 10:43, Acts 13:38 and 39, Acts 16:31 all make it clear that one who comes to believe in Jesus Christ as his own Saviour, that is, to rely upon Christ, depend upon Christ, to trust Christ, to risk Christ for forgiveness and salvation, is instantly saved. "He that believeth on the Son hath everlasting life." This simple faith in Christ, this committing of one's self to Christ's mercy, is the deciding matter in the salvation of a soul.

It is true that a sinner who trusts in Christ must repent. That is what was meant in saying that everyone who would be saved must realize that he is a sinner and so, of course, must turn his heart away from his own resources and ways, and turn to Christ. Honest heart-turning from sin is a part of saving faith. Repentance and faith cannot be separated. But this is most often expressed in the Scriptures by that simple term "believe." Do you know that the moment a poor sinner honestly turns from his sin and believes on Christ, that is, relies upon Christ for salvation, he is saved? If you know that, you know the great decisive factor in getting sinners saved.

4. It Follows Naturally That One Who Would Win a Sinner Must Teach Him Not to Rely Upon Any Human Merit.

Christ alone does the saving, and He does it when a lost sinner depends upon Him and commits himself to Christ. Moral goodness does not save and does not *help* save. Church membership and the rites of the church cannot save and cannot help save. The soul winner must be able to teach the sinner that Christ alone can save and that salvation is on the basis of God's love and mercy which provided the atoning sacrifice on the cross to pay for man's sins.

V. The Soul Winner Must Be a Surrendered Christian, Willing to Give Up Any Known Sin to Please Christ and to Have God's Power for Soul Winning

Some Christians are vessels to honour, and some really saved people are vessels to dishonour. In II Timothy 2:19-21 Paul, by divine inspiration, discusses this matter:

"And, Let every one that nameth the name of Christ depart from iniquity. But in a great house there are not only vessels of gold and of silver, but also of wood and of earth; and some to honour, and some to dishonour. If a man therefore purge himself from these, he shall be a vessel unto honour, sanctified, and meet for the master's use, and prepared unto every good work."

Every Christian should depart from iniquity. One who does purge himself from iniquity shall be a "vessel unto honor, sanctified," (or set apart) "and meet for the master's use, and prepared unto every good work." A Christian who does not judge his sins, who does not honestly turn from known sins, loses the power to win souls and the ability to win souls, as well as the heart for soul winning. The greatest honor that could ever come to a Christian is to be enabled of God to win souls. But one who does not purge himself from iniquity by honest confession and turning from sin, will be a vessel not of gold and silver, but of wood and earth; not a vessel unto honour, but a vessel unto dishonour.

Paul constantly remembered this truth, that if one would be continually blessed in soul winning he must remain a vessel "meet for the master's use." In I Corinthians 9:27 Paul said: "But I keep under my body, and bring it into subjection: lest that by any means, when I have preached to others, I myself should be a castaway."

What was it Paul feared? He feared that after he had preached to so many, he would be laid aside and be cast away as a soul-winning instrument. And for fear of this, Paul buffeted his body and kept down the old sinful nature so that he would be fit for the Master's use.

One of the holiest motives that any Christian could have for living a separated and holy life is that he might thus be fit to win souls. And if you should give up incidental pleasure of one kind or another that is questionable; if you should give up a habit in which you would have pleasure; or if you should give up some dear idol of your heart in order that you might have the power of God and win souls, then how great will be the reward in Heaven! Thank God for the privilege of keeping a soul out of Hell a billion years and then a billion times a billion years more! Who would not be willing to give up any of the pleasures of sin, as Moses did, to have such a blessed reward!

Salt can lose its savour; at least the natural salt collected around the edge of the seashore with various impurities in it could lose its savour. Even so a Christian may lose his saving power. Jesus said, "Ye are the salt of the earth: but if the salt have lost his savour, wherewith shall it be salted? it is thenceforth good for nothing, but to be cast out, and to be trodden under foot of men" (Matt. 5:13). Christians who dally with sin, who keep bad company, who are wrapped up in money-making, may become salt without savour. They may put their light under a bushel. I do not say that Christians who drift into worldliness and sin have lost their souls, but I do say that they lessen the power to win others to Christ. They lose their joy here and eternal rewards hereafter.

Oh, to the soul-winning Christian, the will of Christ must be the most important thing in the world! No place is too hard if it is where God wants the surrendered Christian. One who would be a soul winner must learn to make Jesus Christ the Lord of his life. He must set his affection on things that are above and seek first the kingdom of God and His righteousness. Surrender to Christ so that one is willing to leave any known sin and do the will of God is essential to one who would be a soul winner.

Then the soul winner must have some real compassion in his heart for sinners. "God so loved the world, that he gave his only begotten Son," we are told. Well, how could one enter into that blessed work of saving sinners, which cost Christ and the Father so much, unless he enters into that compassion, that burden of concern. That is another way of saying the soul winner must be sincerely concerned to keep people out of Hell.

Then the Christian, to win souls, must have the power

of the Holy Spirit. This is too big a business for human wisdom, human personality, human devices, and for the logic of the schools.

In other chapters we will take up in detail these great requirements of the use of the Bible and the compassion of heart and the power of the Holy Spirit, but it is only fair to number them here and now as absolute essentials for one who would turn men and women from darkness to light and from sin to salvation and from Hell to Heaven.

2. Value and Importance of Personal Work

"One of the two which heard John speak, and followed him, was Andrew, Simon Peter's brother. He first findeth his own brother Simon, and saith unto him, We have found the Messias, which is, being interpreted, the Christ. And he brought him to Jesus. . . . The day following Jesus would go forth into Galilee, and findeth Philip, and saith unto him, Follow me. . . . Philip findeth Nathanael, and saith unto him, We have found him, of whom Moses in the law, and the prophets, did write, Jesus of Nazareth. . . ."—John 1:40-43, 45.

"And he said unto them, Go ye into all the world, and preach the gospel to every creature."—Mark 16:15.

THE WINNING of individuals by individuals in personal conversation is the main way to win souls.

The New Testament type of Christianity has been so perverted and misshapen that now people generally consider Christian work to be primarily done in a church house, in formal services, conducted by preachers. The simple truth is that in New Testament times there were no church houses (not a single one mentioned in the New Testament). The public meetings were informal and more or less incidental to the main work of carrying the Gospel all over town, yes, all over the world, speaking to individuals.

Seminary professors and others without much practical experience sometimes discuss the relative merits of personal soul winning and mass evangelism. The truth is that they are essential parts of the same thing. The right kind of gospel preaching sends Christians out to win souls, and bombards the hearts of sinners, dynamites the hard ground, and arouses the conscience, and makes a climate for personal soul winning. And the personal soul winning is best done, always, where there is plain Bible preaching, evangelistic preaching. No man who is against mass evangelism is ever a very good personal soul winner, and the greatest soul winners have been the best advocates of mass evangelism. Who ever did better personal soul-winning work than D. L. Moody and R. A. Torrey? And who ever developed personal soul winners like these great evangelists and other evangelists?

In an evangelistic ministry of nearly forty years, and having seen tens of thousands of people come to Christ, I can say that personal contact, personal invitation, had a part in winning nine out of ten of all those I have seen come to Christ.

The best gospel preaching and the best personal soul-winning effort go together.

It is good to preach to great crowds the Gospel of Jesus Christ. But the simple truth is that many a lost sinner will never come to hear a sermon unless some Christian brings him, will not respond to the invitation unless some Christian encourages him to go forward and claim Christ, and would not know how to trust Christ and have the assurance of salvation if some personal worker did not show him from the Scriptures.

D. L. Moody said that if he had to win one thousand souls in order to make sure of Heaven himself, he would certainly choose to risk it by personal soul winning without public preaching rather than to attempt it by public preaching without personal soul winning.

Dr. Charles G. Trumbull, long-time editor of *The Sunday School Times*, after many years as editor of a magazine with an average circulation of a hundred thousand copies, after preaching for many years to good crowds, said that he felt sure he had won more souls to Christ in personal conversation than all those saved through his influence in other ways.

I am saying that personal soul-winning effort with individuals is the main way to win souls.

I. The Winning of Individuals by Individuals Is the Way Most Clearly Commanded in the Bible

Let us examine the marching orders which Jesus Christ left for Christians, His "Great Commission" left to churches and individuals.

Consider Mark 16:15, "Go ye into all the world, and preach the gospel to every creature." We generally think of "preaching the Gospel" as preaching a sermon to a crowd. But a little examination of this Scripture will show that that is not the principal meaning of the Great Commission. We read that Great Commission as if it read, "Go ye into all the world and preach the Gospel in every church auditorium and to every congregation." But the Great Commission does not mention any auditorium and it does not mention congregations. No, the Lord Jesus here is talking about individuals. We are to preach the Gospel "to every creature," that is, to every individual. Christ did not die for congregations; He died for individuals. The Great Commisson is not to preach the Gospel to congregations, but to individuals.

I freely grant that it is a blessed thing to preach the Gospel to as many as we can, whether a Sunday School teacher talks to ten, or a preacher preaches to fifty in a rescue mission, or to a thousand in a great congregation, or to a million in a radio broadcast. But the only way that a group or congregation fulfills the Great Commission requirement is that in the Sunday School class, or in the rescue mission, or in the church congregation, or in the radio audience are poor lost individuals who need to hear the Gospel. And every preacher ought to remember that he is not preaching to a crowd, but to individuals.

I think we preachers often have a wrong conception of the ministry to which we are called. We say, "God has called me to preach," by which we generally mean He has called us to prepare a sermon with a good outline and Bible truth and an exposition of Scriptures, and to preach this in a public address or sermon to a congregation. Now the call to preach may include preaching to a congregation, but that is not the primary meaning of the word as Jesus used it in the Great Commission. Actually we preachers are called to keep people out of Hell. We are called to get the Gospel to individuals. A preacher is doing exactly what Jesus commanded in the Great Commission when he talks to one poor sinner in his home, or on the street, or in the shop. And I say it with deep concern, I doubt if most of us preachers who preach formal sermons to congregations are really "preaching the Gospel to every creature" in the sense in which Jesus meant it. We are not called to preach sermons primarily. We are called to keep sinners out of Hell. In some cases sermons will help to do that. In other cases the individual contact is the only way we can get people saved.

And so since I am called to get the Gospel to people, to get people saved and keep them from eternal destruction, I edit a paper, I hold revivals, I have conferences on evangelism, I teach people to win souls, I write songs, I carry on a 40-station radio broadcast. By God's mercy I have spread my books and pamphlets with over twenty-one million copies around the world in thirty languages. All this simply means that any way in the world we can get the Gospel to sinners and keep people out of Hell, we are obeying the Great Commission. But certainly the Great Commission in Mark 16:15

commands us to deal with individuals as individuals. We are
to get the Gospel "to every creature."

Consider the Great Commission as given in Matthew
28:19 and 20: "Go ye therefore, and teach all nations, baptizing them in the name of the Father, and of the Son, and
of the Holy Ghost: Teaching them to observe all things
whatsoever I have commanded you: and, lo, I am with you
alway, even unto the end of the world. Amen."

Here the disciples were commanded to go and make disciples. Then they were commanded to baptize the converts.
And then they were commanded to teach these same converts to do exactly what Jesus had commanded them, the
apostles, to do! We are to get people saved and get them
baptized, that is, get them publicly committed, get them to
take an open stand, get them branded for Jesus. And then
we are to teach them to observe all things which Jesus
taught us to do. Every lost sinner is called to be saved.
As soon as he is saved he is called to win souls. Every Christian in the world has exactly the same command to win
souls that the apostles had. They had apostolic authority in
doctrine and over churches before the Scriptures were completed, which we do not have. But they did not have any
more command to win souls than we have.

Then if every Christian is commanded to win souls, it is
obvious that the Great Commission is not primarily to
preachers. It is obvious that one cannot obey the Great Commission only publicly expounding the Word of God to congregations. No, God does not call everybody to be a pastor,
does not call everybody to be an evangelist, does not call
every Christian to take charge of a congregation and proclaim the Word. The women are to keep silence in the
churches, not to usurp authority over the men, not to teach
men, but to be in silence. And many a man likewise is not
called to take authority over a congregation nor to expound
the Word publicly with the authority of an elder or a bishop,
to use New Testament terms. But every Christian is to win

souls. And that proves then that the Great Commission is primarily concerned with every Christian dealing individually with lost people. Personal soul winning is the main thing taught in the Bible and is the main duty of Christians.

In Luke 14:16-24 Jesus told the story of a man who made a great supper and bade many, "And sent his servant at supper time to say to them that were bidden. Come; for all things are now ready." Please notice that the only servant God has in the parable is the one carrying personal messages to individuals. The servant knocks at one door of a man who is already invited, but he excuses himself, saying, "I have bought a piece of ground, and I must needs go and see it." He knocks at another door and that man has bought five yoke of oxen and is about to hitch them up at suppertime to prove them! Another door is that of a newly-married couple and that man says he cannot come because "I have married a wife, and therefore I cannot come." And then the servant is commanded to "go out quickly into the streets and lanes of the city, and bring in hither the poor, and the maimed, and the halt, and the blind." So down the street the servant goes talking to a beggar here, to a tramp there, to a poor destitute family there, and gathering them into the great feast.

But yet there is room, so out in the highways and hedges the master sends the servant to farms and tenant houses to "compel them to come in, that my house may be filled."

This is a picture of how God intends to fill the great tables at the wedding supper! This is a picture of how God expects to get people to Heaven. And that is by individual soul winners going out after individuals.

Oh, the public preaching of the Gospel has its place. It supplements personal soul winning. God calls and equips some men to do that as well as the other.

Personal soul winning, individual dealing with individuals, is the main plan of soul winning taught in the Bible.

Dr. R. A. Torrey calls attention to the wonderful truth

that since everybody is commanded to win souls, then it must necessarily be, with most people, dealing with individuals. And since we are to get the Gospel to every creature, personal soul winning has the great advantage that anybody can do it, that it can be done at any time and can be done anywhere!

Oh, thank God, one can win souls personally when he cannot get people to come out to church to hear the public proclamation of the Gospel. Ten days ago I won two at a wedding rehearsal! I have won hundreds of people at funerals or at the cemetery following funerals. In Dallas, Texas, I had the great privilege of winning grown men as they wept beside the deathbed of their father dying of cancer. One by one he urged them to consider it, and then I took the Scriptures and showed them how to be saved. I won a housewife as she baked cookies, won a twelve-year-old boy after climbing to sit beside him as he sat on the rooftree of a great barn. My son-in-law, the other day, won a young man at Winston-Salem, North Carolina, in a supermarket, with people filling their grocery baskets all about them! Dr. Jack Hyles won a hotel maid as she knelt in the bath tub washing away the bath tub rings!

I remind you again that since the Great Commission commands every Christian to win souls, and individual work is the only way that every Christian can do it, then the main teaching of the Bible about soul winning is the winning of individuals.

II. Jesus Christ Was a Great Personal Soul Winner

It is true that Jesus often preached to multitudes. Some twenty-two times in the first twenty-two chapters of Matthew the words "multitude" and "multitudes" are used about the crowds who heard Him. Sometimes it was five thousand men besides the women and children. At another time it was four thousand. It is true that great crowds heard the Saviour when He "spake as never man spake."

But it is also true, and rather surprising on second thought, that most of the people who were saved under the ministry of Jesus were saved in personal contact, as far as the gospel record shows. I have no doubt that many were saved as they crowded around Him and heard Him preach, but the Bible does not tell about that. It does tell case after case of individuals whom He won personally.

The first day He was announced to Israel by John the Baptist with the clarion words, "Behold the Lamb of God," He won Andrew and John the beloved (John 1:35-39). And the next day we read, "The day following Jesus would go forth into Galilee, and findeth Philip, and saith unto him, Follow me" (John 1:43). Philip did follow Him, and he, too, became a soul winner that day and went and found Nathanael for Jesus, as Andrew had gone to find his brother Simon and brought him to Jesus.

Then in John, chapter 3, we learn that Jesus preached the most wonderful sermon to one timid Nicodemus, in the nighttime. If all the preachers who preach big sermons on "Ye must be born again" would use those words to one individual, no doubt many more would be saved. I am for preaching it in public, but I am also for preaching it as Jesus did, to individuals.

In the next chapter, in John 4, we read the thrilling story of how Jesus approached the woman at Sychar in Samaria, and won her to Himself. Oh, the story of the four Gospels is largely the story of Jesus dealing with individuals—with the woman at the pool of Siloam in John 5, with the woman taken in adultery in John 8, with the man born blind in John, chapter 9. To the man borne of four, let down through the roof top, Jesus said, "Son, thy sins be forgiven thee" (Mark 2:5). About the poor sinful woman who washed His feet with tears and kissed them, Jesus said, "Thy sins are forgiven" (Luke 7:48). The maniac of Gadara had his legion of devils cast out and was saved and commanded to go tell what God had done for him. So Jesus called and won Matthew the publican, and so in Luke 19, He won Zacchaeus, the publican who was up a tree. To the blind beggar Bartimaeus who came to Jesus, He said, "Receive thy sight: thy faith hath saved thee" (Luke 18:42). And even as He was dying on the cross, the Lord Jesus stopped dying long enough to win the penitent thief!

Oh, how much of the life of Jesus we would miss if the Gospel did not tell any of the wonderful stories of individuals with whom He dealt personally, winning them to trust Him!

III. Other Personal Soul Winners in the New Testament

Most of the people whose conversion is related in the New Testament were won in personal conversation.

1. Consider How New Converts Set Out to Win Others.

John stood with two of his disciples, John, the son of Zebedee, and Andrew, the brother of Peter. And he looked at Jesus and said to these two, "Behold the Lamb of God!" They went home with Jesus and the indication is that they trusted Him and were changed in that brief time. And then we are told, "One of the two which heard John speak, and followed him, was Andrew, Simon Peter's brother. He first findeth his own brother Simon, and saith unto him, We have found the Messias, which is, being interpreted, the Christ. And he brought him to Jesus . . ." (John 1:40-42). Here we find that Andrew turned immediately to his own brother and won him the same day that he himself had trusted the Saviour.

Then the next day Jesus won Philip and immediately we read, "Philip findeth Nathaniel, and saith unto him, We have found him, of whom Moses in the law, and the prophets, did write, Jesus of Nazareth, the son of Joseph" (John 1:45). Philip was a new convert. He may have used the term "son of Joseph" to identify Jesus by the term popularly used about Him. Perhaps he did not think of the significance.

He was only a new convert. But he brought Nathaniel to Jesus that day and Nathaniel was saved.

Jesus won the woman of Samaria who had had five husbands and was then living in sin with a man to whom she was not married. That woman, wonderfully saved, left her waterpot and ran to the city, "and saith to the men, Come, see a man, which told me all things that ever I did: is not this the Christ?" (John 4:28, 29). And strangely enough we are told, "And many of the Samaritans of that city believed on him for the saying of the woman, which testified, He told me all that ever I did." And then, when they came and heard Him, we read, "And many more believed because of his own word" (vss. 39, 41).

It is certainly the most normal thing in the world for a young Christian to want other friends and loved ones saved, and to go and urge them to trust the Saviour. So new converts often did in the New Testament.

The description of the conversion of Levi the publican, later called Matthew, who wrote the book of Matthew, is interesting in its charming simplicity and directness. Jesus saw Levi sitting at his job of receiving taxes and said to him, "Follow me." And we read, "And he left all, rose up, and followed him. And Levi made him a great feast in his own house: and there was a great company of publicans and of others that sat down with them" (Luke 5:27-29). We are not given details of what Jesus said to Levi, if He said anything more than "follow me." And we are not told what Levi told the other publicans as he gathered them in to a great dinner and had Jesus as a guest. But we may be sure that he had in mind the salvation of these fellow tax collectors, these friends of his, and that he urged them to love and trust the same Saviour he loved and trusted.

After the Gadarene demoniac was saved and the demons had left him and he was clothed and in his right mind at the feet of Jesus, we read, "Now the man out of whom the devils were departed besought him that he might be with him: but Jesus sent him away, saying, Return to thine own house, and shew how great things God hath done unto thee. And he went his way, and published throughout the whole city how great things Jesus had done unto him" (Luke 8:38, 39).

Oh, what a glorious testimony that man had! And he went throughout the whole city telling people "how great things Jesus had done unto him." He was a personal worker.

Thus we may regard it as normal that young Christians should set out immediately to win souls.

2. Christians After Pentecost Made a Great Deal of Personal Soul-Winning Effort.

It is impressive that at Pentecost the hundred and twenty in the upper room "were all filled with the Holy Ghost" (Acts 2:4). And so not simply the apostles, but all, including the women, were filled with the Holy Spirit and set out to witness for Christ. Those saved at Pentecost were not all saved by Peter's sermon. We may properly believe that every one of the hundred and twenty Christians filled with the Spirit set out to win souls that day and each helped to win some of the three thousand.

Again in Acts 4:31 we are told the same thing: "And when they had prayed, the place was shaken where they were assembled together; and they were all filled with the Holy Ghost, and they spake the word of God with boldness."

Here we are told that "they were all filled with the Holy Ghost, and they spake the word of God with boldness," and that was the whole company of Christians, as we see from verse 23 preceding.

Then the regular pattern of Christian work in the book of Acts is given in Acts 5:42: "And daily in the temple, and in every house, they ceased not to teach and preach Jesus Christ."

Some have supposed that the Lord here speaks of public services in the temple, and then personal soul winning elsewhere. But there was no auditorium in the temple, no seats, no organized congregation. People came individually or in families to offer their sacrifices or to make their vows. There was no preaching in the regular temple services, and no provision for it. People came and went; some sold doves and other sacrifices. Others were money-changers, changing the money from the regular Roman coin to the temple coin, and so the temple porches and temple area resembled a market place with crowds of people coming and going. It may be that someone preached to the throngs assembled there when he could get a hearing, as a street preacher does. There was no organized seated congregation. But just as a man when the streets are crowded in a country town on Saturday afternoon may go to win souls or as one might go about soul winning in a fair or supermarket, so they went "daily in the temple" as well as in every home in Jerusalem! That was personal soul winning, person by person, house by house, and it is indicated as the regular pattern of Christian work in the book of Acts.

In Acts, chapter 8, we are told that "at that time there was a great persecution against the church which was at Jerusalem; and they were all scattered abroad throughout the regions of Judea and Samaria, except the apostles." And then we are told, "Therefore they that were scattered abroad went every where preaching the word" (vss. 1, 4). The apostles stayed at Jerusalem. Everybody else went out running for their lives and winning souls everywhere. They preached, some like Deacon Philip who had a revival in the city of Samaria, but most of them no doubt preaching to individuals more than to crowds. It was primarily personal soul winning.

3. Peter, the Great Preacher, Was a Personal Soul Winner.

We find in Acts, chapter 3, that Peter and John went to the temple and there healed the lame man and taught him to trust in Christ. Then in Acts, chapter 10, we have in great detail the story of how God impressed upon Peter that he must go with the messengers to the household of Cornelius, the Roman centurion, and win the man and his family and some other awakened soldiers. It was preaching, but the preaching to one family is more nearly personal soul winning than it is preaching in the usual formal way.

4. Paul the Apostle Was a Personal Soul Winner.

We know that Paul the apostle preached in synagogues, anywhere he could find a group of Jews gathered. But Paul indicates elsewhere that he was not a great preacher, though he was a great soul winner.

Paul and Barnabas were in a period waiting before the Lord, were set apart by the church at Antioch for a work to which the Lord had called them, as we learn in Acts 13. So they had started on a missionary journey to Seleucia and Cyprus and preached in the synagogue. But at Paphos they found Sergius Paulus and set out to win him. Elymas the sorcerer interfered, but Paul rebuked him and he was struck blind. "Then the deputy, when he saw what was done, believed, being astonished at the doctrine of the Lord" (Acts 13:12).

We know that Paul and Silas went to a women's prayer meeting at Philippi and won Lydia, a seller of purple. They won a devil-possessed fortunetelling girl and got put in jail. Then they won the jailer and his family and baptized them.

In Acts, chapter 20, we have a revealing word which tells us of the regular pattern of Paul's soul-winning ministry. He called the elders of Ephesus together at Miletus, a little seaport town near Ephesus, and reminded them that he had spent three years in Ephesus, "and how I kept back nothing that was profitable unto you, but have shewed you, and have taught you publickly, and from house to house, Testifying both to the Jews, and also to the Greeks, repentance toward God, and faith toward our Lord Jesus Christ" (Acts 20:20,

21). And in verse 31 he says, "Therefore watch, and remember, that by the space of three years I ceased not to warn every one night and day with tears." Night and day, with tears, publicly and from house to house Paul "warned every one." That is, he spoke to men and women, Jews and Greeks, one at a time, testifying to them, showing them how to be saved.

We may well believe that Paul the apostle won more souls to Christ individually than he won by his public preaching alone.

Nearly every evangelist would testify that most of those won to Christ in the great revivals were won partly by the personal testimony and entreaty and instruction of some good Christian.

IV. The Preacher and Personal Soul Winning

It is my strong conviction that personal soul winning will make the difference in the success or failure of any preacher's ministry.

1. First of All, the Pastor or Evangelist Should Train and Organize and Supervise Soul-Winning Visitation.

In most cases the man who depends on the public preaching of the Gospel to win souls does not have many lost people in his services and so does not have much definite results in souls won. Only the preacher who works at getting a crowd and who builds a visitation program inviting people to come to attend the services has many lost people to preach to. The best soul-winning churches have used the Sunday School with regular organized weekly visitation to reach prospects and get them to attend the Sunday School and to attend the preaching services. Nearly all good soul-winning churches require that the teachers visit their absentees and visit other prospects, get them to the Sunday School, and then bring them in to the preaching service. The best churches have one or more specific periods a week in which the visitation is organized, cards are given out to those who will visit from house to house and see prospects already listed. Many churches take a census of the neighborhood for which they feel accountable, and find the names and addresses of prospects who ought to be won to Christ.

Every evangelist should preach soul winning, should lay on the hearts of Christians a burden for souls, show them their duty to win souls, and show them how.

Ephesians 4:11 tells us that God gave evangelists and pastors and teachers "for the perfecting of the saints, for the work of the ministry, for the edifying of the body of Christ . . . maketh increase of the body unto the edifying of itself in love" (Eph. 4:12, 16). So the duty of the evangelist is not only to preach to lost sinners, but it is to stir up Christians to win souls. And so it is the duty of the pastor to teach soul winning, to show how it is done, to supervise it.

2. The Great Soul-Winning Churches Have Most Converts Won Before They Come Forward Publicly.

It has been my very great joy to know most of the very best present-day soul-winning churches in America and their pastors. And I know of the great number of souls won to Christ in these churches, most of them are won in the homes and then brought out to the services where they make public profession, join the church, and are baptized.

Dr. Beauchamp Vick, pastor of the great Temple Baptist Church, Detroit, probably the largest church in the world with some fourteen thousand members and the Sunday School often running nearly five thousand in attendance, tells me that of some fourteen hundred converts who made public profession of faith and were received for baptism in his church in one year, the big majority were won by personal visitation in the homes. *(Written in 1961)*

I have often been on programs together. That church for the last eleven years has baptized more than a thousand new converts every year. And the pastor has said repeatedly that most of these are won in house-to-house visitation, won in a home either by organized visitation supervised by the church, or by individual earnest work of Christians among neighbors and fellow workers and friends and relatives.

3. The Preacher Himself Should Win Many Souls Person to Person.

Years ago I was shocked to hear a pastor of a First Baptist Church say that he had never personally won a soul to Christ. He believed the Bible; he preached the Gospel in the pulpit, but he had never personally won a soul to Christ, dealing with him as an individual, showing him how to be saved, bringing him to trust the Saviour and confess Him! Understandably, there were not many people saved under his public preaching of the Word.

Years ago in an evangelistic campaign in a city auditorium, I, a young assistant pastor, talked to a drunkard, brought him to the front seeking salvation, and I asked the evangelist if he would like to talk to him. The evangelist was embarrassed and said, "No, John, I wouldn't know what to say," and urged me to deal with him myself or take him to the evangelist's father!

In a revival campaign in a Pennsylvania city, a Presbyterian pastor who was officially co-operating in the revival services, said he was converted, said he believed the Bible, but he had never won a soul and did not know how to begin.

An Episcopal rector, about to take over one of the largest Episcopal churches in Ohio, told me sadly with deep conviction that he had a Bachelor of Divinity degree from Yale Divinity School, as well as an A.B. degree from a standard college, and he said, "They taught me to turn a pretty phrase. I can balance a tea cup on my knees and talk to a group of women. But if a drunkard wanted to know how to be saved, I would not know how to tell him!" He was, I am glad to say, greatly concerned about his lack.

I use these illustrations to show that it is shocking for a preacher not to know how to win souls and not to do it regularly.

The preachers who have many people coming forward to claim Christ as Saviour in their services are, almost without exception, preachers who do a great deal of personal soul winning themselves. I know that Dr. Lee Roberson of Chattanooga told me he tries to make ten visits a day when he is in his home city, soul-winning visits.

Dr. Jack Hyles, pastor of the First Baptist Church of Hammond, Indiana, had a remarkable ministry at Garland, Texas, and then in his first year at the large city church where he is now pastor baptized 556 new converts won to Christ in the year. How did he do it? Well, he won 250 of them himself in house-to-house visiting. In the year he made an average of fifty-three calls on lost people per week, and won 250 converts, and in many cases went himself in his car to get them and bring them to the church on Sunday morning to make public profession. And his assistant, Mr. Jim Lyons, won 193 people in the same year. So together they won nearly 450 of the 556 converts who were baptized in the year! A soul-winning preacher makes a soul-winning church.

There are some great preachers who are not good soul winners and the results of their ministry are mediocre. There are some great soul winners who are not great preachers, but they are great workers and God blesses their personal contact with men.

Long ago I resolved, as an evangelist, that I would never have a fruitless revival effort, that I would never preach long in any place attempting to win souls without winning some. But if I waited for others to bring lost people to the services and waited for others to bring them down the aisles, I could not always be sure that some would be saved. So I resolved that always I would win some. And praise the Lord, in every circumstance where God leads me to go, I find there are some people who can be won to Christ.

And oh, what a difference it makes in the public preaching of the Word when a man's heart is warmed and freshened by the sweet consciousness that Christ has just helped him to win a soul! And how easy it is to give a public invitation when one knows that there are some present who have already decided for Christ and have taken Him as Saviour and are ready to come down the aisle and openly claim Christ.

Let me say again that the main way souls are won is by personal work. Every Christian can do it, every Christian ought to do it. It can be done anywhere and any time. It will reach thousands who would never be reached by the public preaching of the Word alone.

I remember how I was so burdened for one lost man and prepared special sermons to win him Sunday after Sunday. Then one day when I had preached my best and had most earnestly pleaded at the close of the sermon for those who were lost to come forward to take Christ as Saviour, and he did not come, I had the closing prayer and rushed around the building to the front door and there when I met him in the vestibule I asked him why he was not saved. In a moment his heart was tender and he quickly trusted the Saviour. In three minutes of conversation I got the result I had failed to get in a number of sermons aimed at his benefit! Oh, God help our preachers and our churches to call every Christian back to the main business of personally winning souls to Christ.

I had just carefully read over and corrected the typed manuscript of this chapter when I felt a great urge to go out and prove it again, that personal soul-winning effort can always find someone to win, and can win souls who perhaps do not attend the public service. Engaged in a tent revival campaign in an Iowa town, preaching twice daily, I laid aside the manuscript, earnestly prayed for the Lord to guide me, and set out. That first afternoon I won a man to Christ in a filling station. The Lord moved my heart to go back and speak to him again. The day before I had approached him, but there were other customers; I could not find a convenient time to press the matter of his salvation. As I drew near, I saw one man get in a pickup truck and drive away, and another walked away in another direction. The man was alone. Yes, he was a church member. I said, "You say you are a member of the Methodist church. Have you ever truly been born again? Were you really converted to Christ?"

He shook his head. "No," he said, "and I never go anymore." It was simple and easy to win this man forty-nine years old to the Lord.

A day or two later I went with a pastor out to see another man on a farm miles away. His wife had been happily won to Christ in the service. The home had almost been broken with dissension. Now she said, "I think I can go on and be happy." We found the man on the hay baler. He left the tractor motor running idly while we talked with him long and earnestly. Yes, he was a sinner. His heart was tender. The unhappiness in his home had burned deeply into his conscience. He agreed to ask the Lord for forgiveness in his heart while we prayed. Then he claimed the Saviour, took our hands gladly, and agreed that now he could count himself a child of God, and on the authority of John 3:36, could claim everlasting life, depending on Christ.

The next afternoon I went eighteen miles away to visit with another pastor. A woman in her home joyfully took Christ. When her son, twelve or thirteen years old, came in, she told the son, "I have accepted Christ as my Saviour." In another home two boys, one a big burly seventeen-year-old, and the other thirteen, listened carefully. Only the mother and the little girl were Christians. The father refused Christ and would not be saved. But the two boys, in their father's presence, bowed their heads to pray and then openly claimed Christ as Saviour.

The next day I went with another pastor. We had two remarkable experiences. In one home an old man berated us. The preachers only came because they wanted something out of him, he said. They thought if they could get him in the church, they could get some of his money! He didn't need any help, he said, and he had his own opinions. Then as I pressed upon him the wickedness of his course, he ordered us out of this house!

But the same afternoon God wonderfully paid us back. We went into one home where the man listened so kindly, so tenderly. He needed the Saviour. Yes, he knew he was a sinner. He was willing for us to pray with him. Then he took Christ as his Saviour openly. And so did his little girl.

We went on to make another call or two, and here came the little girl running down the street. "Mamma wants you to come back and pray with her!" she said. The mother, who had been in a back room, when she learned after we had gone that her husband had been converted, now wanted the Lord Jesus as her Saviour, too! How simple and easy it was to win her! And in another home a thirteen-year-old girl, with no one else at home, stood at the screen door and opened her heart to Jesus.

Oh, we cannot win everybody, but personal soul winning will reach people who can never be reached through preaching from the pulpit.

3. The Main Business of Every Christian

"Go ye therefore, and teach all nations, baptizing them in the name of the Father, and of the Son, and of the Holy Ghost: Teaching them to observe all things whatsoever I have commanded you: and, lo, I am with you alway, even unto the end of the world. Amen."—Matt. 28:19, 20.

"The fruit of the righteous is a tree of life; and he that winneth souls is wise."—Prov. 11:30.

"And daily in the temple, and in every house, they ceased not to teach and preach Jesus Christ." —Acts 5:42.

EVERY CHRISTIAN ought to be a soul winner. Soul winning ought to be the main business of every Christian, as well as the main business of every preacher, every missionary, every Christian worker. No born-again Christian is excused from the solemn duty to win people to Jesus Christ. No excuse is acceptable. It cannot be left for ministers of the Gospel and professional soul winners. One simply is not a good Christian if he is not a soul winner. He is not obeying orders, not obeying the plain commands of Jesus Christ. If he does not win souls, then he is not following Jesus, he is not filled with the Spirit, he is not abiding in Christ, he does not love Jesus Christ supremely. That is what I will prove in this chapter.

Reader, I want to show you by incontrovertible proof that, according to the Word of God and every holy obligation, you ought to make soul winning the main thing in your life. Getting people to know Jesus Christ as Saviour, to trust Him for forgiveness of sins, and thus keeping poor lost sinners out of Hell, ought to be your supreme aim, your constant employment. If you will read this chapter in the fear of God, and are willing to know and do the will of God, you will set out to be a soul winner and make that your supreme business.

I. Soul Winning Is the Thing Dearest to the Heart of Christ

It was to keep sinners out of Hell that Christ Jesus died. It was to save sinners that the Lord Jesus came into this world.

Paul was inspired to write: "This is a faithful saying, and worthy of all acceptation, that Christ Jesus came into the world to save sinners; of whom I am chief" (I Tim. 1:15).

What was the purpose of Christ's coming into the world? It was to save sinners!

The Lord Jesus stated this matter very clearly when He explained why He loved and sought Zacchaeus, the despised tax collector. "And Jesus said unto him, This day is salvation come to this house . . . . For the Son of man is come to seek and to save that which was lost" (Luke 19:9, 10).

When the Pharisees asked Jesus, "Why do ye eat and drink with publicans and sinners?" Jesus answered, "I came not to call the righteous, but sinners to repentance" (Luke 5:30, 32; Mark 2:17).

Oh, the coming of the Lord Jesus Christ in human form to this world has been the most civilizing and exalting impact that human society ever had. One can never finish tracing the influence of Christ upon the laws of the nations, the moral standards, the art, the literature. Christianity has raised the value of human personality till slavery is unthinkable in a civilized country. Womanhood has been exalted. The poor, the sick, the homeless, and little children have benevolent care because of the impact of Christ on men. But all these things are incidental and are by-products. They are not what Jesus came for. He came to save sinners! He came to keep people from going to eternal ruin in Hell! Oh, there are countless blessings wrapped up in the bundle with salvation, but the saving of a soul is the one great purpose that brought Jesus to the world, the one cause that took Him to the torments of the cross, the separation from Heaven, the abuse and hatred of men.

I wonder why some people think that they know the Lord Jesus well, these people who never win a soul, who have no tears for the unsaved, who have no holy compassion, and who are occupied about ordinary matters all the time, and never concerned about the supreme matter. How can anybody know the heart of the Lord Jesus who doesn't get concerned about and busy about the one thing dearest to Christ's heart?

And I boldly say that I know what Christ wants and what is dearest to His heart.

In Isaiah 53:11, after a wonderful prophecy of Christ as the despised and rejected Man of Sorrows who will have borne our griefs and carried our sorrows, who will have been wounded for our transgressions and bruised for our iniquities, and by whose stripes we are healed, the Scripture tells us how the Lord Jesus will feel about the souls He has won. In that far and eternal future, it is said, "He shall see of the travail of his soul, and shall be satisfied . . . ." As a mother sees her lovely baby and forgets the sorrow of travail since she has the child she loved and longed for, so Christ endured the tortures of the cross and did it gladly, looking toward the time when He would see the fruit of His sufferings in the salvation of millions! In Heaven the Lord Jesus looks forward with increasing gladness to the redemption of all who are brought to Him for salvation, all who trust Him in saving faith.

In Hebrews 12:1, 2 we Christians are told to "lay aside every weight, and the sin which doth so easily beset us, and let us run with patience the race that is set before us, Looking unto Jesus the author and finisher of our faith; who for the joy that was set before him endured the cross, despising the shame, and is set down at the right hand of the throne of God."

What was in Christ's mind and heart when He was on the cross? He endured the cross because He had a great idea. He despised the shame and ignored it because He looked forward to a glad reward. What was in the heart of Christ then? What was "the joy that was set before him" mentioned here? It was the joy of seeing multitudes redeemed forever through His precious blood!

And what now does the Lord Jesus think about? Well, we know that the Lord Jesus has not changed. He is "Jesus Christ the same yesterday, and today, and for ever" (Heb. 13:8). If He looked on Jerusalem and wept over it when He was here in the flesh standing on the Mount of Olives overlooking the temple, do you think He never weeps now over sinners? If the Lord Jesus looked on the assembled multitude and had compassion on them since they were like sheep without a shepherd, and admonished His disciples to pray for more reapers for the white harvest, do you think He feels any different now about the multitudes unsaved, stumbling in the dark about us? I make bold to say that the dear Lord Jesus has tears on His face now in Heaven for poor sinners unsaved. At least He has the tears in His heart. His compassion is unchanged.

And what makes the Lord Jesus happy? In what does He rejoice? He Himself told us. He told how the shepherd who finds the lost sheep brings it home on his shoulder and calls together his friends and neighbors saying, "Rejoice with me; for I have found my sheep which was lost"; then he adds, "I say unto you, that likewise joy shall be in heaven over one sinner that repenteth, more than over ninety and nine just persons, which need no repentance" (Luke 15:6, 7). Note it is not just the angels who rejoice in Heaven over sinners saved. It is also those others among the angels, the redeemed saints. But the principal rejoicing is done by the Lord Jesus Himself. It is the Lord Jesus who rejoices most and who urges others to the happy hand clapping, to the songs of praises, to the holy rejoicing in Heaven over a sinner saved!

A song of mine says:

The Saviour will see the travail of His soul,
And be satisfied fully o'er souls He's redeemed;
Compared to that reaping, He scorned all His suffering,
To be paid at the reaping up there.

Well, every soul saved now is a coupon of rejoicing which Jesus clips as a dividend from His suffering. And we are foolish and worldly and spiritually shallow and heartless if we are unconcerned about the one thing so dear to His heart.

Let me leave this with you now. If you want to understand the Saviour and know His joy and feel His heartbeat, you must enter into His compassion and into the great business to which He has set Himself—the keeping of souls out of Hell at an infinite price. The sufferings of Jesus on earth and His compassionate concern now in Heaven ought to be enough to set every Christian in the world to soul winning.

If you love the Lord Jesus, then for His dear sake win souls, win all you can, and do it now!

II. Jesus Christ Commands Every Christian to Win Souls

One of the most moving events in human history took place many years ago on a hill north of Jerusalem and overlooking the temple. The Lord Jesus stood on the Mount of Olives with His disciples. After the birth of Christ, His crucifixion and the resurrection, the next most important event in human history was there taking place. The Lord Jesus was about to ascend in His glorified body straight to Heaven. He was to go up, up, up, and the clouds would receive Him out of their sight. Two angels were to stand by and promise that this same Jesus would return again. But before going, Jesus must give the marching orders for Christians for the whole world and for the whole age. There Jesus gave the disciples the Great Commission. He gave the basic plan for Christian work, the central outline for all Christianity, for all the centuries to come. Jesus gave the Great Commission in the following words:

"Go ye therefore, and teach all nations, baptizing them in the name of the Father, and of the Son, and of the Holy Ghost: Teaching them to observe all things whatsoever I have commanded you: and, lo, I am with you alway, even unto the end of the world."—Matt. 28:19, 20.

Note the following important facts about this Great Commission:

1. The Gospel was to be preached in all nations. In Mark 16:15 Jesus even said, "To every creature."

2. Those saved were to be baptized as a public profession of their faith, so marking them as Christians before the world and starting them publicly on a new life after they had been converted, born again.

3. The new converts were then to be taught to do exactly what Jesus commanded the apostles to do: "Teaching *them* to observe all things whatsoever I have commanded *you*." Every convert ever saved since the Great Commission was

given had the same command passed on to him that Peter
and the other apostles got that day!

4. This command was to continue "even unto the end of
the world," and Christ promised to be with every Christian
obeying Him in this soul-winning command.

So Christ clearly commands every Christian to win souls.

In 1918 I was in training as a soldier at Camp Travis,
San Antonio, Texas. One day as acting corporal I was drill-
ing my awkward squad on the drill ground, as were all
the other would-be corporals of the company, under the
driving supervision of our martinet captain. Striding vigorously, the captain approached my squad. I said abruptly,
"Halt!" My squad of beginning soldiers shuffled to a halt
and tried to line up.

Abruptly the captain said to me, "Did you give the correct command then?"

"No, sir."

"What should your command have been?"

"I should have said, 'Squad, halt!' in two counts."

"Then why didn't you give the correct command?"

"Sir, I was scared."

He continued with specific instructions. One soldier must
button the pocket flap on his blouse. I was to hold my head
up straighter. When he had ended his brief instruction and
turned to go, I saluted smartly and said, "Thank you, sir."

His steely gray eyes looked at me and he said, "Don't
thank me. I'm not giving advice. Those are orders!"

Christian, did you think Jesus was only giving advice
when He stood on that little hill that day and plainly said
that every convert should be taught to carry out all the
commands He gave the apostles? Did you think that it was
only a mild suggestion when Jesus said that you are to
help to carry the Gospel to every creature, that you are to
save people from Hell by your urgent entreaty? No, Jesus
was not giving advice; He was giving orders. And there is
only one thing for any Christian to do who acknowledges

the authority of Jesus Christ—that is, he is to obey orders and put soul winning in its primal place in his life.

Prefacing that Great Commission, Jesus said, "All power is given unto me in heaven and in earth. Go ye therefore . . . . " Do you bow before that authority of Jesus Christ which He claims over every creature in Heaven and earth? Do you acknowledge His lordship? Then today set out to keep that holy command! Every Christian is commanded to be a soul winner.

III. New Testament Christians Were All Expected to Win Souls

Not only was it the command of Jesus for that little group to set out to win souls and for all their converts to win souls, but that was the actual practice of New Testament Christians.

John the Baptist himself started it. Although a mighty preacher with enormous crowds waiting on his ministry day after day, he took time to point out Jesus to two of his disciples. "And looking upon Jesus as he walked, he saith, Behold the Lamb of God!" (John 1:36). John and Andrew followed Jesus that day, and then followed in their hearts forever!

But one of the most thrilling examples is that of Jesus Himself. Jesus "findeth Philip, and saith unto him, Follow me" (John 1:43). Jesus personally won Nicodemus, as recorded in John 3; the woman at the well of Sychar, in John 4; the woman who was a sinner in the house of the Pharisee (Luke 7:36-50). He won the maniac of Gadara (Matt. 8:28-34), the woman with the issue of blood (Matt. 9:20-22), the woman taken in adultery (John 8:1-11). He won the man born blind (John 9:1-38). He won Zacchaeus the publican (Luke 19:1-10). The Gospels are replete with instances of how the dear Lord Jesus, though preaching to multiplied thousands, sought out lost people and won them, or took time to prove Himself and to remove difficulties for those who sought Him. Oh, Jesus was the master soul winner, a personal soul winner every day of His ministry!

And New Testament Christians followed the example as well as the precept of Jesus.

Andrew was saved and immediately went and found his brother, Simon Peter. "He first findeth his own brother Simon, and saith unto him, We have found the Messias, which is, being interpreted, the Christ. And he brought him to Jesus . . . ." (John 1:41, 42).

Jesus won Philip, and then Philip went after Nathanael immediately. "Philip findeth Nathanael, and saith unto him, We have found him, of whom Moses in the law, and the prophets, did write, Jesus of Nazareth, the son of Joseph" (John 1:45). Philip did not know much about the matter. He did not understand the details of the virgin birth, and ignorantly called Jesus "the son of Joseph." But when he was at the end of his strength he challenged Nathanael to "come and see." Nathanael came, and Jesus answered all his doubts and saved his soul. But that young convert, Philip, went after Nathanael and got him, by divine help.

After Pentecost, when the disciples received the great enduement of power from on high, personal soul winning seems to have been the universal practice of Christians. We must believe that every one of the 120 in the pre-Pentecostal prayer meeting were active in the great reaping when three thousand souls were won in a day. Acts 5:42 tells of the activities of the New Testament Christians: "And daily in the temple, and in every house, they ceased not to teach and preach Jesus Christ."

When Jesus won the woman at the well of Sychar in Samaria, she set down her water-filled pitcher, gathered up her skirts, and ran back to the city to cry out to the men there, "Come, see a man, which told me all things that ever I did: is not this the Christ?" (John 4:29). Then people believed the woman. Some were immediately saved before seeing Jesus. Others poured out of the city to see Him and hear Him and decided immediately for themselves that He was the Saviour, and they made Him their own.

When Jesus won Levi, that publican made a supper and invited all the tax collectors to meet Jesus at the meal. In Mark 2 we are told of four men who brought a paralyzed man to Jesus and broke up the roof to let him down before Jesus when there was no other entrance through the crowd. They were examples of holy zeal in personal soul winning. And the Gadarene demoniac when he was healed and sat clothed and in his right mind at the feet of Jesus begged Jesus that he might go with Him, but Jesus told him rather, "Go home to thy friends, and tell them how great things the Lord hath done for thee, and hath had compassion on thee" (Mark 5:19). And he did it! "And he departed, and began to publish in Decapolis how great things Jesus had done for him: and all men did marvel" (vs. 20).

Everywhere Jesus went, scurrying feet hurried to bring to Him the poor, the sick, the blind, the demon-possessed, that He might heal them soul and body. These Christians were soul winners. Oh, yes, soul winning by every Christian is the New Testament pattern.

Some deacons were elected to look after poor widows. But did these deacons, like modern church officials, busy themselves only with the material matters of the church? No, they were Spirit-filled men, great soul winners. Two of them, Stephen and Philip, became mighty preachers of the Word and won multitudes. Stephen was himself the first martyr to the cause.

Please note Acts 8:1 where it is said that "they were all scattered abroad throughout the regions of Judaea and Samaria, EXCEPT THE APOSTLES." The apostles stayed at Jerusalem. The others were scattered abroad. Then verse 4 tells us, "Therefore they that were scattered abroad went every where preaching the word." Simple lay Christians— men, women and children—persecuted, running for their lives, yet went everywhere preaching the Word. That was New Testament Christianity at work.

IV. Soul Winning Is Obviously the Most Important Matter That Can Occupy the Mind and Effort of Christians

In Louisville, Kentucky, a fire broke out and students from the Southern Baptist Seminary gathered to see the fire. A mother screamed and pleaded; her baby was asleep in the third floor room and would soon be burned to death. Firemen put up ladders and tried to reach the window but were beaten back by the smoke. One student wrapped a wet towel around his face, climbed the ladder, found the baby, wrapped it in his coat, then gripped his legs about the ladder and slid with his precious bundle to the ground. The mother seized her baby, and then laughing and crying showered the young ministerial student with kisses. Thus my father, before I was born, saved a little one from horrible death in the fire.

But what is that compared to keeping a soul out of the fires of eternal torment for eternity? One man has been "tormented in flame" in Hell for nearly two thousand years, according to the words of the Lord Jesus, begging even for a drop of water which he has never received. Who can think of anything so important as saving souls?

So in James 5:19, 20 we are told, "Brethren, if any of you do err from the truth, and one convert him; Let him know, that he which converteth the sinner from the error of his way shall save a soul from death, and shall hide a multitude of sins." To "save a soul from death"—what a victory, what a triumph, what a gain! And to "hide a multitude of sins," to stop the stream of sin in one heart and life before it pollutes the whole race—what a victory! Oh, if someone had won to Christ the head of the infamous Jukes family before they let loose on society a succession of criminals, harlots, imbeciles, and paupers! To head off generations of sin and crime is what one does when he saves a soul from death and hides a multitude of sins.

Other gains are measured in terms of time. The gain of a soul brought to Christ and born again, and made into a new creature, and headed for Heaven, can only be counted in terms of eternity!

I am not unaware of the social implications of the Gospel. Christianity ought to help people to do right. But these silly and wicked infidels who reject Jesus Christ as deity, who reject the Bible as God's infallible revelation, and who reject the blood atonement as God's only plan of salvation, never succeed with their so-called "social gospel." Go with me to rescue missions like the Pacific Garden Mission in Chicago; the Chicago Industrial League Mission; the Mel Trotter Mission in Grand Rapids; the Evansville Rescue Mission, Evansville, Indiana; the City Rescue Mission in Memphis, Tennessee; the Bowery Mission in New York City; and the great rescue missions in St. Paul, in Minneapolis, in Los Angeles, and other principal cities. There I will show you more social reform in one night's testimony meeting than the social gospelers can show in a lifetime of their profane, Christ-rejecting social gospel! I will show you drunkards made sober, harlots made pure, tramps and bums made into successful businessmen. I will show you broken homes restored, thieves made into honest men who have restored the stolen goods, escaped criminals who have surrendered to serve out their terms or be pardoned and then live godly lives.

Do you believe in giving money to help the poor? Well, remember that the best help that you can give to a poor home is to give it a husband and father who is born again, who is a changed man in heart and soul, who is now a faithful provider, a true husband, a good citizen, an honest workman.

It is unspeakable folly to think of making people better without bringing them to Christ, or of making people happy without Christ making them good with changed hearts. If there were no Heaven of eternal rewards and blessings, the Gospel of Jesus Christ does more for human happiness and welfare than all other agencies combined. And it has been so down through all the centuries.

People, from good motives, send CARE packages to poor people in Europe, or arrange jobs for displaced persons who immigrate to this country, or give to relieve the victims of a flood or tornado or earthquake. People give to the Community Chest, support homes for orphan children, and give to cancer research and the fight against polio. Thank God for all the tender hearts and for all that is done for others in Jesus' name. But all of it is but a drop in the bucket compared to the ocean of eternal welfare which one gives when he brings a soul to Jesus Christ, and a child of Satan becomes a child of God by the new birth. When one steps out of the darkness of fear and danger and damnation and enslavement of sin and steps into the light and liberty and joy and peace and eternal hope of the Gospel, how wonderful beyond compare!

What wonderous love is this, that Christ has left to us this message of reconciliation! What marvelous condescension that the dear Lord should not give the Gospel to be preached by angels, but to be spread by every born-again child who finds Him and loves Him and trusts Him!

One day I talked to the late William Jennings Bryan at great length. I was a graduate student in the University of Chicago, and William Jennings Bryan came to speak on "The Bible and Its Enemies." The Kent Theater was jammed and overflowing, and soon we ran to the Hyde Park Baptist Church where Bryan spoke to the packed assembly of students. Afterwards Mr. Bryan told me that he would speak that day five times for the Lord Jesus and would lecture once for a livelihood. Officially he was not a preacher, but he had come to the holy conclusion that politics and statesmanship were poor and unrewarding compared with the eternal blessedness of winning a soul to Christ; so he had resolved to spend the remaining years of his life in getting out the Gospel everywhere. He told me that he rejoiced that his public career had opened so many doors for him that he could speak daily to great crowds, often where ordained preachers were not invited. Mr. Bryan had learned this truth, that soul winning is obviously the most important thing that can ever occupy the mind or absorb the efforts of any Christian in the world!

V. Soul Winning Cannot Be Left to Ministers, Missionaries, and Other Professional or Full-Time Christian Workers

We know that Christ commanded not only the ministers, but every Christian to win souls. We know that it was the practice of New Testament Christians to go everywhere telling the story and witnessing for Christ, the poorest layman as well as the ministers. Even new converts who had no training whatever went immediately about this holy task. When we consider the matter well, we come to see that the duty of soul winning is inherent in the very nature of Christianity.

In the first place, every Christian is a bondslave of Jesus Christ. "Ye are bought with a price." "Ye are not your own." We have no right to our own way. We are bound by the holiest ties and duties and love to please the Lord Jesus Christ. Men who turn from sin to Christ necessarily turn to good, away from harm. Men who are saved become good men in their hearts. I do not mean that being born again makes one perfect, but I do mean that one who is really a child of God has a new heart, a new nature, and wants to do right and to help. The hard heart, when born again, becomes tender. I saw a brutal gangster, who had planned to kill his wife and daughter—saw him after he was wonderfully saved. Now he was one of the tenderest, most kindly men. The Lord Jesus had made the lion into a lamb. That is an

old, old story to everybody who has been in soul-winning
work. But if one is made good, with a tender heart, he must
long to see others blessed, and must weep to see souls
damned. How can anybody claim that he loves his fellow-
men when he has no heart of compassion for their lost estate? How can anybody claim to love the Lord Jesus well
who does not set out to love what Jesus loves, and do what
Jesus does, and have concern and compassion over the very
thing dearest to the heart of the Saviour?

In the second place, the job is so urgent that we cannot
wait for professionals to do it.

On the beaches at Dunkirk, in World War II, a great
British Army was about to be slaughtered, annihilated, by
the German blitzkrieg. They were hemmed in on the sandy
beaches, and not only defeat, but utter destruction of the
whole army was inevitable unless rescue could reach them
across the British Channel. So the British people rushed to
the rescue. Every fishing boat, every pleasure launch, every
barge and tug that could be gathered from the coasts and
harbors of England were rushed to the scene by civilians.
In God's mercy, clouds hid them from the bombing and
strafing aircraft. Soldiers waded into the sea and climbed
into rowboats towed by launches, or were lifted into every
kind of vessel; then by their volunteer and unofficial res-
cuers they were taken safely to England. Dunkirk would
have been the symbol of unspeakable tragedy. But the no-
bility of volunteer lay people did what the army and navy
could not do. With their little vessels, their patched-together
and inadequate equipment, they saved the army to fight
again!

A baby lay choking to death with diphtheria. The
phlegm had gathered in a tight membrane in the throat
and nearly cut off breathing. The doctor had been called
but had not come. The frantic mother thrust her finger into
the child's throat and pulled out the plug of mucus so that
the child could breathe. It would have been fatal to wait for

a professional doctor. The child's life was saved. And how can any Christian be willing to see souls dying all about him and going to Hell, and yet be content just because he has paid part of a pastor's salary, although he has done nothing personally to redeem the lost and rescue the perishing?

It is well to have a fire department, but every sensible citizen ought to help put out the fire in his own house or his neighbor's. It is well to have paid life-guards at the beach, but every father with any heart would try to save his own child, or any other. Oh, how terrible it will be for a Christian to face the disappointed Saviour when he has let his own loved ones go to Hell, simply content that he had helped to pay a preacher!

It is the plan of God that every Christian should win souls. Every one of us can win some who will be lost if we do not do our part. God has given to every Christian the key to somebody's heart. This must not be left to full-time workers, to preachers, to missionaries, to evangelists. Of course, every preacher should make soul winning his main business. Every Christian worker should earnestly try to win individuals day after day, as did D. L. Moody, R. A. Torrey, Billy Sunday, and every other great soul winner. But be sure of this: God did not plan for the work to all be done by paid workers, professional workers, full-time workers, trained workers. Such a holy task requires the compassionate labors and tears and prayers and untiring efforts of every Christian.

4. Our Sinful Neglect

". . . Refuge failed me; no man cared for my soul."—Ps. 142:4.

"Then saith he unto his disciples, The harvest truly is plenteous, but the labourers are few; Pray ye therefore the Lord of the harvest, that he will send forth labourers into his harvest."—Matt. 9:37, 38.

ELSEWHERE IN Chapter Eleven we have given the strong Bible truth that one can always win souls, that the harvest is always white. But here I would stress the fact that God always has a man-power shortage when it comes to actual soul winning. The laborers are always few.

It is bad for a man not to believe the Bible. And when the unbeliever, denying the essentials of the Christian faith such as the supernatural authority and the infallibility of the Bible, the deity, virgin birth, blood atonement, bodily ressurection and miracles of Jesus Christ, then claims to be a Christian, it is wicked dishonesty and blasphemy. I do not wonder that Jesus called such men "ravening wolves" who come in "sheep's clothing" (Matt. 7:15).

But what about a Christian who believes the Bible and claims to follow it, one who believes that Christ is all He claims to be—the virgin-born Son of God, Creator, Saviour, Judge—and has trusted in the Lord Jesus for salvation, yet does nothing to get other people saved? Not believing in the

Word of God, the modernists let people go to Hell; but the fundamentalists who do not win souls let people go to Hell likewise. Although they claim to believe the Bible from cover to cover, in the end the practical result is much the same. It is shocking how few people win souls, and how callous and indifferent most of us Christians are about the lost souls around us for whom Christ died, the souls that He commanded us to warn and win!

The psalmist said, "Refuge failed me; no man cared for my soul" (Ps. 142:4). That is a pathetic cry. But most of the lost millions of earth could say the same thing. Most of them never had anyone earnestly seek to win them.

Jesus looked on the multitudes, and they were like sheep having no shepherd. He lamented that the harvest was so plenteous and the labourers few, and He taught us to "pray ... the Lord of the harvest, that he will send forth labourers into his harvest" (Matt. 9:38). Yet most of the unsaved multitudes about us have no one who earnestly warns them, and pleads with them, and tells them what God has said about sin and its ruin, its doom, and its Saviour.

I. Many Hearts Are Hungry With No One Trying to Win Them

Even in Bible times there were hungry hearts all about, waiting for someone to win them.

Down in Ethiopia an important man, treasurer to Queen Candace, brooded in his heart about his sins, about the true God, and about future punishment or forgiveness. He had heard many a tail of the God of Israel in his dealings with Israel. He knew there was a temple of God in Jerusalem. So one day he took leave, took his chariot with a driver and perhaps a mounted escort, and went to Jerusalem to worship. No doubt he went to the temple; perhaps he offered sacrifices according to the instructions of the priest. He inquired about the Word of God and purchased an expensive manuscript, handwritten on vellum, no doubt, and rolled into a scroll, a copy of the book of Isaiah. No one told him how to be saved. No one told him the details of the Saviour who had recently died. Perhaps he heard the name of Jesus, perhaps not; but he had no clear instruction on salvation.

It is rather remarkable that at this time the apostles were at Jerusalem and they did not find this man. Oh, if they had been praying and watching as they should have been, with all the other Christians scattered about, surely someone would have found this man with a troubled heart, this man with a guilty conscience who wanted cleansing and forgiveness! But the apostles were concerned about another matter. They had heard that down in Samaria, Deacon Philip was having a great revival. Perhaps they were afraid that Philip was not adequately teaching the people; perhaps they were afraid of some extreme emotionalism. At any rate, they had some apostolic authority and apostolic responsibility, so they went down to check on that revival and there they laid hands on the converts and prayed for them that they might receive the Holy Ghost. All that was well and good, but the poor, lost man had started back home to dark Egypt reading a scroll of the prophecy of Isaiah which he did not understand.

So God called Philip aside and urged him to go down the road that would intersect the highway from Jerusalem to Gaza. Philip went and God instructed him to draw near the chariot, and he ran. "Understandest thou what thou readest?" he asked. The man, reading Isaiah 53 about the Saviour who went as a lamb to the slaughter, pleaded with Philip to sit in the chariot and explain the Scripture to him. Philip did, and the eager sinner soon became a happy convert, stopped the chariot, and insisted on being baptized!

How strange that a hungry-hearted sinner should come so far and so nearly miss learning the way of salvation, with Christians all about committed to taking the Gospel to every creature!

In the city of Caesarea, we are told there was a centurion, a captain of a hundred men in the group called the Italian band. Cornelius was "a devout man, and one that feared God with all his house, which gave much alms to the people, and prayed to God alway" (Acts 10:2). Yet this earnest, seeking, hungry-hearted man was not saved for the simple reason that he did not know how to be saved! He "prayed to God alway"; so an angel appeared to tell him that his prayers had come for a memorial before God. He should send to Joppa and ask for Simon Peter who lodged at the house of Simon the tanner by the seaside. Peter would tell him how he and all his house could be saved.

It is strange how much trouble it took to get Peter to go to tell Cornelius and his family and his soldiers how to be saved. It was harder to make a soul winner out of Peter than it was to make Christians out of Cornelius and his household! All Peter's Jewish prejudice, his distaste for Gentiles, his fear of what the brethren would think, had to be overcome. But Peter went, after strong insistence and three visions from the Lord.

I have no doubt he expected to preach a long sermon. But at first he made the plan of salvation plain, saying, "To him give all the prophets witness, that through his name whosoever believeth in him shall receive remission of sins" (Acts 10:43). That settled it: Cornelius and his entire household were saved immediately, and later Peter reported, "As I began to speak, the Holy Ghost fell on them, as on us at the beginning" (Acts 11:15).

That woman at the well of Sychar seemed a shabby woman to the twelve disciples. What did Jesus see in that woman and why did He talk to her? Besides, she was a Samaritan and "the Jews have no dealings with the Samaritans." These disciples seemed to have no idea that the town was full of hungry-hearted people. That woman who had had five husbands and was then living with a man to whom she was not married, ran to the city and told her tale. Some men were immediately saved on her testimony. Others came out to see Jesus in person and were saved. Hearts were hungry. The fields were white but the laborers few.

Christians today are even more careless. Even more do Christians neglect the lost sinners around them.

Four years ago a woman living fifty miles below Dayton, Ohio, wrote my office asking when I would be at home. "We have three boys unsaved and I want Brother Rice to win them to Christ," she said. My secretary wrote that I would be at home on three certain days and would be glad to talk to her boys.

So on a Thursday in June, 1957, the family came to my home at seven o'clock in the evening. We greeted them warmly, and I got acquainted with the boys. I took time to win their confidence and to go thoroughly into the matter of sin and salvation. I found one of the boys had trusted Christ in Sunday School some years before, though he had never told his mother and father about it, and he had no assurance of salvation. Soon he got it settled by the Bible that his sins were forgiven, that he had everlasting life and was a child of God.

Then I talked with the other boys. The mother said, "Brother Rice, you are tired. Maybe you had rather wait until tomorrow morning to talk with the boys further, and I have something else I want to talk with you about."

"No," I told her, "we must settle this matter now." So I continued until each of the boys asked God's forgiveness and each put his trust in the Saviour and claimed it, then had assurance from the Word of God that his sins were forgiven.

Then, turning to the mother I said, "You said you had something else you wanted to talk to me about, didn't you?"

"Yes." Pointing to her husband she said, "He and I are not saved either."

So I began again with the plan of salvation and made the Scriptures clear, until both of them could definitely say from the heart that they had trusted Christ and were assured their sins were forgiven.

They went that night to a motel and the next morning they came by the office to see me. We had a glad time of greeting. Their faces were happy. They were saved and had assurance of salvation.

"Now let me see if I know how to tell it," the good woman said. "It seems to me that people ought to know how to tell this so other people can be saved. From the Scriptures you showed me, it seems that if one is sick and tired of sin and wants forgiveness, and if he believes that Christ died for him, then the moment he depends on Christ and trusts in Christ, his sins are forgiven and he has everlasting life. Is that right?"

I assured her that was right. Then we had some goodbys and they went on their way. They had driven some 350 miles, across half of Ohio, across Indiana, and half of Illinois, to get saved. And as I talked to the boys, the woman in deep earnestness had said, "Now listen, boys, this is Brother John R. Rice and you can trust him. He knows the Bible. I have read some of his books and THE SWORD OF THE LORD, and I know he can tell you how to be saved."

I walked back and forth in my study and talked to the Lord. "Lord, wasn't there anybody in the State of Ohio who could tell them how to be saved? Did they have to come 350 or 400 miles to learn Your simple plan of salvation?"

The Lord seemed to answer, "Oh, there are many people within a few miles of them who could have told them how to be saved and would have been glad to do it, but they were not making enough noise about it, and this troubled family did not know where to go, and so they traveled hundreds of miles to talk to the only person they knew who they thought could tell them and would tell them how to be saved!

During World War II, I was on a train from Chicago to Newton, Kansas, on some business with the printer of THE

SWORD OF THE LORD. At Kansas City I got out of my pullman berth and dressed. After some private Bible reading in the book of Hebrews and prayer I went into the dining car and was seated at a table with three men. I had my bacon and eggs and tea. The train was crowded. It was wartime. We talked about war, about business and other things, but I did not say anything about the Lord Jesus. It is true I had my Bible with me and laid it with my briefcase beside my chair when I ate. I did bow my head and silently thank God for the meal.

When I finished breakfast I said, "Now, I must go up into the chair car"; my pullman berth was only to Kansas City. So I arose, paid my bill, took my Bible and briefcase, and went forward to the chair car. The first car I came to was filled, every seat. I went on to the second car and walked through it from one end to the other. Every seat was taken. I turned and saw that one of the men at the table had followed me through the two cars. I said, "I'll have to go back to the lounge car to get a seat." I went back through the coach and he followed; through the next coach and he followed; through the dining car and he followed. In the lounge car I found a seat, and this man came and sat down beside me. I looked up; it was obvious he wanted to talk to me. He said, "Excuse me, sir, but are you a minister?"

I replied that I was an evangelist, John R. Rice, and he told me his name.

"Well, I am in terrible trouble," he said. "I hope you won't mind. My wife died, and I am taking her body out to the West Coast for burial. My wife was such a good Christian woman, but I haven't been a very good husband. I want to know: Do you think she would forgive me?"

"You say your wife was a good Christian?" I asked.

"Oh, yes. Her father is True Maxwell, pastor of the First Fundamental Church in Los Angeles. She was the best Christian I ever knew."

"Did she love you truly?" I asked.

"Oh, yes, I know she did!"

"Then you may be sure that she would forgive all your failures and sins."

"Well, another thing," he said, "how am I ever going to see her again?"

How strange it was! I am an evangelist, and the man had to come seeking me to find out how to be saved! The other two men with him at the dining car had come in and sat across the aisle from us. I learned the bereaved man was a designer for General Motors, that he lived at Rochester, Michigan. General Motors Company had sent these two men with him across the continent to bury his wife. So I took the Scriptures and verse-by-verse I showed him that we are all sinners, that Christ died for sinners, that now all one needed to do, if he really wanted forgiveness and salvation, was to turn to Jesus in his heart and trust Jesus, rely on Him for forgiveness and salvation. Other men around us were all quiet and reverent as I showed the sorrow-stricken man how to trust the Saviour. Then I said, "Now, are you ready to ask Jesus Christ to forgive you and save you?"

He was, he said, and so we bowed our heads. I prayed rather softly for the Lord Jesus to show the man how to trust Him and to forgive him and save him. Then he prayed, only he prayed right out loud.

When the prayer was done, I said, "Will you here and now take Him to be your personal Saviour forever? Will you trust Him and turn your case over to Him now?"

Oh, yes, he was glad to do it and took my hand as a sign between me and him and God. Then I showed him John 3: 36, "He that believeth on the Son hath everlasting life." And he had the glad assurance that his sins were forgiven and that he had everlasting life.

I got off the train at Newton, Kansas, and he and his friends went on to bury the dead body of his wife.

Later I had a letter from the father-in-law in which he

said, "Thank you for talking to our beloved Bob. He told us that he had met you, how he had claimed Christ as his Saviour and went home happy."

Two years later I was in a city-wide campaign at Pontiac, Michigan. One night waiting after the service to see me were two men. One of them spoke to me and said, "Dr. Rice, do you know me?"

"Yes," I replied. "Your name is Bob. I do not remember the last name. You are a designer for General Motors. You live at Rochester, Michigan. You and I met on a Santa Fe train two years ago." It was a happy meeting. Then he said, "Dr. Rice, I want you to meet my pastor." And he introduced the pastor of the First Nazarene Church of Rochester. That pastor told me, "Dr. Rice, Bob is the best member of my church, the best giver, the best soul winner, the best Christian in my church."

Every time I think of that case, first, my heart rejoices at the mercy of God, and second, I feel so ashamed that a poor, troubled sinner with a broken heart had to run me down and follow me about and ask me how to be saved.

Oh, we Christians are shamefully negligent about soul winning.

II. There Are So Few Efforts to Win Souls!

There are millions of Christians in America. There are millions of troubled and hungry hearts all around us. There is really very little effort to win souls. That is a shocking and sinful fact.

Last year I flew to Dallas, Texas, and took a limousine from Love Field to Fort Worth, where I spoke one afternoon and evening at a gathering of Christian workers. Then I had supper at the Texas Hotel, and at 11:20 took a car from Fort Worth back to Love Field. I was the only passenger. As we drove away the driver said, "Are you flying far tonight?"

"To Chicago," I replied.

"Do you live in Chicago?"

"No, I live at Wheaton, twenty-five miles west of Chicago."

"Well," he said, "I am a Christian and I try to give a testimony to everybody I haul in my car, and there is a man at Wheaton who has helped me a great deal. From him I get little booklets on *'What Must I Do to Be Saved?'* His name is Dr. John R. Rice."

I said, "I am John R. Rice." From the front seat he turned his head rather startled and said, "What did you say?"

Again I told him my name.

"Are you making fun of me?" he asked.

I took from my pocket a copy of the little booklet which has been spread in so many millions of copies. How glad he was to see me! We sang songs together and talked of our wonderful Saviour all the thirty odd miles to Love Field. There he brought in another taxi man and yet another friend to meet me before my plane took off for Chicago.

But my heart was so stirred. Up and down this land I have gone all these years preaching the Gospel and telling people about the Saviour. And so I began to count up all the times that anybody had ever approached me about my soul.

I remembered that before she died my mother told us that we must all meet her in Heaven, but nobody told us how to be saved. When I was seven or eight, a godly Sunday School teacher had told all the class, "I am praying for you that you will be saved, and I will never give you up until all of you have been saved." But she did not tell me how to be saved.

Once in a barber shop in Dallas I approached a twelve-year-old boy to get acquainted and make friends before I talked to him about the plan of salvation. I said, "Son, where do you go to Sunday School?"

His mother, who sat nearby waiting with her son, spoke up and said, "Mister, I'll tell you, you need a lot more than going to Sunday School and going to church. You need to be born again. Let me tell you my experience," and she told me a wonderful story of how God had cared for her as a widow, helped her keep her family together, had raised her up from a bed of sickness when the doctors said she would die. "What you need is not just to go to Sunday School and church, but you need to be born again," she said. I never told her that I was a preacher. My heart was so full that anybody should care enough about me that she would want me saved. She didn't go any further and tell me how to be saved, but I was so touched that she went that far.

One other time did someone ask me if I was a Christian. Many years ago in the Pacific Garden Mission in Chicago a young woman, a student at Moody Bible Institute, said to me, "Are you a Christian?"

I assured her that I was.

"Are you from Moody Institute?" she asked.

"No, I am from the University of Chicago," I said.

"Then you are not a Christian," she said. "Out there they don't believe the Bible!" She was right. Leaders at the University of Chicago did not believe the Bible, and I had some trouble convincing her that I was really a born-again Christian. But, thank God, she had asked me.

Those are the only times in my lifetime, as far as I can recall, when anybody has approached me about the matter of my soul, in any form!

I am sixty-five years old when these words are written. I am a member of the "100,000 Mile Club" of American Airlines and my card has on it the designation, "Million Miler," because the records indicate that I have flown on the airlines more than a million miles. I have flown all over America. The airports in Chicago, Los Angeles, Dallas, Denver, Atlanta, Detroit, and New York City are as familiar to me as business houses in my own little city. I have flown over Canada, east and west. I have flown to Honolulu, to Japan, to Korea, and back by Alaska. I have flown to Scotland and back. I have flown to India.

I have practically worn out twelve cars driving many hundreds of thousands of miles, and only three or four people have ever shown any interest in my soul!

It is only fair, then, to infer that Christian people in America do not often approach strangers and talk to them about salvation. When I was about nine years old, I went forward in the First Baptist Church of Gainsville, Texas, and there trusted the Saviour the best I knew. No one took the Bible to see that I had assurance of salvation. But I went home and asked Dad if I might join the church, and he replied, "No, Son. When you have really been convicted and have repented of your sins and have been regenerated, then will be time enough to join the church." Of course, what he said was true, only I did not understand those big words. And I didn't know how to tell him what had happened. If he had taken five minutes, he could not only have assured himself, but could have given me the assurance from the Word of God that my sins were all forgiven. I would have been saved three brokenhearted years with no assurance of salvation and trying to get saved again.

Two or three years later I was so troubled that I asked a good preacher, plain and devoted preacher, in whom I had great confidence, to pray for me. I told him I wanted to be saved. Instead of telling me how to be saved he said, "All right, John, I'll pray for you. Now you pray for yourself tonight before you go to sleep." How strange it seems to me that he went no further with the matter, did not tell me how to be saved, or did not show me the Scriptures. He made no inquiry, gave me no instruction, so I went away still troubled and unsure.

Years ago I taught in Wayland College, Plainview, Texas, and among other duties I was football coach. One day in faculty meeting the president said, "I have been checking and I find some students are not saved. Herbert Gunter, the president of the senior class, is not saved. He will be the honor graduate this year. Mr. Rice, he is halfback on your football team and in some of your classes. Don't you think you ought to talk to him about his soul?"

So I met Herbert Gunter in the hall and asked him to come to my room at eleven o'clock. He came in and I locked the door. Then I said to him, "Herbert, don't you want to be a Christian?"

He replied, "Of course I want to be a Christian. How can I be the kind of man that I want to be unless I am a Christian?" I learned that he had chosen to come to a Christian college when he could have gone to a secular school. His father was a Baptist deacon. He had been to church every Sunday morning and Sunday evening and was regularly in Sunday School. He elected extra courses in Bible and made better grades in Bible than any ministerial student in the class. Yet he was unsaved.

We knelt down together. I showed him some Scriptures and we prayed. Then I said, "If you will take Christ as your Saviour here and now and depend on Him for salvation, will you take my hand?" He seized my hand and we arose together. He was assured that he was saved, his sins forgiven. I expected him to be glad and to rejoice. Instead, he put his head on my shoulder and wept, this football halfback, this president of the senior class. When I inquired why his concern and tears, he said, "No one cared whether I was saved or not! Rufus Brazil mentioned it one time, but nobody else ever mentioned it and no one cared whether I was saved or not." Those words have condemned me as I remember them!

All around us are people who are lost and could be won, but there is almost no effort to win them. Nearly any poor, lost soul could look up to God and make the complaint, "Refuge failed me; no man cared for my soul" (Ps. 142:4).

III. Preachers Generally Do Not Do Much Soul Winning

It is shocking to me to find how many preachers do not make much effort to win souls. Some never preach to the lost, and those who do preach to lost people and give a public invitation to accept Christ usually do very little personal soul winning outside the pulpit. Years ago I was shocked after someone had preached to a group of Christian workers, and the pastor of a First Baptist Church, the largest church in the area, arose and said, "I never did personally win a soul to Christ. I have preached the Gospel from the pulpit and sometimes sinners have been saved under my preaching, but I never did personally win a soul to Christ. I would not know how." I thought then that it was shocking. I think now it is even more shocking than I thought it then!

Once there was a revival campaign in the city auditorium in a town where I served the Lord. One night at the invitation time I brought a poor, wicked, drinking man down to the front. He wanted to be saved. I asked the evangelist, "Don't you want to talk to this man and show him how to be saved?" To my surprise he said, "No, John, you do it or take him to my father. I would not know what to say."

Three years ago we had a conference on revival and soul winning in Chicago. In the evening services the four speakers alternated in four principal churches. In the daytime we met in the Belden Avenue Baptist Church in downtown Chicago. One day in a group including twenty-eight pastors I asked, "How many of you pastors have made as many as ten calls within the last week on lost sinners or unenlisted Christians?" Only two of the twenty-eight pastors had made as many as ten calls on unsaved people, or on unenlisted, out-of-duty Christians! It was not surprising that most of those pastors had small crowds, few converts.

All my life I have had the most profound respect, almost reverence, for foreign missionaries. Yet in Japan and Korea and in India, I was shocked to find that many missionaries win very few souls. I found that many missionaries spend their time in teaching in the schools, or in getting out literature, or doing translation work, or hospital or relief work, and almost never make a personal effort to win souls. I found missionaries who had been on the foreign field three years and had never learned the language enough to be understood.

In 1956 I went to Japan as the guest of the Evangelical Foreign Mission Fellowship and spoke at a conference at Karazawa to some six hundred missionaries. A missionary leader wrote me that some missionaries had been greatly offended at my article in THE SWORD OF THE LORD in which I said that the Lord's work should be supported at home and abroad, or not supported, on the basis of whether or not it was winning souls, and that only by souls won could a foreign missionary justify the support of the churches. This missionary leader thought some would resent my coming, though he said I should come ahead.

However, the week before I was to speak, at a deeper-life conference one of the missionaries rose and with many tears confessed his failure. He had been in Japan three years and had never yet won a Japanese to Christ! He begged the prayers of others. He said that the churches supporting him would be shocked if they knew he had never won a soul in Japan. So the missionaries who might have been angry with me were somewhat chastened and subdued, and God gave a wonderful reception as I poured out my soul to missionaries about soul winning.

Years ago I preached with Dr. Theodore Epp for a month on the Back to the Bible Broadcast. A missionary leader was there, and he said to me, "Brother Rice, why don't you support a foreign missionary?"

I replied that I had long wished to do so, and if I could find someone who would do on the foreign field the same kind of work I was trying to do, getting sinners saved everywhere, putting soul winning first, I would like to support such a missionary.

"I have just the young man you want," he said. "He is here with me now." And so he introduced me to a young man, graduate of a Bible institute, who was prepared to go to Africa as a missionary.

I asked him some questions. I found him sound in the faith, well-taught in the Bible. Had he ever won souls?

"Yes," he said, "I think that I have a right to claim that I have won souls. I sang in a male quartet two summers and we visited in many churches. Two different people were saved in services in which I sang, and I think I have a right to claim part of the credit for their salvation."

I was shocked. He had never personally won a soul, yet he planned to cross the ocean and spend his lifetime as a missionary. I knew that a three-thousand-mile ocean voyage would not make a soul winner out of a man who had never won a soul in America. I told him frankly that I could not honestly use God's money to support the missionary who had never won a soul.

I was present and was a guest speaker at a large meeting of Baptists. One night before I spoke, a missionary candidate spoke. He was the best possible missionary material. He was born on the foreign field where his father had been a missionary for years. He already knew the language of the field to which he was going, knew the customs of the people, and was adjusted to the sacrifices that were necessary. He had come back to America, had graduated from a Christian college, had married a beautiful and talented girl. Now they were going to the mission field, and he told that large congregation, "I realize that we are in the last days. I know it is getting harder all the time to win souls. So we won't expect any great ingathering of souls, yet I think I ought to give my testimony where I can before Jesus comes."

He went to the foreign field not expecting many to be

saved. He spent some years there. He and his wife were not happy in the work. Few souls were saved. They generally did routine work connected with the mission, but not directly winning souls. After some time on the field, he came back to the States and is now in a secular profession. He is a noble, good man. But unfortunately, it seems to me, he did not succeed in the mission field to a degree acceptable to himself because he did not spend enough time in actual soul winning and he had not been taught that everywhere there are souls who can be won.

Because of the great founder, Hudson Taylor, and many noble missionaries connected with the movement, I have loved what was the China Inland Mission. My own daughter and son-in-law volunteered to go to Tibet under the China Inland Mission. But China was closed later, and they could not go. However, I was shocked to find that the China Inland Mission in its last years in China won only thirteen souls per year per missionary. That is, a missionary full-time at the work, with all the national workers and local churches already established, altogether could win only thirteen souls per year, for each missionary employed. My wife wins more souls than that in a year; my secretary wins more souls than that in a year; and they have many other duties. Mrs. Rice has won as many as one hundred souls in a year's time.

In Lake Louise, Toccoa, Georgia, at a conference on revival and soul winning in July, 1959, I told the story of the family that drove 350 or 400 miles from Ohio to ask me how to be saved and told how all five of the family went home happy in the Lord. When the services dismissed for lunch that day, I saw a tow-headed boy working his way through the congregation, and he came to me on the platform and said, "Brother Rice, that sure was a good sermon you preached."

Then he scuffed his foot on the floor, embarrassed, and

he said, "Brother Rice, ah—I want to—ah—no, not join the church, you know!"

"Do you mean you want to be saved?" I asked.

"Yes, that's it," he said. "You said you did not mind telling that family from Ohio how to be saved, and so I thought you wouldn't mind telling me."

He was soon saved. I found that his father was a preacher. He had sat by his father throughout the service. He had left his preacher-father's side to come and ask me how to be saved!

I find that many preachers never do any visitation except among their own members or others who have moved into the community and are prospective members, already converted. I find that many churches have no visitation program.

In a large church in Wheaton, Illinois, in a Wednesday night meeting, a committee presented the name of a man as a prospective pastor. Evangelist Walt Handford rose and asked the chairman of the committee, "How many converts were baptized in this man's pastorate which he is leaving? Does he win many souls to Christ?"

The chairman, mildly condescending to the young evangelist, said, "Brother Walt, we are not so much concerned with numbers in this church."

And the young evangelist said, "I am convinced of that. I have noticed the records and for the last year there have been only four people who professed faith in Christ in this church."

That church was supporting in whole or in part some forty missionaries, but in at least two different years they had had only four converts to come for membership, and they had agreed on a rule for the church, that there would be no public baptizings in any of the regular services of the church.

I am saying that there are many preachers who do not

win souls, many churches where soul winning is not stressed.

IV. How Many Excuses People Make for Not Winning Souls!

Those who do very little soul winning, in order to live with themselves must either admit it is sinful and wrong not to win souls, or they must make up excuses for their sinful negligence. They rationalize their sinful neglect in various ways. Let me name some of the excuses often heard:

1. "We are in the last days. Wickedness abounds more and more. It is getting harder to win souls."

The answer to that is very simple and easy. If we knew it were true that Jesus Christ were coming tomorrow (as indeed He may!), that would not change a particle our duty to win souls. The Great Commission command to take the Gospel to every creature is still binding. The promise of Jesus Christ, "Lo, I am with you alway" (Matt. 28:20) in soul winning is still good. The Holy Spirit still convicts sinners. The Gospel is still the power of God unto salvation. There would not be a particle of difference in the opportunity to win souls if Jesus Christ were to come tomorrow. He may come tomorrow. He may come today. But the truth is that nobody knows when. There is not any way anybody can know when this age will close. It is foolish and unscriptural to declare that we are in the closing days of the age. All this defeatist talk about "these dark days" is wholly unscriptural. The darker the days, the more the opportunity for soul winning. Where sin abounds, grace does much more abound. All God's resources are still available. Souls are still all about us to be won.

2. "But so many of the people around me are Catholics or Jews or Lutherans. And so many are modernists, and so many are open infidels who do not believe the Bible."

Again, this is an excuse. The simple truth is that Christ died as much for Catholics, He died as much for Jews, He died as much for infidels, as for anybody else. Missionaries often say that it is practically impossible to win a Mohammedan. That, too, is an excuse. The simple truth is that "the gospel . . . is the power of God unto salvation to every one that believeth; to the Jew first, and also to the Greek" (Rom. 1:16).

Those who were saved in the revival at Pentecost and following at Jerusalem were Jews. Most of those saved in Paul's missionary journeys were Jews. Again and again in major campaigns I have seen Jews converted. I think I saw between thirty and fifty Catholics converted in two weeks in Bombay, India, last January. In a recent eight days of services in a Colorado city, six adult Catholics turned to Christ. The sad truth is that sometimes people do not love Catholics and Jews and those of false religious cults as they ought. At Hastings, Minnesota, a Jehovah's Witness visitor came by to give or sell some of Judge Rutherford's books. I won the man to Christ. He immediately went after his twelve-year-old son and brought that son and commanded him to stand still and hear while I told him how to be saved, and the boy was saved, too.

A few weeks ago I won a Catholic woman to Christ in Norfolk, Virginia, a woman I had never seen before as I simply called at house after house down the street. I did not set out to show her the folly of the pope and the mass and prayers to Mary and Catholic dogma. I simply showed her that all of us were sinners, that Christ died for sinners, that she needed forgiveness. I made friends with her beautiful little girl and so made friends with her. Catholics or Protestants, Jews or Gentiles, old or young—people everywhere are sinners who need to come to God for mercy and trust in Jesus and the atoning blood of Jesus Christ.

3. "But I am busy at other work for God."

So someone says who uses that as an excuse for not doing the main work that God has called him to do.

I remember a young minister, a graduate of a Bible institute, graduate of a Christian college with an A.B. degree and then taking three years of theological seminary work, who told me, "If you like evangelistic work, that is fine. You go ahead and do it. I do not like that so much. What I want is to be pastor of a church—not too large, because I don't want to have to do much visiting. But I want to be pastor of a church and have a good library and spend plenty of time in my study."

I told him, "There is nothing wrong with you that couldn't be fixed if you would just come like drunkards and harlots and others do, to a mourner's bench of confession and tears, and beg God to revive your heart and help you do right."

I know some people give out tracts and use that as a substitute for soul winning. I am for Christian literature, but a little leaflet of two or four or six pages is not enough attention to give to a lost soul. And giving out a tract does not take the place of personal testimony and entreaty and an explanation of the Scriptures.

Many a preacher who spends a great deal of time and preparation of his sermons would do well if he spent part of that time going from house to house after lost sinners. There would be a warmth and joy and freshness and glory about his preaching, a compelling sincerity which he will lack if all his sermon comes from the study and none of it from practical contact with souls.

4. "I do not have the personality and the talent for soul winning," some people say.

A pastor said to me the other day, "I know I am not scholarly. I am not gifted. I don't have the abilities some men have." I said to him, "Then you are just the kind of man God wants, for ". . . not many wise men after the flesh, not many mighty, not many noble, are called" (I Cor. 1:26), and "God hath chosen the foolish things of the world to confound the wise; and God hath chosen the weak things of the world to confound the things which are mighty" (I Cor. 1:27).

Soul winning is not a matter of human talent or logic or personality. It is a matter of the supernatural Word of God and the supernatural power of the Holy Spirit. God chooses weak vessels so that He will get the glory. Some of the most gifted men I ever heard preach are poor soul winners. There is more moving eloquence in a tear, in a deep concern, in a holy compassion and love for sinners than all the flowery phrases and all the back-slapping personality of an extrovert.

5. *"But I do not have a gift of gab," says another.*
Then a gift of the Holy Spirit will fix that!

Any so-called reason we may give for letting people all about us go unwarned into death and Hell is simply an excuse for which we will have to answer to God.

IV. How to Conquer Negligence and Failure to Work at Soul Winning

Negligence, indifference, halfheartedness, inattention to soul winning—these sum up the most glaring sin and failure of present-day Christians. We make some suggestions as to how one may conquer this sin and become an alert, always-at-it soul winner.

1. *Face your sin and failure honestly.*
In a quiet time before God confess that sin. Accept as a basic part of your Christian philosophy that soul winning is the first duty of every Christian, the most important activity anybody can pursue, the one work with the greatest eternal rewards, the one Christian business that Heaven most rejoices over. Pressure of every kind is on the Christian— duty to family, to his job, to his friends, rest and food and the care of his body and home, routine church activities—

but you should honestly face it that everything in your life ought to be subordinated to the one main business of keeping souls out of Hell. Get this settled in your mind: See your excuses for what they are. Make honest confession of your sin and failure to God, and pleading His constant help, set out to be a consistent, daily, working soul winner.

2. That means that you should give soul winning priority.

The preacher should face the fact that winning souls is more important than preaching a sermon that would not win a soul. The Sunday School teacher should face the truth that to win one of her pupils is more important than teaching the lesson. The church visitor should face it that it is far more important to win a soul than it is to get someone to attend a service or to join the church. Of course the preaching service, the Sunday School class, the visit in the homes, all properly may be used to win souls or to lead toward soul winning. But the end itself, soul winning, is more important than any of the means. You will have to give soul winning priority.

3. That means that the Christian should definitely schedule a time for soul winning.

One should have a time when regularly, as regularly as he eats or goes to his job or attends church services, he gives some time to seeking out sinners. Every really consecrated Christian hopes to do some soul winning. But too often it is left to convenience, left to some casual meeting where, we hope, the lost soul will be put in our way. But the Christian should set aside a certain evening every week or certain morning or more time when he definitely sets out to win somebody to Christ. It may be that you have prospects in mind, or that you go to your own relatives and friends first. With most soul winners, there ought to be a time when you set out to go from house to house to meet new friends, and earnestly pray that God will guide you to someone you can win. I have tried it again and again in strange cities with blessed results. Even in recent weeks in Winston-Salem, North Carolina, in Norfolk, Virginia, and in Centerville, Iowa, I have gone out greeting people, getting acquainted, and have in each case found someone I could win to Christ, someone I had never seen before. Put soul winning in your schedule.

4. Be Soul Conscious, Always Alert to Find a Lost Sinner.

Aside from a regular scheduled time when you set out to do nothing but seek to win souls, the spiritual Christian should be always on the alert. Every morning one should pray for an open heart, so that, as Jesus found the woman by the well of Samaria, and as He found the man born blind, and the poor, cripple by the pool of Bethesda, you can win souls. In church, be careful to meet every stranger possible or every Sunday School pupil who might be unsaved. If there is a sermon and a public invitation, you might plan if possible to sit near a lost person and offer to go forward with him if he will take Christ as Saviour and claim Him openly. After the service, take time to seek out those who may be lost. People who come to church should expect someone to talk to them about the Lord. God has helped me to win hundreds as I found them in the crowds leaving a church service. In business one seeks to make friends. If the worldly man would drink a cocktail with a business acquaintance as a social gesture, why should not a Christian approach him on the basis of his family and where he goes to church, and does he know Christ as Saviour? Business contacts are often a wonderful opportunity to win souls.

On vacation people have a little leisure, they are often friendly. It is often easy to get on intimate terms, to find out about people's families, their work, their hobbies, their plans, to find out if they are saved.

5. Daily, Constant Prayer That One May Find the Right Person.

One cannot be always on the alert and successful in soul winning unless this becomes a serious part of daily prayer life. Dr. R. A. Torrey tells how he would seek a seat on a train or street car and then pray for God to send someone to sit beside him that he might win to Christ.

Once I flew from upstate New York to a Carolina city. That involved a flight down to Washington on a small airline, a wait there, and then continuing flight.

In the morning flight I had a blessed time with my Bible. I had been working very hard and felt the need of waiting on God. So I read the Bible, prayed about my work and my friends, and had the dear Lord lift my burdens and comfort my heart. Then I pleaded with Him as I sat in the Washington airport, after we had had such a precious time together with the Word and with prayer and meditation, that I might win someone to Christ on the next flight.

I got a seat on the Eastern Airline plane, and here came a lad in uniform in the armed services. He was flying down to Virginia. The airplane hostess announced that the flying time would be twenty-eight minutes to the next stop. I had only that long to talk to the boy. I sat and prayed for God to make clear to me how to approach him, and then God led to the third chapter of John. I said, "Do you know the most popular, the best-known verse of Scripture in all the Bible?"

He meditated a bit and then said, "No, I don't know much about the Bible. I lived on a farm in Maine, eight miles from Bangor. I went to Sunday School some as a boy, but I don't know any Bible."

I showed him John 3:16. I told him that Martin Luther called this "the little Gospel." I went over it carefully and said, "Did you ever hear that before?"

He wrinkled his brow and said, "Yes, it seems like I heard that in Sunday School when I was a little boy."

I prayed for God to make the story sweet, the story of

God's love and Christ's sacrifice and the promise of eternal life. In a little bit of time he was ready to admit he was a sinner and needed such a Saviour. I asked him if I might pray for him, and I said, "God knows what is in your heart. If honestly you will ask Him to forgive you, to change your heart, and if you will in your heart depend upon Him, He will do it right now."

He agreed to pray silently. We bowed our heads and he whispered a prayed and then he told me yes, that he would take Christ as his Saviour. He took my hand on it in a solemn handclasp. He gave his name and address, and then the hostess was saying, "Please fasten seat belts. We are approaching the landing at Norfolk." He went gladly on his way and so did I. But there is no way to be an alert, constantly active soul winner without putting that as a major part of your prayer life.

A few years back I preached at a big youth meeting in Buffalo, on New Year's Eve night. I spoke to some 1,200 young people, I suppose, at one o'clock, the first service in the New Year. Then I walked to my hotel for a few hours of sleep. On New Year's morning I took a plane back to Chicago.

But my own heart was deeply stirred. "O Lord Jesus, please help me to win some soul this first day of the New Year!" I prayed. The plane came down at Detroit for a bit, and an air force man sat down beside me. He was glum. He was leaving his wife and baby, flying to the West for duty. He was not talkative, but when I inquired about his family he soon warmed up. Was his wife a Christian? Oh, yes, she was a good Christian; she attended the Methodist church at Albion, Michigan. Did he have any children? Oh, yes, he had a wonderful little boy. Was he himself a Christian? No, he was not. He had often thought he should be, but he was not.

So there on the plane I said, "It is New Year's Day. It is the time for new starts, new resolutions. Would not your wife be happy if you could tell her that today on New Year's

Day you have taken Christ as your Saviour, you have set out to serve her God and help her have a Christian home? Wouldn't that be sweet to her?"

He was deeply moved. "Yes, nothing would make my wife happier, I know. A man with a family ought to be a Christian."

So there on the plane we bowed our heads and I whispered a prayer, and he in his heart asked God to forgive him and save him. We had a solemn handshake on the matter. Then I showed him the Scripture, "He that believeth on the Son hath everlasting life . . ." (John 3:36), and he had assurance that in trusting Jesus he now had everlasting life.

But a strange thing happened. The hostess had come through serving dinner on the plane. But I waved it aside gladly. I said, "No, I am to have dinner with all my loved ones today. My daughter, Mary Lloys, is having dinner and they will wait until I get there. It will be after one o'clock, but we will all be together." So the passengers all ate their dinner on the plane and I waited.

However, we arrived over the Chicago airport and circled and circled, and finally an announcement was made. The Chicago airport was closed in. We were flying back to Detroit. Then I asked the hostess, "Do you have any of those dinners left?" She did, and I ate my dinner.

We landed at Detroit. The air force boy called his wife with the good news and arranged for a car to take him to the next city. I took a taxi to Lansing, caught a train, and did not get into Chicago until midnight that night. But God had rearranged all of our plans in answer to prayer so that I might win that hungry-hearted air force boy!

Oh, this must become a matter of passion and constant burden and attention, and above all, a matter of constant leading of the Spirit and constant anointing with His power, if you would win souls, day and night, regularly, working at this great business and not neglecting your opportunities.

5. "GO"; the Main Essential

"GO ye into all the world, and preach the gospel to every creature."—Mark 16:15.

"So that servant came, and shewed his lord these things. Then the master of the house being angry said to his servant, GO out quickly into the streets and lanes of the city, and bring in hither the poor, and the maimed, and the halt, and the blind. And the servant said, Lord, it is done as thou hast commanded, and yet there is room. And the lord said unto the servant, GO out into the highways and hedges, and compel them to come in, that my house may be filled."—Luke 14:21-23.

"He that GOETH FORTH and weepeth, bearing precious seed, shall doubtless come again with rejoicing, bringing his sheaves with him."—Ps. 126:6.

THE FIRST GREAT essential in soul winning is to go after sinners! This is the simplest part of soul winning, but the one on which most people fail. Most people do not win souls simply because they do not work at it. They do not go after sinners. One may cry, and pray, and read his Bible, and go to church, and have family altar, and give his tithes, and pay his honest debts, and yet 'his own family may go to Hell and all his friends around him, because he simply does not go after them, does not take the Gospel to them, does not urgently try to win them to Jesus Christ. No one ever becomes a soul winner who is not willing to work at it. Aggressive efforts are blessed of God in soul winning. One who does not make the effort will not get people saved.

I. The Bible Everywhere Puts Going After Sinners As the First Requirement

The first word in the Great Commission as given in Mark 16:15 is, "Go." "Go ye into all the world, and preach the gospel to every creature," Jesus said. Again in Matthew 28:19, 20 in the Great Commission Jesus said, "Go ye therefore . . . ." The go is first. Going is before preaching. Going is before baptizing.

The Bible command is not, "Build a church house and preach." The command is not, "Settle down and preach." The Bible says, "Go . . . and preach." Preaching without an earnest effort to reach sinners and get them to hear the Gospel does not fulfill the plain command of Jesus Christ.

That wonderful passage in Psalm 126:6 puts going first in soul winning. "He that goeth forth and weepeth, bearing precious seed, shall doubtless come again with rejoicing, bringing his sheaves with him." Of what use would be the weeping over souls if I did not go after them? Of what use would be all the good seed if I did not go forth and sow it? Going is the first requirement in soul winning.

We are commanded to "put on the whole armour of God, that ye may be able to stand against the wiles of the devil" (Eph. 6:11). In that armour Christians are exhorted to put on the girdle of truth, the breastplate of righteousness, to take the shield of faith and the helmet of salvation. But often we forget the plain exhortation that the Christian must have "your feet shod with the preparation of the gospel of peace." What a ridiculous picture a man would be with a heavy coat of armour on—helmet, breastplate, shield, a heavy sword—but barefooted! A soldier for God is no good if he doesn't go. The first grass burr he would step on would incapacitate the warrior! But God wants a Christian to put on the shoes of "the preparation of the gospel of peace." In other words, all the armour of a Christian is no good as far as fighting the Devil if he does not have his feet consecrated to going for God.

I suspect that we overemphasize talking as a means of serving God, though certainly we ought to speak up for Jesus. But the Bible has some pretty bad things to say about our talking apparatus. Of the whole human race it is said, "Their throat is an open sepulchre; with their tongues they have used deceit; the poison of asps is under their lips: Whose mouth is full of cursing and bitterness" (Rom. 3:13, 14). It is important to use the tongue for God, yet we should remember, "And the tongue is a fire, a world of iniquity: so is the tongue among our members, that it defileth the whole body, and setteth on fire the course of nature; and it is set on fire of hell" (James 3:6). Again, "But the tongue can no man tame; it is an unruly evil, full of deadly poison" (James 3:8). Every Christian needs the greatest humility about his speech, needs to watch carefully that the tongue be conquered and curbed and dedicated. God does not brag much on the human tongue.

We may say a preacher is a "silver-tongued orator." We may say, "winsome personality," and "radiant charm." We may exalt a preacher's "scholarly bearing," or speak of his "charming style." But these are not the things about a soul winner which are most important to God. The Bible tells us what God loves best of all and what He praises most of all in a Christian's personality. "How beautiful," says He, "are the feet of them that preach the gospel of peace, and bring glad tidings of good things!" (Rom. 10:15). Oh, beautiful feet that go out to carry the gospel message to sinners!

A wonderful example of Christ's teaching on this matter of going after sinners is given in the parable of the great supper in Luke 14. In the parable only one servant of God is illustrated—the servant who is busily working to get people to the heavenly supper! And that servant does more walking than talking! Listen to these words: "Then said he unto him, A certain man made a great supper, and bade many: And sent his servant at supper time to say to them that were bidden, Come; for all things are now ready" (vss. 16, 17).

It is important to note that the servant did more going than saying. I do not know how many miles he walked to get to all the people, but he had the same simple message, "Come; for all things are now ready." It did not take much brains to give the message. It did take loyalty and faithfulness to take all those steps.

But those first invited made excuses enough to discourage anybody. And the servant very properly came back to report and get further orders. And what were those orders? They were, "Go out quickly into the streets and lanes of the city, and bring in hither the poor, and the maimed, and the halt, and the blind" (vs. 21).

Again it was mainly *going*. And the servant must "go quickly," for time was short and the matter of desperate importance. This time he was to go down every street, and search out every back alley in the town, and find every poor person, every pauper, every crippled beggar, the least likely persons to come to his lord's great supper. Again his work was primarily walking, not talking. It was more going than saying.

Then the servant, after his expedition searching out through the whole city for every single person who might come to this supper, came back for further orders. He said: "Lord, it is done as thou hast commanded, and yet there is room" (vs. 22).

This time the orders are still to go, and go further, and go more urgently. "And the lord said unto the servant, Go out into the highways and hedges, and compel them to come in, that my house may be filled" (vs. 23).

Again he is to go, this time down the highway, turning to follow every country lane, and out to every cottage on a hedge row. He must go with compelling haste to furnish guests for the great supper!

Oh, may God give us urgent and consecrated feet that we may hurry after sinners!

The main thing about soul winning is going. The number of guests at the great supper in Heaven will be largely determined, humanly speaking, by how faithfully we go after people to invite them.

II. We Make Many False and Sinful Excuses for Not Going After Sinners

This Bible idea of going after sinners, seeking them, running them down, hunting for them, pleading with them, being aggressive in seeking to save them, does not suit our carnal nature and our worldly ideas. We offer all kinds of substitutes for God's plan of going after sinners.

1. We Provide a Church and Preacher and Say, "Let Sinners Come and Be Saved If They Will."

But we need to remember that church houses themselves are more or less an afterthought in New Testament Christianity. There is not a record of a single church house being erected in New Testament times for the preaching of the Gospel and for the regular meeting of a congregation. People met in synagogues, in the porch of the temple, in private homes, in upper rooms, in courtyards, on mountains, on the seashore. I think church buildings are a great convenience, and it is well to use them for the Lord; but let no one think that when he has provided a church building and a preacher, he has then fulfilled his part in getting sinners saved. The things that most church people are interested in— Gothic buildings, learned preachers, robed choirs, stained glass windows, pipe organs, rich altars—are incidentals not even required in the Bible and utterly ignored by the apostles and other New Testament soul winners!

There is a familiar saying that all of us have heard,

"Sinners just don't come to church any more." Well, back-slidden Christians have been saying the same thing down through all the centuries! The simple truth is, the Bible did not command sinners to come to church. It commands the church to go to sinners. God's plan is not that sinners should seek out someone to tell them how to be saved. God's plan is that Christians should seek out sinners and win them.

Dr. A. J. Gordon in *When Christ Came to Church* tells of a life-transforming dream he had in which the Lord Jesus came to the Clarendon Avenue Baptist Church where Dr. Gordon was pastor. In the remarkable dream Dr. Gordon saw for the first time how foolish were the pew rents, the worldly but talented hired singers, the emphasis on wealth, culture, and dignity in the services. So Dr. Gordon set out to bring common people into the church, to seek out sinners and get them saved in the church. And every church ought to be glad to leave the robes off the choir, or to omit the anthem or organ solo, or to displease the cultured and leave unsatisfied the aesthetic feelings of the few in order to bring in lost people and win them to Christ and have a soul-winning church. I do not say that organs and choirs are necessarily against soul winning. But when they become ends in themselves, then they become a disgraceful hindrance to the cause of Christ.

The whole idea that we are to provide a church building and a preacher, then if anybody wants to be saved he may come and be saved, but our hands are clean and our responsibilities are ended, is utterly foreign to the Great Commission and to the practice of New Testament Christianity. For this reason every church should go to the jails, go to the parks, should conduct street meetings, should have visitation in hospitals, should have door-to-door invitations for sinners, should follow up prospects. No church is filling its place that is not primarily occupied with going after sinners.

2. Some Christians Say, "Well, I Try to Live Right and I Expect My Christian Example to Lead Men to Christ."

But that is a false philosophy and contrary to the Scriptures. It is true that Jesus said, "Let your light so shine before men, that they may see your good works, and glorify your Father which is in heaven." But the Lord is not talking about paying your debts. That is not gospel light shining. Many sinners pay their debts: of course you ought to be honest and right. But you can't let your light shine without taking the Gospel out to sinners. You are not even living a good Christian life if you don't go after sinners, because you are living in rebellion and disobedience to the main command that Jesus has given to His people.

It has been a sad experience often repeated when I preach in jails, or when I preach to drunken bums, down-and-outs in rescue missions, to find that many a man will tell me, "Yes, I know all that. My father was a Baptist deacon," or, "My father was a Methodist preacher," or, "I grew up in a preacher's home." Many a man who has gone to the depths of sin, and many a sinful woman has told me that they came from homes where Mother and Father went to church, where they had a family altar, where they had thanks at the table, where they tithed their income regularly; yet these same Christians did not aggressively win their own children to Jesus Christ!

If living a good, moral, religious life would get loved ones saved, then all the Pharisees in the time of Christ ought to have been wonderful soul winners! But they were not. God's way is that the Christian should live right, yes; but he should do right about the *main* thing and that is about personal soul winning. He should go after sinners and seek them with heartbroken entreaty and consuming passion! There is no substitute for going after sinners if we would win them.

3. Many Christians Pray Very Earnestly for Sinners to Be Saved, and They Feel That That Is Their Part in Soul Winning.

But that is wrong, dead wrong. God has appointed a way to get sinners saved, and the very first element in it is to go after them. God wants us to take the Gospel to sinners. He wants us to urge them to be saved. He wants us to show them how to be saved. He wants us to use every means to get them to trust Jesus Christ for salvation.

I have heard men pray most earnest and fervent prayers for sinners. They would say perhaps, "Lord, send the Holy Spirit over to that sinner and convict him so he can't sleep, so he can't eat. Convict him deeper than sin has ever left a stain, so that he will have to come and be saved." But I have known such men who have prayed so earnestly and eloquently, who never lifted a finger to keep anybody out of Hell, and who sat at home and read the newspapers while they wanted to send the Holy Spirit, like a Western Union messenger boy, over to do the work which God had commanded them to do. I am not minimizing the work of the blessed Holy Spirit. I know that no sinner will ever be saved who is not convicted and enlightened by the Spirit of God. But God's plan is that the Holy Spirit shall work through Christians. He is to make His appeal through the heart, and the voice, and the tears, and the handclasp, and the earnest entreaty of a Christian who loves Him.

Think what one is really saying to God when he ignores the command that we are to go after sinners and compel them to come in, the command that we are to take the Gospel to every creature, and yet prays for sinners to be saved. In effect, the man is saying, "God, I don't like your plan, and I want you to change it and save people my way. I don't want to go as you commanded me to go, but I want you to send the Holy Spirit anyway and save the sinner." Such a prayer is presumptuous, when it is not ignorant. Certainly

God is not going to change his wonderful plan that Christians are to go after sinners.

"It pleased God by the foolishness of preaching to save them that believe" (I Cor. 1:21). It does not please God to save people by praying, without preaching. It does not please God to save people any way in the world that leaves out a presentation of the Gospel to the individual heart. Preaching here, of course, means the preaching of a mother to her child, of a man to his neighbor, just as much as the preaching of an ordained minister in the pulpit. The point is that though it may seem foolish to the world, God will not save people except that some human being takes them the Gospel! You can pray until you are black in the face, but God will not change His plan. Your prayer in that case is a wicked rebellion against God's own plan, and God's clear commands! The Christian must go after people and must take the Gospel to them if he would have them saved. And when we pray, we must pray with the plan of God and in obedience to God's command instead of praying contrary to His plan and in rebellion against His command. I am for praying, if you do something about it.

In revival campaigns I often have people make requests for loved ones they would like to see saved. But I have found it necessary to require this simple stipulation. I do not allow people to make public requests for prayer for loved ones to be saved if they are not willing to speak to those loved ones and earnestly try to win them. I believe that God does not hear favorably the prayer of rebels, of disobedient people who are not willing to do what God said to do. Dear friend, if you want your loved ones saved, then pray by all means. But then let your concern for souls and your burden reach your feet as well as your voice, and go after them. There is something insincere and hypocritical about one praying for a loved one to be saved when the one praying is unwilling to take the Gospel to the sinner and urge him to take Christ as Saviour.

4. I Have Heard Christians Say, "If They Ask Me, I Will Be Glad to Tell Sinners How to Be Saved."

But that presupposes that a Christian has no responsibility in the matter. That presupposes that God has not given us a clear command to go after sinners. Many a timid Christian wishes to avoid any rebuff, and the fear of man holds him back from doing the plain will of God. He is willing, if some sinner should ask him, to tell the plan of salvation. But that is utterly contrary to God's plan in soul winning.

In Hammond, Indiana, a timid woman held her hand for prayer one Sunday morning after I had preached in a revival campaign. She wept as she sat silently at her seat. We gave a brief invitation for people to come forward and claim Christ as Saviour, but she did not come. Timidly she halted between two opinions, longing to come, but lacking courage. After the benediction I went to her as she stood in the pew and found her eager to be saved. We had a quiet prayer, and with many tears she took my hand to claim Christ as Saviour and said that I might tell the waiting friends. Others came to rejoice with her, then she said, "I wanted so badly to go forward during the service and claim the Saviour, but I felt so timid. I couldn't go by myself. Had I had someone to go with me, I would have gone."

Her older brother who had been a Christian many years and who had come to rejoice when she was saved, spoke up quickly and said, "Sister, why didn't you come and tell me? I would have been glad to go with you down to the front to claim the Saviour."

I turned to him, I fear pretty sternly, and said, "You ought to be ashamed of yourself! You have been a Christian for many long years. Yet when your own sister is lost and wanted to be saved and held her hand for prayer, you would not even step across the aisle to encourage her to come to Christ. Then you suggest that she ought to have come and asked you to walk down the aisle with her. Why didn't you *offer* to go?" It is a silly and unscriptural idea that we ought to expect sinners to come to us to find out how to be saved. God has plainly commanded us to go to sinners, and we sin when we do not do it.

5. *"I Like for People to Make Their Own Decision Without Outside Influence," Some Christians Say.*

The other day after I had won a fourteen-year-old boy to Christ and he gladly went with me to tell his father that he had accepted Christ as Saviour, the father said, "Well, I didn't say anything to him about it because I do not believe in forcing such matters. I wanted to leave it to him to decide." That hungry-hearted boy—I can see now his dark serious eyes and the hunger in his face as I remember how quickly he turned to Christ and joined me in prayer for his own salvation when I spoke to him. I thought in my heart, as I faced the father, If no one else had cared more about that boy than his father did, the boy might well have gone to Hell!

The father would not have left to the boy as to whether he should go to school or not, as to whether he should get up on time, as to whether he should lie or steal. The father would feel responsible for teaching the boy what was right on every other important matter in the world. But about the boy's immortal soul, the father said nothing. He said he wanted the boy to make his own choice. Actually, he was giving an excuse for his own timidity and his own sin in neglecting the boy. I do not believe in pressing anybody to make a public stand who has not made an honest decision in the heart. But I know that every human tie in the world ought to be used to bring sinners to decide for Jesus Christ.

In a revival campaign where I preached, a man stepped out quickly to come forward and take my hand and claim Christ as his Saviour. Later someone said to me, "I'm glad he came without anybody talking to him. I would so much rather see sinners come to Christ without anybody bothering them. Then I know that they mean business."

But I replied, "I would much rather that every sinner would have somebody talk to him. Then I know that Christians are doing right. It is God's appointed way that Christians should win sinners, not that sinners should come without Christians winning them." For Christians to leave lost sinners in a congregation to make their decision alone seems to me to shift all the burden to the preacher, and by ignoring their own duty Christians let many precious souls slip away unsaved who might have been won by a kindly and tactful and unobtrusive bit of encouragement.

The idea that a man will be a better Christian if nobody encourages him to be saved is silly. No boy turns out to be a more honest man because nobody ever told him it was wrong to steal. No girl makes a more virtuous woman because her mother did not warn her of the pitfalls of immorality.

It is God's plan that Christians should go after sinners, should seek sinners, should win sinners. We must face God one day and give an account as to how well we have kept His plain command to go after sinners and bring them to trust in Christ.

The Lord Jesus likened soul winning to going fishing. He said to Peter and Andrew, "Follow me, and I will make you fishers of men" (Matt. 4:19). People do not fish without "going fishing." No one expects a fish to get up on the bank and come to the fisherman of his own will. No one expects to hang a fishing line out of his car as he drives along and catch anything but pedestrians! I wish we were as sensible about soul winning as we are about fishing. The first thing you must do if you would fish is to go fishing. The first thing you must do if you would win souls is to go after sinners.

We go hunting if we want to find game. The good shepherd went and sought the lost sheep until he found him. Jesus told how the woman who lost one piece of silver lighted a candle, and swept the house, and sought diligently till she found it (Luke 15:8). And that is the way Christians get lost sinners, too, for Jesus. We must go and seek them until we find them.

Agents go from house to house selling insurance. No one expects all the people who can be sold insurance to come and seek out the agent and persuade the agent to sell. No, it is the other way round. God expects Christians to seek out sinners and "sell" them the Gospel!

Politicians have learned to make a diligent house-to-house canvass to get votes. Not only newspaper advertising, but the personal contact is used. And those who would be willing to vote for the favored candidate are furnished a car to go to the polls, or whatever help is necessary. If we Christians get as anxious to see sinners saved as politicians are to get elected, we will go after sinners with all our hearts and with all our might.

III. Bible Examples Prove That Simply Going After Sinners Is the Greatest Essential

How did Bible Christians win souls? That is easy to answer. They simply went after them. I know that soul winners need compassion of heart. I know they should use the blessed Word of God. I know that they must have the power of the Holy Spirit to change hearts and make dead men live. But it is still true that no other equipment will help the soul winner who does not *go* after sinners.

Andrew won his rough, cursing, loudmouthed brother, fisherman Peter. How did he do it? We are told, "He first findeth his own brother Simon, and saith unto him, We have found the Messias, which is, being interpreted, the Christ. And he brought him to Jesus" (John 1:41, 42). It was a very simple thing that Andrew said to Peter. Anybody could say that. But Andrew went and sought out Peter and found him, to tell him the good news and to bring him to Jesus!

Jesus won Philip, and this new convert then won his

friend Nathanael. How did he do it? We are told, "Philip *findeth* Nathanael, and saith unto him, We have found him, of whom Moses in the law, and the prophets, did write, Jesus of Nazareth, the son of Joseph. And Nathanael said unto him, Can there any good thing come out of Nazareth? Philip saith unto him, Come and see" (John 1:45, 46).

Nearly anybody I know could do better than this poor, ignorant new convert Philip did in talking to Nathanael. He called Jesus "the son of Joseph." He was not denying the virgin birth of Jesus. Possibly he was only using the generally accepted term since Joseph acted as foster father to Jesus and was so known to the public. Very possibly the new convert did not really know much about the virgin birth of Christ. At any rate, he made a big blunder. But in his sincerity God overruled his blunder and Nathanael was saved. He was not saved immediately; he had problems and questions. And Philip the new convert could not answer all the questions, but he had the right answer nevertheless. He said, "Come and see." He brought him to Jesus and Jesus fixed everything up with Nathanael, just as He will do with every sinner who honestly comes to find Him.

You see, the main thing is that Philip went after Nathanael and brought him to Jesus. Philip did not know all about it, and Philip made some mistakes, but he did not make the tragic mistake of neglecting his friend's soul and letting him go to Hell. There is no mistake in the world as bad as leaving people alone in their sins, unwarned, uninvited, and untaught about Jesus and salvation. Nearly anybody could do as well as Philip did. But he did do the one essential thing. He went after Nathanael and found him and got him to come to Jesus.

That is a wonderful story of soul winning we read in Acts 8:26-40. Philip was in a great revival at Samaria when the angel of the Lord told him to "arise, and go toward the south unto the way that goeth down from Jerusalem unto

Gaza, which is desert," and Philip went. That is one of the big secrets of this soul winner's power. He obeyed orders. He was always willing to go. So he went and at the crossroads he found the Ethiopian eunuch, treasurer under Candace, queen of Ethiopia. And this great statesman was reading from a handwritten scroll the prophecy of Isaiah, and pondering the message in the fifty-third chapter where Christ is pictured as bearing our sins. It was really not difficult to win the Ethiopian eunuch to Christ. He insisted that Philip get into the chariot and ride with him and explain the Scriptures. So Philip "began at the same scripture, and preached unto him Jesus." Then the eunuch, trusting Christ and sure of his salvation, asked to be baptized. And after the baptism, Philip was caught away.

There was nothing remarkably difficult about winning the man. He was already under conviction, he was already reading the Bible, he asked what the Scriptures meant. He had gone to Jerusalem to worship, and his heart was hungry. Nearly anybody who was at hand and ready could have taught the man how to be saved. It is rather shocking to think that the twelve apostles at Jerusalem had not found the man, nor had a single Christian there told him how to be saved. But the great virtue in Philip's action was that he simply went after the man and won him. You see, *going* is the main part of soul winning.

It was so about the conversion of Cornelius in Acts, chapter 10. Cornelius and his household were all convicted. They were all feeling their need of salvation. They were fasting and praying. Anybody could have told them how to be saved. Just as soon as Peter said to them, "To him give all the prophets witness, that through his name whosoever believeth in him shall receive remission of sins," they were all converted and Peter never did get to preach the big sermon he had prepared! You see, the deciding thing was that Peter, though with great reluctance, had gone to tell them how to be saved. It was harder to get Peter ready to win Cornelius than it was to get Cornelius and his household saved.

Naaman the Syrian, the great captain of the host who was a leper, was saved because a little Hebrew captive maid insisted that there was a prophet of God in Samaria who could recover him of his leprosy. Naaman went for healing of his leprosy and found also the healing of his soul (II Kings 5). We do not suppose that there was any special eloquence in the little girl's talk, nor any wonderful logic in her argument. But she took up the matter and urged until it was brought to Naaman's attention, and the man's body was healed and an immortal soul was saved! You see, the initiative must be with the Christian. God wants saints to seek for sinners.

IV. The Greatest Soul Winners Are Those Who Simply Work at Soul Winning

It is sometimes almost comic the way people try to account for the success of great soul winners. How many learned men marveled about D. L. Moody! They could never see the secret of his power! Since he seemed not to be a great preacher by human standards, since he did not have much education, and since his language was often ungrammatical and his voice rather abrupt and sharp, they could not understand how he won so many souls! You see, people nearly always want to think that soul winning is done by human talent or by eloquence or personality. Actually, D. L. Moody won many, many souls because he worked hard at that business. For long years he earnestly tried to win one soul a day in personal contact. Even after he was a great preacher winning multitudes, he earnestly sought out individuals and tried to win some every day in personal conversation. And that directness and urgency he carried over into his preaching.

An English newspaper said that Mr. Moody "had the faculty of precipitating decision." Actually, in every ser-

mon he plunged right into the main point, either getting
Christians to win souls, or getting sinners to trust Christ.
He was so direct and urgent and enthusiastic and inisistent
that the blessed Holy Spirit could use him in getting people
saved.

Somebody has said that Billy Sunday was "God's joke
on the preachers." He evidently meant that the things most
preachers value so highly, such as scholarship, dignity,
clerical bearing, etc., seemed foreign to Billy Sunday; yet
Billy Sunday got the work done that multitudes of other
preachers would have liked to do. I think God meant to
show that it is not learning, not scholarship, not human
eloquence, not stained glass windows and pipe organ music
and robed choirs and Gothic cathedrals that get people
saved. God simply blesses every honest effort where willing
feet and a burning heart go after men and run them down
for Jesus Christ! If you really believe that a holy urgency
of heart—along with the power of the Holy Spirit put in
eager hands and feet and voice that are willing to go to any
extreme to get the Gospel to people and to urge them and
compel them to decision for Christ—is the main things God
wants, then you can understand all the great soul winners.
The great soul winners are simply people who work hard at
getting people saved and have God's power to bless their
tremendous toil.

One of the greatest soul winners America has seen was
John Vassar. He was not a preacher; he simply called himself the Master's shepherd dog, sent to seek out lost
sheep. Pastors would invite him to come to their town to
help in revival services. The pastor would do the preaching,
but John Vassar would talk to every soul in town. He would
weep, he would plead, he would be insulted; but he plodded
on from house to house cheerfully, lovingly, in relentless
pursuit of sinners! In the public services he might exhort or
start an old song and plead for sinners to come to Christ.
But mainly his work was with individuals. He really ran

men down for God. Multiplied thousands were won by that simple, rather unlettered soul, in the last half of the last century.

In Dallas, Texas, on the evening of June 25, 1933, I preached in an open-air revival campaign on "How We Can Win One Thousand Souls by Christmas." I suggested that in the six months, from June 25 to December 25, we should set ourselves, in that young church recently organized, to win a thousand people to Christ. I told my people it could not be done in the Sunday services alone. Probably it could not be done in our open-air revivals alone. We planned to have Sunday afternoon open-air services in Marsalis Park by the zoo. We planned visitation in the tuberculosis hospital and the city hospital. We planned street services. We planned house-to-house visitation. But mainly I insisted that each Christian must set himself a goal and dedicate himself to the soul-winning business. I called for volunteers, and thirty-three people that night stood, agreeing, each one, to set a goal for himself and try to win a definite quota of people to Christ within the six-month period.

I remember that my good wife, deeply moved, agreed to try to win fifty people in the six months. She had five children in the home, and she taught a class of young women, besides other duties as a pastor's wife; but she felt that she ought to win at least fifty people in six months' time, in personal contact. When the six months had ended, she had a record of about 101 or 102 people whom she had led to trust in Christ, or backsliders who had returned from their life of sin to live for God.

One seamstress, a little woman with only high school education and no special Christian training, had a burden of heart to win one hundred souls. She had never even taught a Sunday School class. Yet she began a vigorous plan of personal visitation in the homes winning souls. By Christmas time she had won a few more than 150! Two or three days after Christmas, when reports were all in, I had a record of 1,005 people who had confessed Christ as Saviour or who had returned from a life of backsliding and sin to serve the Lord anew. And most of them had been won by earnest, pursuing Christian workers who sought them out and found them, and pleaded with them to be saved, and showed them how from the Word of God.

In our watch-night service on New Year's Eve the little seamstress made a vow to God. She had learned what could be done by earnest, personal soul-winning effort. She said she felt she ought to win five hundred souls within the next year. And what joy she was all the year to her pastor's heart! How many, many people she brought to the services and then brought to the pastor to make public profession of faith in Christ. She won men and women, young people and children. At the year's end, in another New Year's Eve watch-night service she rose and with many tears confessed that she had failed the Lord. She had hoped to win five hundred souls. "And I could have done it, too, if I had been as faithful as I should have been," she said. She had won only 360 people to Christ in the year's time, and she felt very sad! And as I think about it, my heart is deeply shamed for all the preachers who in a life-time ministry hardly win that many, and that Christian woman who had never been to a Bible institute, nor had any special training, and did not even teach a Sunday School class, had won some 360 people to repent of their sins and avow their faith in Jesus Christ as Saviour and Lord! I am saying that great soul winners are simply people who work hardest at the business of going after sinners.

May I mention Hillus Gas, now with the Lord, another soul winner in the great church of which God made me the pastor in Dallas, Texas. I baptized him. He was a young man of ordinary background. He finished high school, I believe, but with only ordinary grades. He had had no special Christian training. However, under my preaching of the urgent duty of every Christian to win souls, his own

heart had taken fire and he began to work at soul winning.
In how many ways he put me to shame! He would go down
to domino parlors, interrupt men at their play and their
drinking, give them tracts, and talk to them about their
souls. He seemed to me to be even untactful, and I feared
he would repel some. But his sincerity, his urgency, rather
compelled respect instead.

When the Texas Centennial World's Fair began at
Dallas, he longed to be able to do personal soul winning
among the crowds who attended. He would work a few days
and save a little money, then go and spend a day at the Fair
and do personal work. At first I furnished him the booklets
to give away. Later his brother-in-law said, "If you will do
that work for you and me both, I want to furnish your
board. You stay at my house, eat at my table and work at
soul winning." I was so convinced of Hillus's faithfulness
that I bought him a season ticket to the fair grounds. So
he did every day a full day's work in the fair grounds. With
another young man of like mind, he would spend the entire
day talking to people and giving out the booklet *What Must
I Do to Be Saved?* to all who would agree to read it. A Jew
running a concession of dancing girls protested vigorously
against the young man's giving out the booklets and talking
to people about their souls in front of his show. "You will
hurt my business!" he said excitedly. But my young friend
talked to him so earnestly and fervently about his own
soul that the Jewish man threw up his hands and said, "Go
ahead! Talk to anybody you want! You are doing more good
than I am."

A policeman protested that he must not give out the
booklets to the general crowds in the fair ground. My young
friend showed him his paid ticket, said that he had the
same right there that everybody else had, and then talked
to the policeman about his soul for half an hour and the
policeman was converted!

At the end of the season, my young friend and his partner brought me a list of more than five hundred people, with names and addresses, who had claimed to trust Christ as Saviour under their personal work. How many of them went on to serve the Lord? Of course I do not know. But I know that the impact on many was the touch of God that meant the difference between life and death, between Heaven and Hell. I baptized many of the converts he won.

I wish I could impress it tremendously on your heart, that people go to Hell because we do not go after them.

V. Is This Failing to Go After Sinners Your Sin?

We make all kinds of alibis and excuses for not winning souls, but I wonder if usually this is not the real reason we do not win souls—that we do not work at it?

The other day a dear man wrote me and said that he was praying day and night to be filled with the Holy Spirit. He has never won a soul he said, but as soon as he felt the mighty power of God upon him, he was going out to win souls. Let me tell you, along with this dear brother, that you ought not to wait even for the fullness of the Spirit. How will you know whether the Spirit of God is with you in soul-winning power unless you do what God has said? And why should you expect God to be willing to give you His Holy Spirit when you are not doing the one business that the fullness of the Spirit comes to aid? I say, go ahead and try with all your heart to win souls. Go in Jesus' name. Use the Word of God. Weep over sinners. Call on God to do His part. And I doubt not that more and more as you go, the Spirit of God will go with you and give you soul-winning power.

Someone says to me, "But I do not know the Bible. I am not familiar with the Scriptures. I do not know how to win a soul." To such people I often say that if they will bring me their Bibles, I will show them where John 3:16 is. They can mark that, learn that, and use that one precious verse.

I have won many hundreds to Christ on that one verse alone.

No, ignorance of the Bible is no excuse for not winning souls. Certainly I believe that every Christian should love his Bible passionately, read it every day and delight in it and learn it. But anybody who is born again can, in a few minutes' time, learn enough Scriptures to win many souls. You will need to learn more in order to win some cases, but your main trouble is not ignorance of the Bible. Your trouble is laziness, disobedience. You do not win souls because you do not go after them.

Someone says, "But Brother Rice, I don't have the gift of speech. I am not eloquent." Bible students will remember that that is an old, old excuse which Moses himself made to God. But it is not a valid excuse. God made the tongue. And even if you speak with stumbling and halting words, God can use you if you earnestly go to seek sinners. What man ever failed to propose to the girl he loved because he felt he was not eloquent? No man would let insurance prospects go without a sales talk just because he felt he was not eloquent. Whatever you lack in "a gift of gab" can be remedied by a gift of the Holy Spirit. And whether you speak eloquently or speak in plain and stumbling words, if you go with a broken heart for the Lord Jesus and do your best, you can win souls. God does not want so much eloquent words as honest words. God does not want a gifted tongue so much as willing feet.

"But," says one, "I do not feel the leading of God. I would go talk to sinners, but I do not feel impressed." Whose fault do you think it is that you do not have the leading of the Holy Spirit? Do you believe that it is God's fault, or yours? Your trouble is deeper than that. You are not surrendered to do the will of God. You do not have the holy urgency in your heart to go after sinners. If you did, you would find that God would give instructions.

When I was in the United States Infantry during World

War I, I learned that there are two kinds of orders that a soldier may have. He has general orders that are always in effect. Then he has special orders for special occasions. Every soldier on guard duty had to learn his general orders and then some special orders to fit special occasions.

Now the Lord has certain general orders that are for every Christian and are always in effect. The general orders are that I am to get the Gospel to every creature in the world. So unless I have clear leading to contradict it, I am under obligation to try to get everybody to be saved. Oh, I know that there must be a holy wisdom from God. I know that one must have direction and leadership of the Holy Spirit. But it is still a fact that God has already committed Himself to the plan of Christians going after sinners, and it is a general principle that anybody I have a good chance to win, I ought to try to win. Often I ought to warn even those I have little chance of winning. If you, dear reader, will get a burden of soul and will set out to try to win everybody you can, then you may go to God with clean hands and ask Him for the leadership of His Spirit and He will give that leadership. But I fear your trouble is a calloused, hard, disobedient heart in that you do not run after sinners to seek them and find them for God and get them to trust in His dear Son, our Saviour.

Why Preachers Fail.

May I say a word here about why so many revival efforts fail? I believe that more often revival efforts fail for lack of work than for lack of gospel preaching. I believe that the publicity, the visitation, the advertising, and wholesouled activity to enlist Christians in going after sinners are more often the lack which lead to failure than the quality of the preaching.

I have seen many, many preachers stand up and preach an earnest gospel message, making plain the plan of salvation, but preaching to a congregation which did not include a single unconverted sinner. That is putting the *preaching* in the Great Commission before the *going,* and it does not work.

And let me suggest further to my preacher friends that many a preacher who preaches good sermons is nevertheless a failure because he does not win souls. The reason is usually just this: he does not definitely go after sinners. No man should feel that his duty is done when he preaches a sermon in the pulpit. Certainly if one did not get sinners out to hear the Gospel in the church house, then he ought to go after them.

I preached as earnestly as I knew how once, hoping to win a man to Christ whom I loved and for whom I had prayed much. The service came to a close and he was still unsaved. At the door as he left the building I shook hands with him and earnestly urged him to take Christ as Saviour. In five minutes of conversation he was soundly converted. Preaching from the pulpit, long-range soul winning, did not do it. Definite, persistent, personal effort did.

Dear preacher, do not hide behind the pulpit. In Jesus' name I beg you to go after sinners. Find them in the hospitals, find them in the jails, find them in the rescue missions. Find them in the homes of your members. Find them next door to your church.

I was in a revival campaign in a good church in Chicago. Very few unconverted people came to the services. The church members were self-satisfied. They were good, sound people. They believed the Bible. They lived clean lives. But in a residence jammed against the side of the church building lived an unsaved woman. She sat on the steps of her home, and there in the eventide, just before the church service began, Mrs. Rice and I won her to Christ. How guilty that church full of Christians would have been had that poor neighbor woman gone to Hell unwon! I beg every Christian to leave the ninety-nine good sheep in the wilderness if need be and go after that which is lost until you find it, like the good shepherd did about whom Jesus told us. The one great essential of soul winning is going after sinners. Do it today. You have already prayed. You have waited for a more favorable opportunity, or for others to do it. Wait no longer! Do not sin longer in this matter. Today go try to win that loved one or friend to Christ!

6. Soul-Winning Compassion

"They that sow in tears shall reap in joy. He that goeth forth and weepeth, bearing precious seed, shall doubtless come again with rejoicing, bringing his sheaves with him."—Ps. 126:5, 6.

"As soon as Zion travailed, she brought forth her children."—Isa. 66:8.

"But when he saw the multitudes, he was moved with compassion on them, because they fainted, and were scattered abroad, as sheep having no shepherd."—Matt. 9:36.

"I say the truth in Christ, I lie not, my conscience also bearing me witness in the Holy Ghost, That I have great heaviness and continual sorrow in my heart. For I could wish that myself were accursed from Christ for my brethren, my kinsmen according to the flesh."—Rom. 9:1-3.

TEARS, HEART SORROW, heaviness, travail, compassion—these must be part of the character of the soul winner. A soul winner is not primarily one who works at the soul-winning task, but one who is the kind of person who can and will and *must* win souls. One cannot win souls unless he is a soul winner and has a soul winner's heart. And nothing is clearer in the Bible than that the soul winner must know a broken heart, the compassion, the travail of soul, the burden for sinners that will see them saved.

"They that sow in tears shall reap in joy," says the psalmist (Ps. 126:5). And the next verse tells us that weeping is as much a part of soul winning as the seed of the Word which we carry and the obedient going after sinners! Dr. L. R. Scarborough used to say to us in his great class on evangelism at Southwestern Baptist Seminary, "No sowing, no reaping; no weeping, no rejoicing!" We might as well face our problem honestly. In soul winning, the cold heart, the dry eye, the commonplace attitude will not succeed! A soul worth Christ's dying for is worth any man's weeping for! Preaching and testimony from cold hearts and with dry eyes are like barren wombs and dry breasts. Children are never born without travail, and many of us lack spiritual children because we have not learned this lesson!

How little is thought of the heart broken over sinners, the tears of compassion in these days! I looked in a dictionary of illustrations for preachers. In over six thousand illustrations there was not one on weeping, not one on tears, not one on travail. The only one on burden had nothing to do with concern for sinners, and the only one on compassion referred to having mercy on beasts! I wonder if in six thousand sermons there would be one on compassion for souls, concern over lost sinners, and burden for the redemption of the lost!

The late Dr. Scarborough said, after quoting many Scriptures:

"These Scriptures tell us the *heart* of the Three in the Godhead. The Father *loves* us, and *gives* us His best, His only Son. The Saviour weeps with *longing compassion* and *dies* a cruel death on the cross for us. The Spirit *intercedes* with *unutterable groanings* for us. The Psalmist says we must weep if we win. The Prophet says we will rise out of obscurity and be watered gardens if we *draw out our souls* to the lost and needy. The Apostle, *weeping* over a lost city for three years, tells us he has *great heaviness* and *continual sorrow* in his heart and is willing to be *accursed* that his brethren might be saved. The lawgiver and leader stood in the breach between the people and God's wrath, and saved them from the consequences of their sins. In Ezekiel 22:30 God searches for someone to stand in the gap before Him lest He should destroy the land. But He fails to find any. So He pours out His indignation and the fires of His wrath. No prophet nor priest with compassion! In Ezekiel 34:1-19 God makes awful charges against the shepherds of His people, 'You feed *yourselves* with the fat, you clothe *yourselves* with the wool, but you do not feed the flock. The diseased you do not strengthen, the sick you do not heal, neither bind up the broken, nor bring back those who were drawn away, neither have you *sought that which was lost.*' Then He says, 'Behold *I am against* the shepherds, and I will require my flock at their hand and cause them to cease from feeding the flock.' He says with burning words, 'I will seek that which is lost.' This He did in the life, death, and ministry of Jesus Christ, and by the persistent calls of the Holy Spirit and by the efforts of His people through the centuries. A compassionless Christianity drifts into ceremonialism and formalism and dries up the fountains of life and causes the world to commit spiritual suicide. A compassionate leadership in the Christian movements of the world is now our greatest need. Every niche of this lost world needs the ministry of a fired soul, burning and shining, blood-hot with the zeal and conviction of a conquering Gospel. Spiritual dry rot is worse than the plagues of Egypt, the simooms of a thousand Saharas, to the churches of Jesus Christ throughout the world. Many a minister is in a treadmill, marking time, drying up, living a *professional life,* without power, not earning his salt because he has no passion for God or souls and no power for effective service. May our God kindle holy fires of evangel-

ism in all churches and pulpits where such are needed"
(from *With Christ After the Lost*).

May the dear Lord speak to our hearts together, both
yours and mine, and teach us to have compassion such as
He has for sinners!

I. Soul-Winning Compassion for Sinners Naturally Expected of Sincere Christians

When one meditates about the matter a bit, it seems
strikingly clear that a compassion for poor, lost sinners in
danger of eternal ruin and torment ought to well up in the
heart of every Christian. How can anybody be a good
Christian, be spiritually-minded, be near to Christ, who
does not care about the doom of sinners and long with unceasing burden to see them saved? Consider the following
evidences of the fitness of tears and heart burden on the
part of every one who would win souls.

*1. Why Should a Sinner Be Moved When the Christian
Who Talks to Him Is not Deeply Moved About His Soul's
Need for Christ?*

A young drunkard knelt one night in a room in the
Capitol Hotel, in Amarillo, Texas, with four preachers. I
will never forget the tears that flooded down his face.
Twenty-six years old, he had made $26,000 the year before,
but was such an incurable drunkard that his wife had left
him and he had tried to commit suicide. Now he pleaded with
us to pray. He had heard me speak that night and afterward called the room to ask our help. There he was, on his
knees in the room, with the four preachers around him. He
told how his grandfather was a famous Presbyterian
preacher. He called by name a half dozen other well-known
ministers whom he knew. But he said, "Yes, I know lots of
preachers, but I have to have somebody to pray for me
who means it!" I do not accuse the other preachers he
knew, but oh, I felt that night that they had failed God and

failed this sinner in not having tears and compassion enough to convince this wayward and enslaved sinner that they "meant it." He trusted Christ that night, and I saw him reunited with his young wife. Oh, I have thought so many times, God forgive us preachers and Christian workers for not "meaning it" enough to convince everybody.

We sometimes critically suggest that sinners are hard-hearted these days. But I think that hard hearts are just as likely to be found in the breasts of preachers and deacons and stewards and elders and Sunday School teachers and parents. When Christians learn to weep so that there can be no doubt of their holy concern, God will give the increase. Surely there is a fundamental insincerity in Christians who accept, theoretically, all the great doctrines of the Bible, and glibly repeat that they believe in Heaven, in Hell, in the atoning work of Christ, in eternal damnation of those who do not trust Him, in the eternal blessedness of those who do receive Him and believe Him, yet who have never learned compassion for sinners! All such orthodoxy is head orthodoxy, but heart treason to the Gospel. Many Christians may be as orthodox as Paul in their heads, but in their poor, cold hearts they may be as tragically wrong as Judas Iscariot.

Once I heard Gipsy Smith speak to a great crowd in Dallas, Texas. My heart was so tremendously moved that I vowed to God that I would thenceforth take every opportunity to win souls. I was moved by the tears of Gipsy Smith and by his earnest pleading. In the service I had the joy of helping to win a woman to Christ. I then solemnly decided that when I left the building I would talk to the first man I should see, about his soul. That enormous crowd filed slowly from the big First Baptist Church auditorium. Outside I found a cab waiting and spoke to the cab man. "Are you a Christian?"

"Yes. I believe I am."

I asked him when he had been converted, when he had

been born again, and he replied, "Just a minute ago. A short gray-headed man with a mustache came out the door back yonder and urged me to be saved. He was so earnest—he said I might die and go to Hell if I didn't do it today—so, well, I just felt I had to do it! So I trusted Jesus as my Saviour." Gipsy Smith had come out the door near the pulpit and had won this cab man before I could get to him! I have never forgotten how the taxi man told me that Gipsy Smith was so earnest that he felt he must be saved.

I remember when I bought a soul from the Devil for fifty cents! I was a student in Seminary and very poor. One night with other students I was at the Union Gospel Mission in Fort Worth on Main Street. That November night two men had drifted into the rescue mission to get warm. They were really young bums who had come in that day from Denver. One was nominally a Catholic, and when I began to talk to him about his soul, he was greatly interested in the New Testament. He asked me, "Say! Is that a Bible?"

I showed him that it was the New Testament, part of the Bible. And he said, "Well, I've always wanted to see a Bible! So that is what the Bible is like. I wish I had one!"

I turned to Scripture after Scripture on the plan of salvation, but his charming childlike enthusiasm for the Bible led me to say, "Didn't you ever see a Bible before?" He answered that he never had.

"But didn't you ever go to church?" I asked him.

"Yes," he said. "I went to church with my mother twice, a Catholic church, but I didn't see any Bible."

After I showed him Scripture after Scripture, he was deeply concerned. It was all so new and strange. He had never heard a sermon, never seen a Bible as far as he remembered. No one had ever said a word to him about how to be saved. All he knew about spiritual matters was that as a boy he had twice attended a Catholic church with his mother. When I pressed upon him to decide for Christ, he said to me with obvious sincerity, "Buddy, that sure sounds good. I suppose it's true; I don't know. I never heard of it before. But you'll have to give me a little time. It seems so strange that one can be saved like that, have all his sins forgiven in a moment and be made a child of God, and I never heard of it. I'll have to study about it. If this is all so, why didn't I ever hear it before?"

When it seemed that I could not get him to decide for Christ at the moment, I gave him my New Testament. I marked certain passages, and he promised to read them faithfully, and earnestly to seek the Lord. Then I asked him where he would spend the night.

"My buddy and I will find a boxcar that's open, or maybe a basement grill where some heat comes up. Sometimes we wrap in newspapers and crawl in a culvert. We'll get by some way until tomorrow, and then we'll get down to my buddy's home at Kaufman."

"But you will freeze tonight," I said. "You don't even have an overcoat." He told me that he and his buddy would manage somehow. They would wake in the middle of the night nearly frozen, then they would get up and wrestle and run and box until they got warm again. But my heart convicted me. I had a warm bed, poor though I was. So I said to him, "Come with me. I'll take you upstairs to a cheap rooming house and get you a bed." Another ministerial student took his companion and we rented each of them a cot for fifty cents. That half dollar seemed as big as a wagon wheel to me, but I paid for the boy's bed; then I told him goodby, begged him to read the New Testament which I had given him and to decide for the Saviour. But as I turned away, he seized my arm. I turned to find him weeping. He said, "Buddy, I didn't think I would settle this matter yet. It is all new and strange. I never heard about it before. But you wouldn't buy me a bed if what you said were not true. I won't wait until I learn more about it. I'll risk what you say. I'll give myself to Jesus now and trust Him to save me." There we shook hands together on his solemn pledge to trust Christ now and forever and to live for Him, and I went away. Often I have wished I could invest every half dollar I ever find in my possession so well! But actually, of course, what won that poor, benighted soul was a holy compassion and urgency in my heart. I loved him. I could not bear for him to be in trouble. He was a poor lost soul for whom Jesus died. Out of my poverty, my compassion made itself known in the simple act of buying him a bed.

God forgive us; how many souls we let go away unsaved because we do not love them, do not yearn over them! It was not fifty cents that won that soul. It was the loving heart, the burden, the compassionate attitude that any lost person must respect. How can we expect lost people to be moved when we are not moved? How can we expect them to be burdened about their sins when we are not burdened?

2. How Can the Unburdened, Unconcerned Worker Expect God to Bless His Soul-Winning Efforts?

Lukewarmness is the sin that makes God spew out His people, He says (Rev. 3:14-16). The proud, the self-satisfied, the self-righteous, the self-contained and self-sufficient person has little claim on God. "The Lord is nigh unto them that are of a broken heart; and saveth such as be of a contrite spirit" (Ps. 34:18). One who would have the help of the dear Lord must seek the broken heart. Again, as David said, "The sacrifices of God are a broken spirit: a broken and a contrite heart, O God, thou wilt not despise" (Ps. 51:17). The would-be soul winner who wants the seal of God's blessing upon his labor should cultivate the broken spirit, the broken and contrite heart which God does not despise.

It is well to remember how King Hezekiah won the favor of God. God had sent Isaiah to say, "Set thine house in order; for thou shalt die, and not live" (II Kings 20:1). Heze-

kiah turned his face toward the wall and prayed. "And
Hezekiah wept sore" (vs. 3). Then the Lord called Isaiah
and sent him again to say to the sick king, "I have heard thy
prayer, I have seen thy tears: behold, . . . I will add unto thy
days fifteen years" (vss. 5, 6). We do well if we weep sometimes when we pray. And certainly, if we want God's help,
we need to weep when we try to keep people out of Hell.

I remember in my early ministry I preached on Psalm
126:5, 6: "They that sow in tears shall reap in joy. He that
goeth forth and weepeth, bearing precious seed, shall
doubtless come again with rejoicing, bringing his sheaves
with him." I wondered why the Lord there should outline
the conditions of soul winning as going, and weeping, and
using the precious seed, the Word of God, but not mention
the enduement of Holy Spirit power. How strange that this
great, indispensible equipment, the power of the Holy Spirit, should not be mentioned in that verse which tells how to
win souls! But the Spirit spoke to my heart and taught me
a lesson. The broken heart, which goes forth weeping over
sinners as it uses the Word to win them, has already met the
requirements for the fullness of the Spirit. The blessed Holy
Spirit has an affinity for the broken heart! The blessed
Holy Spirit can speak better through tears than through the
complacent and well-poised personality of one who has
no deep burden of soul for the unsaved. I say all this to
show that there is little hope of God's putting His blessing,
the power of the Holy Spirit, upon our soul-winning efforts
unless we learn to weep, unless we learn to care with a holy
compassion for the souls of men.

*3. The Gospel Message Naturally Requires Compassion
for the Lost.*
There is a divine compatibility between the Gospel and
tears. The supreme sacrifice of the dear Lord Jesus, His
dying love, ought to melt our hearts. The story of how the
Saviour left Heaven, of His poverty, His humility, His be-

trayal, His bloody sweat in Gethsemane, His dying agony on the cross, are such themes as cannot be discussed properly except with the deepest moving of the soul. What floodtides of love, of gratitude, of holy surrender, of glad service they awaken in the true believer!

In like fashion, the state of the lost as revealed in the Bible should drive any earnest Christian to tears and to the extreme effort to win people. The word *lost* describes the sinner. No little child lost in the mountain among wild beasts is in the pitiful condition of a lost sinner headed for Hell. No ship lost at sea without compass or without engine, with sails blown away in a storm and outside the traffic lanes of the sea, blown off her course and drifting the voyagers know not where, is in as pitiful a state as one who is lost to God, lost to Heaven, lost to forgiveness and salvation and everlasting blessedness! If a mother should weep over her lost baby, if a young bride should weep over her soldier husband missing in action, why should not a Christian weep over a lost soul?

Think of the terminology of the rich man in Hell—"I am tormented in this flame." He begged for only a finger dipped in water to cool his tongue. And the same man, I suppose, has gone on these nineteen hundred years since Jesus first told the story, and has never yet had a drop of water to cool his parched tongue. He has never yet had the word of forgiveness to cleanse his vile heart and appease his burning conscience. Any Christian who says he believes all the Bible, who believes that people are saved when they put their trust in Christ, who believes that people are lost if they reject Christ and will not repent of their sins, ought to learn to weep over sinners. Any Christian who says he believes that a poor, doomed sinner after rejecting Christ and dying impenitent must raise his fruitless cries in Hell forever, is proven a heartless wretch if he does not care with a deep, heartbroken compassion for lost souls! Think of eternity and what it means to the unsaved. Think of all that the sinner misses. Think of all the agony he suffers. Think of the sins whose memory hounds him, the opportunities whose neglect haunts him as he remembers them. Think of the loved ones he will never see again. Think of the open door of mercy once opened and, scorned, now closed forever. All the facts of the Gospel necessarily demand that a Christian have the deepest burden of soul to keep people out of Hell.

We hear it frequently said by lost sinners, "There are so many hypocrites in the church." Well, I am sorry to say that I fear they are right. No doubt there are many hypocrites in the church. One of the twelve apostles was a hypocrite. But no doubt many others are weak Christians who appear to the unsaved about us as hypocrites.

Do you know the one thing more than anything else that makes Christians appear like hypocrites? I think it is not the worldliness which is too prevalent in the churches. I think it is not the careless habits, the worldly amusements. Rather, I believe that unsaved people sense what they do not fully understand nor put into words, that if Christians were what they ought to be and what they often claim to be, they could not be indifferent about such holy matters as the salvation of sinners. I think that lost sinners everywhere know that if there is a Heaven to gain and a Hell to shun; if death and eternity and salvation and damnation are the themes of such magnitude as the Gospel of Christ teaches, then surely every born-again child of God should weep over sinners and with a holy abandon pay any price to keep poor, doomed sinners out of Hell! Indifference, lukewarmness on this matter of winning souls, cannot but brand a Christian as a backslider and as unspiritual and unsurrendered!

4. Concern for Sinners Is Put in the Heart of New Converts By the Holy Spirit.

We are trying to show that a holy compassion for sinners, a heart burden for their salvation, comes naturally to spiritual Christians. One of the best evidences of this is the fact that new converts, however untaught they may be in theology, usually have a deep concern for the salvation of loved ones and friends from the very first.

I found Christ when I was about nine years old, in the First Baptist Church of Gainsville, Texas. The Lord had been after me, then, for years. But on a Sunday morning the beloved pastor preached on the prodigal son. When the invitation was given to accept Christ as Saviour, I slid off the pew, walked down the aisle, and took the preacher's hand. I was not taught much of the Word. I am sorry that no one took time to show me the Scriptures and make the assurance of my salvation clear by the Word of God. But I went home that day glad in the Lord.

My father, a country Baptist preacher and one of the best men in the world, was out preaching that morning and was not present when I found the Lord. So when I saw him, I immediately asked him if I could join the church. I had no words to explain what had happened in my heart. My father did not know that for five years the Lord had been speaking to me—through my mother on her deathbed, through a Sunday School teacher, and through a deep conviction of sin. So my father said, "Well, Son, when you are really convicted of your sin and repent, and are regenerated, then will be time enough to join the church." I did not know what all those big words meant, but I simply knew that my father did not think I was saved. My father was, I was sure, the smartest man in the world. If he did not think I was saved, then I supposed I was not. But the next morning as I started to school, I stopped in the creek bottom under a willow tree and prayed. I asked the dear Saviour if, since I was too young to be saved, He would not save others anyway. So many were lost!

For three years I did not overcome the discouragement I received about my own salvation. Then one day I found that one who trusts in Christ has everlasting life. How sweet were John 3:36 and John 5:24 when I found them, at the age of twelve, and knew that when I had trusted Christ, I was really born again. But I now know that all the evidences of a new heart were manifest when I had that deep concern for sinners. If I had but known it, my earnest prayer that others might be saved was the best evidence that I myself had found the Saviour, the seeking Saviour who loves sinners and puts that love into the hearts of those who trust Him.

In Spearman, Texas, I once had revival services. The French war bride of an American soldier attended the services. She was a Catholic, very devout and religious, though she had never heard the Gospel of salvation by faith in Christ. Yet she came with her husband to the services and, of course, she always claimed to be a Christian. One day I preached on, "Ye Must Be Born Again" and made very, very plain that no matter how religious and prayerful, how moral and outwardly good one might be, he still must have a new heart or be lost forever. That day she did not raise her hand as a Christian. Instead, when our heads were all bowed, she lifted a hand to seek prayer. Then she slipped away from the service. But that afternoon she brought her husband to see me. She must have this matter of her soul's salvation settled. I remember how quaint was her broken English and how eager she was to know the whole matter of salvation. When I read the Scriptures and explained them to her, it was all clear and she was ready to ask the Lord Jesus to come into her heart and save her soul. I suggested that we kneel to pray. She said, "But I always pray in French. I don't speak English very well; I don't know how to pray in English." I assured her that God understood French and it would be all right to confess her sins and tell the Lord Jesus that she would trust Him as her own Saviour, speaking in French. How tearful, how earnest, how glad was that prayer claiming Christ as her Saviour, beseeching Him, then thanking Him for salvation!

We arose from our knees, and since I had an appointment to talk to two young men who were lost, I excused myself. I remember that the young couple went out the gate together. They turned one way and I went the other. Then she called, left her husband, and came running back up the sidewalk. With tears streaming down her face, she took my hand in both of hers and said, "Oh, I do pray that you will be able to win those two young men!" The blessed Saviour had put some of His own compassion for sinners into the heart of this new convert. That goes to show how natural, how fitting, how inevitable it is that any Christian who is really near the Lord and led by the Spirit of God has a holy compassion and concern for sinners.

It may be that one reads this who does not have any soul burden for sinners. It may be that you do not know what it is to wet your pillow with tears in the night, sleeplessly pleading with God to save some dear one. It may be you do not know how to pray for sinners because you have no burden for them. It may be you do not know how to speak to them because you do not have the urgency of heart, the travail of soul, that makes one speak even with blundering words sometimes, if one can do no better, to keep people from eternal ruin. Then, dear Christian, I ask you to consider whether or not you are just a backslider. Have you not lost your first love? Where is that heart union with Christ that would make you love what He loves, want what He wants, and be ceaselessly concerned about poor souls for whom He died? How can anyone claim to be a good Christian if he does not have a genuine burden of soul for sinners?

II. Great Bible Examples of Soul-Winning Compassion

We are not surprised to find in the Bible that the great men of God were men of tears. Those who had most power with God and most usefulness with men knew the broken heart, the burden of soul for sinners about which we write.

1. Consider the Compassion of Moses for Israel.

"By faith Moses, when he was come to years, refused to be called the son of Pharaoh's daughter; Choosing rather to suffer affliction with the people of God, than to enjoy the pleasures of sin for a season."—Heb. 11:24, 25.

Exodus 2:11 tells us, "And it came to pass in those days, when Moses was grown, that he went out unto his brethren, and looked on their burdens. . . ." Moses was reared in a palace and they were slaves, but "he went out unto his brethren, and looked on their burdens." He was in line for the throne, but when he saw his people beaten by taskmasters, he took his side with them and killed an Egyptian who was beating a Jew. Then he ran for his life. After forty years God brought Moses back to Egypt to lead the people of Israel out of bondage. On Mount Sinai God gave Moses laws for the people. But when he came down from the mount, he found the people naked, drunken, dancing about a golden calf in shameless idolatry. Moses took vigorous steps to correct the sin and punish the people, then went back up to stand in the breach before God lest God should destroy the nation, the people whom Moses loved so well! That story is told in Exodus 32.

Before Moses came down from the mount, "the Lord said unto Moses, I have seen this people, and, behold, it is a stiffnecked people: Now therefore let me alone, that my wrath may wax hot against them, and that I may consume them: and I will make of thee a great nation" (vss. 9, 10). But Moses pleaded with God, claimed God's promises, reminded God of His own good name which would be hurt if He should destroy these Jews. "And the Lord repented of the evil which he thought to do unto his people" (vs. 14). All this happened on the mount before Moses came down. Then after Moses came and disciplined the people, he returned to the mountain to pray. We can see the broken heart of Moses as he faces the people and then faces God.

"And it came to pass on the morrow, that Moses said unto the people, Ye have sinned a great sin: and now I will go up unto the Lord; peradventure I shall make an atonement for your sin. And Moses returned unto the Lord, and said, Oh, this people have sinned a great sin, and have made them gods of gold. Yet now, if thou wilt forgive their sin—; and if not, blot me, I pray thee, out of thy book which thou hast written."—Exod. 32:30-32.

It is hard to put in cold type the broken heart of Moses for his people. But notice that broken place in the sentence where Moses said in verse 32, "Yet now, if thou wilt forgive their sin—." I think that dash means that Moses stopped to weep. I think his words were broken words because his heart was broken over his people. God offered to make Moses the great nation that He had promised. But Moses said, "No! If you blot out this people, then blot me out of your plans, too. If you will not take them to the land of Canaan and make of them a great nation, then you are not to take me and my family and make of us a great nation. I am one with my people." And God relented and forgave the people; then upon further intercession by Moses, God brought back the pillar of fire and cloud to the midst of the camp and led them into the Promised Land. Only the loving compassion of Moses prevented God from destroying the nation.

Does God have someone to stand in the breach and keep away destruction from your town, your city, your state, your nation?

2. Jeremiah Was the Weeping Prophet.

He said, "Oh that my head were waters, and mine eyes a fountain of tears, that I might weep day and night for the slain of the daughter of my people!" (Jer. 9:1). He wrote the book of Lamentations as well as the book called by his name. His many tears and his burden of soul mean that his very name has become a synonym for the broken heart. A tearful complaint, a prophecy of doom, is called a jeremiad. Jeremiah preached plainly against the sins of Israel in the days preceding their captivity and following it. But he loved the people. He warned them and wept over them. When the captivity came, he stayed with the remnant. When they insisted on going down to Egypt, he warned them of the disaster that would come, but went with them. Jeremiah had a broken heart. He knew the burden of soul for lost sinners.

3. Queen Esther Fasted and Prayed and Then Risked Her Life to Save Her People.

The book of Esther is one of the most beautiful books in the Bible, though strangely enough, the word *God* is not mentioned. Yet it is full of God's tender care of His people, of answered prayer, of the blessings of God on the righteous.

Wicked Haman hated Mordecai and so set out to have all the Jews destroyed. Haman was the favorite of the great king, Ahasuerus, and so had the decree signed that every Jew was to be slaughtered.

But Queen Esther and her maidens fasted and prayed and then came before the king to plead for the Jews. The rule was that if one came before the king uninvited, he should be killed unless the king in mercy held out the golden sceptre. But Esther came, found mercy, and then pleaded for her people who were to be destroyed: "For how can I endure to see the evil that shall come unto my people? or how can I endure to see the destruction of my kindred?" (Esther 8:6).

How good it would be if we like Esther would come to the place where we feel we could not endure to see the destruction, the eternal destruction of those we love and of neighbors about us!

4. Reuben and Judah, Sinful Men, Yet Were Strangely Moved With Great Compassion for Their Brothers.

Joseph's elder brothers hated him and rejected him.

Reuben was not a strong character, but he did not want to break his father's heart, and he kept the other brothers from killing Joseph and intended to deliver him to his father again. But alas, Ishmaelites came and the other brothers sold Joseph into slavery. When Reuben found that the boy was gone, he was heartbroken. "And Reuben returned unto the pit; and, behold, Joseph was not in the pit; and he rent his clothes. And he returned unto his brethren, and said, The child is not; and I, whither shall I go?" (Gen. 37: 29, 30).

A like tender case is that of Judah's feeling about the child Benjamin. He had been surety to old Jacob for the baby boy. When Joseph said that he would keep Benjamin in Egypt, Judah came and interceded. He said that he knew his old father would die if the boy did not return. He offered to become a servant, a bondslave himself, so that Benjamin could be released and sent home to the fond father. "For how shall I go up to my father, and the lad be not with me? lest peradventure I see the evil that shall come on my father" (Gen. 44:34).

Oh, when we think of how the dear Lord Jesus loves sinners, how can we bear to come and face Him and leave loved ones, and even those unknown, but dear to Him, to die in their sins?

5. Deacon Stephen Was Like His Saviour in Compassion for Sinners.

This Spirit-filled man, "full of faith, and of the Holy Ghost," preached with great power and won multitudes. Even the Jewish leaders ". . . were not able to resist the wisdom and the spirit by which he spake" (Acts 6:10). So powerful was his testimony and his preaching that they determined upon his death. He was arrested, brought before the council, and there preached a great sermon, recorded in Acts 7. Many things about Stephen remind us of the Lord Jesus whom he trusted and loved as we do. He was so filled with the Spirit that sinners could not answer him, so they hated him and determined to kill him. "When they heard these things, they were cut to the heart, and they gnashed on him with their teeth" (vs. 54). Psalm 22 says about Jesus, "They gaped upon me with their mouths, as a ravening and a roaring lion" (vs. 13). Perhaps Stephen and Jesus received the same treatment here. Then they dragged Stephen out of the city to stone him. Stephen was the first Christian martyr, the first person to die for Jesus, after the crucifixion. The Lord Jesus on the cross had said, "Father, into thy hands I commend my spirit" (Luke 23:46). And Stephen died, "calling upon God, and saying, Lord Jesus, receive my spirit" (Acts 7:59). On the cross Jesus had prayed, "Father, forgive them; for they know not what they do" (Luke 23:34), and Stephen, beaten with stones, dizzy, and about to die, "kneeled down, and cried with a loud voice, Lord, lay not this sin to their charge" (Acts 7:60). Even in his death Stephen begged for the forgiveness of those who killed him. He learned the compassionate heart from the Saviour he loved. I hope we may do the same.

6. Paul the Apostle Is an Outstanding New Testament Example of Soul-Winning Compassion for Sinners.

I had long supposed that Paul was a tremendous preacher, mighty and eloquent. I imagined that the multiplied thousands saved in his ministry, which changed the complexion of the whole Roman Empire, were evidence of Paul's pulpit eloquence. However, I learned that I was mistaken. Paul was not counted a great preacher even in his own day. Second Corinthians 10:10, speaking of Paul, says, "For his letters, say they, are weighty and powerful; but his bodily presence is weak, and his speech contemptible." Paul did not have the gift of fluent speech. His delivery was, perhaps, uninteresting. He was not magnetic in personality. His bodily presence was weak and his speech was contemptible in the eyes and ears of those who heard him. No, Paul had some other secret besides human eloquence and personal magnetism. He had the power of God!

But how was this power of the Holy Spirit manifested in Paul? It was manifested in a holy earnestness, in a broken-hearted burden for sinners. Paul was a weeping preacher, a weeping personal worker.

"I say the truth in Christ," he says. "I lie not, my conscience also bearing me witness in the Holy Ghost, That I have great heaviness and continual sorrow in my heart. For I could wish that myself were accursed from Christ for my brethren, my kinsmen according to the flesh" (Rom. 9:1-3). Paul had a deep sorrow in his heart, great heaviness over lost sinners. He could have wished himself accursed from Christ to see others saved. That was the secret of Paul's success.

For three tremendous years Paul had wrought at Ephesus. He had won hundreds and, we suppose, even thousands of souls. In the great church there were many elders, most of them won by Paul himself. After ministering elsewhere, Paul returned to Miletus, the little seaport town near Ephesus, and called for the elders of the church to meet him. There on the sands he gave them solemn warning. He reminded them of how blamelessly he had preached the whole Gospel. "Ye know," he said, "from the first day that I came into Asia, after what manner I have been with you at all seasons, Serving the Lord with all humility of mind, *and with many tears*, and temptations, which befell me by the lying in wait of the Jews: And how I kept back nothing that was profitable unto you, but have shewed you, and have taught you publicly, and from house to house" (Acts 20:18-20). Paul was going up to Jerusalem he said, and knew that there bonds and imprisonment awaited him. And none of these things moved him; he was ready to die, he said, but warned them, "Wherefore I take you to record this day, that I am pure from the blood of all men" (vs. 26). These preachers must take heed to themselves. "Therefore watch, and remember, that by the space of three years I ceased not to warn every one *night and day with tears,"* he said (Acts 20:31). Paul had served the Lord "with tears," he reminded these preachers. He had gone publicly from house to house. He had gone "night and day with tears." I would that God would call together every ministerial association so that some Paul could come among us and warn preachers to preach night and day with tears, as we go publicly from house to house.

We see, then, the secret of Paul's great ministry. His holy compassion led him to stoning, to fight the wild beasts in Ephesus, to risk his life again and again, to suffer long years in jail with a chain on his wrists, and then to die, beheaded in Rome. You see, one who is as burdened for sinners as Paul was does not mind suffering or dying to get sinners saved.

7. The Lord Jesus Himself Is the Supreme Example of Soul-Winning Compassion.

Webster's dictionary says, "COMPASSION . . . Literally suffering with another; fellowship in feeling; hence, sorrow or pity excited by the distress for misfortunes of another; commiseration; sympathy. . . ." Jesus, who never knew sin, entered into the sufferings of our sins. Jesus, who as the mighty God created the heavens and the earth, at the word of the Father humbled Himself and took on Himself the form of a servant, was born of a woman, nursed at a woman's breast, lived in a home of poverty in an obscure village, grew up to be despised and rejected of men, and died a shameful death on the cross. All this was a picture of the love of the Lord Jesus for sinners and the holiest urgency with which His heart longed to save them.

Many times in the New Testament the "compassion" of the dear Lord Jesus is mentioned.

"But when he saw the multitudes, he was moved with compassion on them, because they fainted, and were scat-

tered abroad, as sheep having no shepherd."—Matt. 9:36.

"And Jesus went forth, and saw a great multitude, and was moved with compassion toward them, and he healed their sick."—Matt. 14:14.

"Then Jesus called his disciples unto him, and said, I have compassion on the multitude, because they continue with me now three days, and have nothing to eat: and I will not send them away fasting, lest they faint in the way."—Matt. 15:32.

"So Jesus had compassion on them, and touched their eyes: and immediately their eyes received sight, and they followed him."—Matt. 20:34.

"And Jesus, moved with compassion, put forth his hand, and touched him, and saith unto him, I will; be thou clean."—Mark 1:41.

"And Jesus, when he came out, saw much people, and was moved with compassion toward them, because they were as sheep not having a shepherd: and he began to teach them many things."—Mark 6:34.

"I have compassion on the multitude, because they have now been with me three days, and have nothing to eat."—Mark 8:2.

"And when the Lord saw her, he had compassion on her, and said unto her, Weep not."—Luke 7:13.

Again and again the yearning heart of the Lord Jesus was moved with compassion when He saw lost people around Him. They were like sheep having no shepherd. Let no one think that God the Father drove Jesus, the Son, to the cross. The Lord Jesus came to this world to die, brought by brokenhearted love. He had exactly the same spirit every day of His ministry as He had when He hung on the cross and prayed, "Father, forgive them; for they know not what they do" (Luke 23:34).

In Luke 19:41 we are told that when Jesus was come near, "he beheld the city, and wept over it." What a sight for men and angels! The Son of God, the Creator, weeping over a city that hates Him and rejects Him and will kill Him! That is the kind of spirit that Christians must emulate. As our Saviour feels burden of soul for sinners and weeps over them, may we too learn to weep!

If anyone who reads this longs to please the Saviour, then I know well what will please Him. You have but to keep sinners out of Hell. You have but to take them the message, life-transforming and soul-saving, that Jesus offers them forgiveness and mercy. But you need to go with the same holy concern and pleading tears which the Saviour Himself knew so well. Now at the right hand of God, the Lord Jesus loves sinners the same way. In Heaven they ring the joybells, start the Hallelujah chorus, and praise God aloud when a sinner on earth repents and is saved. "I say unto you, that likewise joy shall be in heaven over one sinner that repenteth, more than over ninety and nine just persons, which need no repentance" (Luke 15:7). How strange for Christians to be so absorbed in things that do not interest Heaven! How strange for Christians to be like ungodly people, thinking mainly of food for the belly and clothes for the back and new model cars and hardwood floors and tile baths and fine clothes and sumptuous dinners, when the dear Lord Jesus has such holy concern to keep people out of Hell!

We may be concerned about place and salary, honor and ease and security. The Lord Jesus is concerned about having every place filled at the heavenly wedding banquet! The Lord Jesus says to us what the lord said to his servant in the parable, "Go out into the highways and hedges, and compel them to come in, that my house may be filled" (Luke 14:23).

I think that if we ever get the concern that we ought to have for sinners, we will care less what men think, and with

Christ-given compassion we will plead with men and women and children and persuade them and will compel them by one means or another, with our pleading and our tears and our holy urgency, to come to Christ.

After graduating from Baylor University, I was an instructor in Wayland College and later did graduate work in the University of Chicago. There I visited the Pacific Garden Mission and God helped me to win an old drunken bum and laid on my heart the great privilege and duty of preaching the Gospel. I gave up my plans, resigned my contract as a college teacher, and began the gospel ministry. I entered seminary.

I had been an active layman. I had been a college debater, had won a scholarship in oratory, had given high school commencement addresses, had made speeches for the Red Cross. So when I gave myself in answer to God's gracious call, I thought, "Well, this is right down my alley! I'll prepare a sermon as I prepared a college debate speech or an oration." I planned to get all my material together, to perfectly digest it, to organize it and outline it. My debate speeches I would write out in full, then memorize them and practice them before the mirror. So I gained a certain fluency and assurance. I thought I had learned how to speak. I had spent three years in the study of speech and had a good deal of experience.

But in spite of all my foolish notions, I had, planted in my heart by the blessed Holy Spirit, a deep concern for the salvation of souls. So when I began to preach, I stood before the congregation and wept. I forgot my outline and pleaded with sinners to be saved. With holy urgency and with arguments and Scriptures that I had not called to mind until they were brought to my remembrance by the Holy Spirit in the pulpit, I begged men to come to Christ and be saved. This was not the polished, carefully-prepared speaking of the literary society, of the college debate, of the commencement address. This was impassioned pleading for men. I went away from a service somewhat shamed. I said to myself, "That doesn't sound like a college teacher. That doesn't sound like a trained speaker. I cried like an ignorant beginner!" I asked God to let me speak with more dignity, and He did. I went back to the pulpit later with a well-prepared message, and followed my outline through. But the thing was dead. My own heart had no response to the message. My words were correct words, but there was no holy passion in them. I could hardly get through the message, for I had no joy in my heart over the matter. The Gospel was like dust and ashes in my mouth, and when I left the pulpit I felt that I could wish I would never have to preach again!

I went back to my room and begged God to give me the broken heart. I promised God that without thought for dignity or the praises of men I chose to have the boldness and urgency and consciousness of His presence that comes with soul-winning compassion. God gave me back the tears. Praise Him, I have preached with tears these long years. I have talked to tens of thousands of individuals, talked with trembling lips, with tears in my eyes and with a pain in my heart. I have come to believe that cold-hearted preaching and cold-hearted personal testimony is sinful, presumptuous, wicked, and unchristian. O God, forgive us for our matter-of-fact attitude toward a sinning world and a yawning Hell and the torment of flames and the eternal damnation that sin brings to the impenitent!

Modernism does not begin with the denial of the deity of Jesus Christ, His blood atonement and His bodily resurrection, nor with the denial of the infallible accuracy of the Scripture. Real modernism begins in the heart with a coldness that has no tears over sinners and has no holy and melting compassion to make us do the will of God in winning them. A man has gone wrong in his heart before he goes wrong in his head. The danger of the church today is not primarily modernism of doctrine, but the wicked modernism that precedes the falling away in doctrine. The danger is that coldness of heart which is essentially unchristian and denies all the sentiment and heart of the Gospel because it does not weep over lost sinners and urgently, at any cost, seek to save them.

7. "Power From on High"

"And, behold, I send the promise of my Father upon you: but tarry ye in the city of Jerusalem, until ye be endued with power from on high."—Luke 24:49.

But ye shall receive power, after that the Holy Ghost is come upon you: and ye shall be witnesses unto me both in Jerusalem, and in all Judea, and in Samaria, and unto the uttermost part of the earth."—Acts 1:8.

". . . And he shall be filled with the Holy Ghost, even from his mother's womb. And many of the children of Israel shall he turn to the Lord their God."—Luke 1:15, 16.

"And when they had prayed, the place was shaken where they were assembled together; and they were all filled with the Holy Ghost, and they spake the word of God with boldness."—Acts 4:31.

"For he was a good man, and full of the Holy Ghost and of faith: and much people was added unto the Lord."—Acts 11:24.

AT NORTHFIELD, Massachusetts, a multitude gathered around an open grave on a hill called Little Round Top. There was a mingling of sadness and glory, of tears and blessing, as the body of D. L. Moody was to be laid away. But the loss could not erase the gain, for this humble lay preacher had won a million souls to Christ.

141

At the funeral Dr. C. I. Scofield said: "He was baptized with the Holy Spirit, and he knew it!"

How can one explain D. L. Moody? How could this man without even high school training hold the multitudes spellbound, and break the hardest hearts, and turn hundreds of thousands to the Lord? How could he build institutions, revive churches, and change the lives of thousands of preachers? There is one simple answer—the breath of God was upon him! He was endued with power from on high. He was filled with the Holy Spirit. His power was supernatural power.

Satan has taken great advantage of God's people in getting us to put second things first. However useful education and money and personality and human influence and organization may be and sometimes are, they are still secondary and even incidental in comparison with the main thing, the power of God! Believe me, oh thou would-be soul winner, there is no equipment, no training, no methods that will give you success in soul winning without the mighty power of the Holy Spirit upon your testimony!

Good men, we believe, have often been misled into putting a false emphasis on what happened at Pentecost. Satan no doubt has in mind to obscure the one principal lesson God meant us to learn there. If soul winning is the main purpose and concern of God, we may be sure that to hinder soul winning is Satan's chief object. So he constantly seeks to confuse Christians about the power of the Holy Spirit, the enduement of power from on high. He turns people back with the fear of fanaticism, the fear of being queer. He causes them to miss God's emphasis by distracting their attention.

Thousands, when they think of Pentecost, assume wrongly that it was simply a dispensational matter, never to be repeated and having only doctrinal importance. They are wrong. In the first place, the day Jesus rose from the dead He breathed on the disciples and said, "Receive ye the Holy

Ghost" (John 20:22). So the indwelling of the Spirit promised when Christ should be glorified (John 7:37-39) was fulfilled on the day of the resurrection, and not at Pentecost.

In the second place, if the church, the body of Christ, began at Pentecost, then the Bible never mentions it. In fact, that "general assembly and church of the firstborn, which are written in heaven," of Hebrews 12:22, 23, seems certainly to contain all who will be called out at the rapture, including Old Testament saints, too—all "whose names are written in heaven."

Others think of Pentecost as a "second work of grace" when God's people were "sanctified" or given "perfect love," and "had the sin principle eradicated." Now there is a Bible holiness, and it is important, though I would differ with those who think God's people may have all the carnal nature removed now. But holiness is not the meaning of Pentecost. No, neither the tongues, nor those visible "tongues like as of fire" that sat upon the disciples, nor the sound of the rushing mighty wind, nor any other of the incidental trappings which God used at Pentecost—none of these are the meaning of Pentecost.

God has a meaning for us in His account of Pentecost. It is simply that the apostles and the women and others were commanded to "tarry ye in the city of Jerusalem, until ye be endued with power from on high." And they did tarry; "these all continued with one accord in prayer and supplication, with the women, and Mary the mother of Jesus, and with his brethren" until the day of Pentecost was fully come, and then they were all filled with the Spirit and that day, in God's power, they saw some three thousand people turn to Christ and added to them! It was true as Jesus promised in Acts 1:8, "But ye shall receive power, after that the Holy Ghost is come upon you: and ye shall be witnesses unto me. . . ." As prophesied in Joel 2:28-32, it came to pass that God poured out the Holy Spirit on all kinds of people, and they prophesied or witnessed and people heard and were saved.

I. All Bible Soul Winners Had a Special Enduement of Power From on High

The Bible uses several terms in referring to the special enduement of power in soul winning. For example, in referring to the enduement of power which came upon the disciples at Pentecost, the Bible uses the following terms:

"Baptized with the Holy Ghost" (Acts 1:5).

"Ye shall receive power" (Acts 1:8).

"Filled with the Holy Ghost" (Acts 2:4).

"I will pour out of my Spirit" (Acts 2:17, 18).

"This Jesus . . . hath shed forth this, which ye now see and hear" (Acts 2:32, 33).

"The gift of the Holy Ghost" (Acts 2:38).

"These . . . have received the Holy Ghost as well as we" (Acts 10:47).

"And as I began to speak, the Holy Ghost fell on them, as on us at the beginning. Then remembered I the word of the Lord, how that he said, John indeed baptized with water; but ye shall be baptized with the Holy Ghost" (Acts 11: 15, 16).

The usual term for the enduement of power from on high is "filled with the Spirit." That is used of John the Baptist in Luke 1:15, of Peter in Acts 4:8, of all the disciples (Acts 4:13), etc., and in the command to all of us in Ephesians 5:18. Ananias came and laid his hands on Saul "that thou mightest receive thy sight, and be filled with the Holy Ghost" (Acts 9:17). And in Acts 10:47 Peter said that Cornelius and his household "received the Holy Ghost as well as we." In Acts 19:2 Paul asked certain disciples, "Have ye received the Holy Ghost since ye believed?" I assure you that in all these cases, the Scripture speaks of an enduement of power from on high. Elsewhere it is called an *anointing*, and we believe that the anointing of King David and the anointing of Aaron the high priest symbolized the same pouring of the Holy Spirit upon them as they typified the Lord Jesus, coming King and Priest.

There are other ministries of the Holy Spirit which in some measure every Christian shares. All Christians have the Holy Spirit dwelling in their bodies. He is the Comforter, the Guide in understanding the Scriptures. He is the prayer helper. In some measure every born-again Christian has the ministries of the Spirit. But the fullness of the Spirit, the anointing of the Spirit, the power of the Holy Spirit, is an enduement of power for soul winning!

1. The Apostles and Others at Pentecost Were Endued With Power From on High for Soul Winning.

The eleven disciples and others who waited with them had a clear command from the Lord Jesus: it was that they were to be witnesses, and repentance or remission of sin was to be preached in all nations beginning at Jerusalem, but they were plainly warned, "But tarry ye in the city of Jerusalem, until ye be endued with power from on high" (Luke 24:49). They wanted to talk with Jesus about His return and the regathering of Israel and the restoration of the kingdom, but He turned them away from that. The Father had kept that in His own power, "But ye shall receive power," He said, "after that the Holy Ghost is come upon you: and ye shall be witnesses unto me both in Jerusalem, and in all Judea, and in Samaria, and unto the uttermost part of the earth" (Acts 1:8). And the Apostle Peter, when the flood tide of power came upon them all, stood up and reminded his hearers that this pouring out of the Holy Spirit on all kinds of people—old men and young men, sons and daughters, servants and handmaidens—was prophesied in Joel 2:28-32, "And they shall prophesy."

So the anointing of the Holy Spirit was given that they might prophesy, that is, witness for Jesus, whether in public or private, whether to a few or many; and that prophecy concluded, "And whosoever shall call on the name of the Lord shall be saved." The fullness of the Holy Spirit is for witnessing, and the witnessing is for soul winning. What God has joined together, let not man put asunder.

At Pentecost they were filled with the Spirit, they witnessed with power, three thousand people were saved. Everything else at Pentecost was incidental besides this fact that now, in the beginning of carrying out the Great Commission, the disciples received soul-winning power and saw a multitude saved.

2. But the Same Christians on Another Occasion Prayed Again, and Were Endued With Power Again, and Won Souls Again.

So many feel that Pentecost was a never-to-be-repeated occasion. The simple truth is that it was repeated again a few days later. Acts 4:31 says, "And when they had prayed, the place was shaken where they were assembled together; and they were all filled with the Holy Ghost, and they spake the word of God with boldness." The same people prayed again. Again, they were filled with the Holy Spirit. The same nine words are used in Acts 2:4 and in Acts 4:13, "And they were all filled with the Holy Ghost." It is only fair to believe that the same thing happened. In each case the disciples received an enduement of power. In each case they spoke for God. And in each case the result of their bold witnessing was the salvation of souls. So what a soul winner needs is not simply one grand experience that will forever equip him for all the future in soul winning. No, rather the soul winner needs to learn to come again and again to the fountain and drink deep. He needs to come again and again before the throne of God in penitent waiting and pleading till God gives power for the work He commands us to do. The disciples could be filled with the Holy Spirit at Pentecost and could witness with great power. Then they could pray again a few days later and be filled with the Holy

Ghost again, and could witness with boldness and power again. And so may we.

3. John the Baptist, Being Filled With the Spirit, Won Many.

The ministry of John the Baptist was peculiar in that he was filled with the Holy Ghost from his mother's womb. He was filled with the Spirit in the first instance as a result of the fervent, believing prayers of Zacharias and Elizabeth, his father and mother, for thirty years or more. In later years the power of God was upon him because he himself sought that power, of course.

But the Scripture clearly connects the fullness of the Spirit and soul-winning power in Luke 1:15, 16: "For he shall be great in the sight of the Lord, and shall drink neither wine nor strong drink; and he shall be filled with the Holy Ghost, even from his mother's womb. And many of the children of Israel shall he turn to the Lord their God."

He should be filled with the Holy Ghost, "and many of the children of Israel shall he turn to the Lord their God," the angel told Zacharias. "And he shall go before him in the spirit and power of Elias . . ." (vs. 17). Here it is suggestive and interesting to note that the same power that was on John the Baptist was on Elijah in the Old Testament. That mighty prophet of God was filled with the Spirit. So while the indwelling of the Holy Spirit in the believer's body is a dispensational matter which Old Testament Christians did not know, yet the anointing, or the enduement of power for witnessing, was the same with Elijah and with John the Baptist, the same in the Old Testament and the New Testament.

4. Even the Lord Jesus Himself Never Won a Soul, Nor Worked a Miracle, Nor Preached a Sermon Till He Was Endued With the Power of the Holy Spirit.

In Luke 3:21, 22, we have the story of how when Jesus was baptized and prayed, "the Holy Ghost descended in a bodily shape like a dove upon him. . . ." And if we read carefully a harmony of the Gospels, we will find that up to this time Jesus had never had any act of public ministry. Later he went to Cana of Galilee and turned the water into wine at the wedding, and "this beginning of miracles did Jesus," we are told. Oh, even the Lord Jesus did not win souls without enduement from on high. And now after He was filled with the Spirit, He went back to the synagogue in Nazareth and read to the people Isaiah 61:1: "The Spirit of the Lord God is upon me; because the Lord hath anointed me to preach the gospel. . . ." And He said to them, "This day is this scripture fulfilled in your ears" (Luke 4:16-21). Jesus never preached until He was anointed to preach. He did not win souls until He was anointed to win souls. His power was the power of the Holy Spirit, which we, too, may have— yea, *must* have if we would win souls.

5. The Apostle Paul Saw and Received the Fullness of the Spirit and Immediately Began His Soul-Winning Ministry.

In Acts, chapter 9, we have the story of Paul's conversion on the road to Damascus. There he surrendered to Jesus Christ, called Him Lord, saying, "Lord, what wilt thou have me to do?" That there was penitence, faith, surrender, and salvation, we can have no doubt. And when Ananias came to him, he called him "Brother Saul." So Saul was converted when he met Jesus on the road.

But for three days he fasted and prayed. And what was he praying for? Ananias said, "The Lord, even Jesus, that appeared unto thee in the way as thou camest, hath sent me, that thou mightest receive thy sight, AND BE FILLED WITH THE HOLY GHOST" (Acts 9:17). And three verses later we read: "And straightway he preached Christ in the synagogues, that he is the Son of God." The burning, cutting words were so powerful and his testimony so strong that people set out to kill him. Thus Saul began that mighty

Spirit-filled ministry in which he won so many, many thousands to Christ!

6. Barnabas, too, Won Souls Because He Was "Full of the Holy Ghost."

In Acts 11:24 we have a revealing word about good old Barnabas: "For he was a good man, and full of the Holy Ghost and of faith: and much people was added unto the Lord."

There is a familiar ring to the words "full of the Holy Ghost . . . and much people was added unto the Lord." So it was with John the Baptist. So it was with Jesus. So it was with the apostles at Pentecost. So it was with all the same crowd in Acts 4:31. So it was with Paul, and so it was with Barnabas. The only way to be an effective soul winner is to have the power of God, to be endued with power from on high, to be filled with the Holy Spirit!

Mark you, I do not speak of signs. The Bible does not discuss any signs by which one may know when he is filled with the Holy Spirit. It speaks of one great result. If one is endued with power from on high, he can speak or witness for Jesus Christ with boldness; he has soul-winning power. When the apostles had three thousand souls at Pentecost, they did not need any signs to know that the promised power had come upon them.

How will you feel? I do not know. The Bible does not even discuss that. It is a mistake to be thinking about signs. God chose at Pentecost to have the sound of a rushing, mighty wind. He chose in Acts 4:31 to have an earthquake: "The place was shaken where they were assembled together." If one man understands English, then you need to preach the Gospel to him in English. If a man can understand only German, then you need to preach the Gospel to him in German. But the one central fact is that the Holy Spirit's enduement of power is given to witness for Jesus. The Holy Spirit is His own witness, His own evidence.

When He deals with the hearts of sinners, speaking through these lips of clay, that is enough. Why should anybody fret about signs and feelings and evidences and something to boast about and take pride in, aside from the one thing dearest to the heart of God, getting people saved? Is it not enough to rejoice about if people are kept out of Hell? Is it not enough sign of God's blessing if He saves souls and prospers the Word of God from your lips? Is it not a blessed plenty if He answers your prayer and saves those to whom you witness?

In a few spectacular cases like those of D. L. Moody and Charles G. Finney, the coming of the Holy Spirit in witnessing power was striking and definite and obvious. So it was in Acts 2:4 at Pentecost and in Acts 4:31 later when the same group was filled with the Holy Spirit again. But a man may be filled with the Spirit without any striking evidence other than soul-winning power, and he may not know just when that occurred except that God's power was on him to win souls.

That seems to have been the case with Apollos. We are plainly told that he was "mighty in the scriptures . . . instructed in the way of the Lord; and being fervent in the spirit, he spake and taught diligently the things of the Lord, knowing only the baptism of John" (Acts 18:24, 25). Note carefully he was "fervent in the spirit." That is, the fervor of the Holy Spirit's anointing was upon him. So many were saved. But he needed further instruction, and Aquila and Priscilla expounded to him the way of God more perfectly. And he did not himself understand the fullness of the Spirit which he obviously had, and in the next chapter we learn that some of the people he won to Christ did not understand the fullness of the Spirit either.

Barnabas was filled with the Holy Spirit but there is no mention of when that fullness began. John the Baptist was filled with the Holy Spirit, but he had no personal knowledge and remembrance of the thing since it was from his birth. The Bible does not mention that there is any sign, any special emotional experience in connection with being filled with the Holy Spirit. It is simply an enduement of power for witnessing. And if God gives souls saved, that ought to be evidence enough.

I have diligently thought back through my own life. When was I first filled with the Holy Spirit? Perhaps it was when a boy of fifteen, I first found the marvelous story of Pentecost in the book of Acts, and my heart was moved at the thought that one could have the mighty power of God and win many souls. I thought then, as now, that the one tremendous fact of Pentecost was that some three thousand people turned to Christ and were saved. I was led to pray for soul-winning power and soon won my first soul. So I think that the Holy Spirit came upon me in some measure then. I had no feeling about it except a concern to win souls. There were no signs or evidences, no emotional experience, except the deep compassion and burden for lost people.

The whole matter of looking to the emotions and looking inside instead of looking at poor lost sinners for whom Christ died and looking to God to give you the enablement and enduement to reach them—I say the looking inward for your own pleasures and feelings—is wrong. If you are really working to get people saved, you will rejoice when they are saved. If the end you seek is the salvation of sinners, then you will know when you have received what you seek, when you see them turn to Christ.

II. Great Soul Winners Have Had Supernatural Power

The great soul winners have all sought and had a special enduement of power of the Holy Spirit.

Some godly women told D. L. Moody they were praying for him to "have the power." He got concerned and for two years his heart was begging God for power. Then he tells us:

"My heart was not in the work of begging . . . . I could

not appeal. I was crying all the time that God would fill
me with His Spirit. Well, one day, in the city of New York
—oh, what a day!—I cannot describe it, I seldom refer to
it; it is almost too sacred an experience to name. Paul
had an experience of which he never spoke for fourteen
years. I can only say that God revealed Himself to me, and
I had such an experience of His love that I had to ask Him
to stay His hand. I went to preaching again. The sermons
were not different; I did not present any new truths, and
yet hundreds were converted. I would not now be placed
back where I was before that blessed experience if you
should give me all the world—it would be as the small dust
of the balance."

R. A. Torrey in the book, *The Holy Spirit: Who He Is,
and What He Does*, pages 107 and 108, says:

"The address of this afternoon, and the addresses of the
days immediately to follow, are the outcome of an experience, and that experience was the outcome of a study of the
Word of God. After I had been a Christian for some years,
and after I had been in the ministry for some years, my attention was strongly attracted to certain phrases found in
the Gospels and in the Acts of the Apostles, and in the
Epistles, such as 'baptized with the Holy Spirit,' 'filled with
the Spirit,' 'the Holy Spirit fell upon them,' 'the gift of the
Holy Spirit,' 'endued with power from on high,' and other
closely allied phrases. As I studied these various phrases in
their context, it became clear to me that they all stood for
essentially the same experience; and it also became clear to
me that God has provided for each child of His in this present dispensation that they should be thus 'baptized with the
Spirit,' or, 'filled with the Spirit.'

"As I studied the subject still further, I became convinced that they described an experience which I did not
myself possess, and I went to work to secure for myself the
experience thus described. I sought earnestly that I might
'be baptized with the Holy Spirit.' I went at it very ignor-

antly. I have often wondered if anyone ever went at it any more ignorantly than I did. But while I was ignorant, I was thoroughly sincere and in earnest, and God met me, as He always meets the sincere and earnest soul, no matter how ignorant he may be; and God gave me what I sought; I was 'baptized with the Holy Spirit.' And the result was a transformed Christian life and a transformed ministry."

Charles G. Finney, a wonderful soul winner in the first half of the nineteenth century, one of the greatest evangelists who ever lived, knew the power of the Holy Spirit and this is his testimony, as quoted by Dr. Oswald J. Smith in the book, *The Revival We Need.*

"I was powerfully converted on the morning of the 10th of October, 1821. In the evening of the same day I received overwhelming baptisms of the Holy Ghost, that went through me, as it seemed to me, body and soul. I immediately found myself endued with such power from on high that a few words dropped here and there to individuals were the means of their immediate conversion. My words seemed to fasten like barbed arrows in the souls of men. They cut like a sword. They broke the heart like a hammer. Multitudes can attest to this. Oftentimes a word dropped without my remembering it would fasten conviction, and often result in almost immediate conversion. Sometimes I would find myself, in a great measure, empty of this power. I would go and visit, and find that I made no saving impression. I would exhort and pray, with the same result. I would then set apart a day for private fasting and prayer, fearing that this power had departed from me, and would inquire anxiously after the reason of this apparent emptiness. After humbling myself, and crying out for help, the power would return upon me with all its freshness. This has been the experience of my life."

Dr. Homer Rodeheaver in the book *My Twenty Years With Billy Sunday* tells how Billy Sunday, no matter what sermon he would preach nor where, always opened his Bible to Isaiah 61:1, and then over the open Bible he laid his manuscript and notes and preached his sermon. Is it not wonderfully suggestive that Billy Sunday always had his Bible open at these words: "The Spirit of the Lord God is upon me; because the Lord hath anointed me to preach good tidings unto the meek; he hath sent me to bind up the brokenhearted, to proclaim liberty to the captives, and the opening of the prison to them that are bound"?

Oh, the testimony of all the mighty men of God is the same: we must have the power of the Holy Spirit if we would win souls.

I hope that the reader will get my book on *The Power of Pentecost or the Fullness of the Spirit,* 441 pages, and study thoroughly the clear Bible teaching on the subject.

III. How to Be Filled With the Holy Spirit

Every Christian may have the fullness of power for soul winning, and there are two simple requirements for that power.

1. Blessed Truth! The Gift of the Holy Ghost Is for Every Christian.

In Ephesians 5:18 we are all commanded: "And be not drunk with wine, wherein is excess; but be filled with the Spirit." If the command against drunkenness is for everyone, then the command to be filled with the Spirit is for everyone.

In Acts 2:38 and 39 Paul said. "And ye shall receive the gift of the Holy Ghost. For the promise is unto you, and to your children, and to all that are afar off, even as many as the Lord our God shall call." The convicted multitude had asked the apostles, "Men and brethren, what shall we do?" (Acts 2:37). I am sure they meant not only "What shall we do to be saved?" but "How can we have what you Christians have, the power and joy and testimony that God has given you?" So Peter told them what to do, not only for salvation, but including obedience that would bring the fullness of the Spirit. And the promise of the Holy Ghost was to all these and to their children and everybody afar off, everybody that God would call to salvation!

The very fact that the plain command to win souls is given every Christian in the Great Commission means, of course, that every Christian can have the power to win souls. The fullness of the Spirit is for every Christian.

At Pentecost we are told, "And they were ALL filled with the Holy Ghost" (Acts 2:4). Again, when the whole company of the disciples prayed, "they were ALL filled with the Holy Ghost" (Acts 4:31). The fullness of the Spirit is for every Christian.

2. The Power of the Holy Spirit Is Given Only to Obedient Witnesses.

In Acts 5:32 Peter said, "And we are his witnesses of these things; and so is also the Holy Ghost, whom God hath given to them that obey him." Will you note that there were two witnesses. First, there were the Christian witnesses. They obeyed God by going out to tell everywhere that Jesus had died for sinners and was risen from the dead and that thus, salvation was offered freely. And then to these obedient witnesses, God gave the Holy Ghost to bear witness also! So in the matter of witnessing for Christ, soul-winning effort, obedience is required if one is to have the power of the Holy Spirit.

There are other ministries of the Holy Spirit, but the fullness of the Spirit is a special enduement for witnessing. This anointing, this fullness, this baptism, is never given to make people happy. It is never given to burn out the carnal nature and sanctify people. It is never given except to obedient witnesses. "Ye shall receive power, after that the Holy Ghost is come upon you: and ye shall be witnesses unto me. . ." is the plain statement of Jesus in Acts 1:8. It is a false doctrine to disconnect these two that God has everywhere connected, that is, the power of the Holy Ghost and soul-winning witness. They go together.

But this book is on soul winning. I take it that the earnest reader intends and longs to win souls and wants to know how. Well, then listen carefully to the next requirement.

3. The Power of the Holy Spirit Is Given in Answer to Persistent Prayer.

In Luke, chapter 11, Jesus gave the lesson on importunate prayer in the story of the man who came to his friend's house at midnight saying, "Lend me three loaves; For a friend of mine in his journey is come to me, and I have nothing to set before him" (vss. 5, 6). Here the Christian is pictured pleading for all the power of the Father, Son and Holy Ghost in order to give the bread of life to a sinner with whom he is in touch. And Jesus said of the Father, "I say unto you, Though he will not rise and give him, because he is his friend, yet because of his importunity he will rise and give him as many as he needeth" (vs. 8). Then Jesus commanded us to "ask, and it shall be given you; seek, and ye shall find; knock, and it shall be opened unto you" (vs. 9). The verbs here are in the present tense. We are to keep on asking, keep on seeking, keep on knocking!

In Luke 11:13 Jesus said: "If ye then, being evil, know how to give good gifts unto your children: how much more shall your heavenly Father give the Holy Spirit to them that ask him?" The giving of the Holy Spirit here refers to the anointing, the enduement of power from on high, that we may take bread to sinners. I am saying that the Holy Spirit power is given in answer to prayer.

So it was when Jesus, standing in the waters of baptism and committing Himself to die, be buried in Joseph's tomb and rise again, prayed; and the Holy Spirit came upon Him.

The disciples went to that upper room and continued ten days in heartbroken prayer. I believe they did not even eat during that time. We are told, "These all continued with one accord in prayer and supplication, with the women, and Mary the mother of Jesus, and with his brethren" (Acts 1:14). The power of the Holy Spirit came in answer to prayer at Pentecost.

In Acts 4:31, the power of God came the same way: "And when they had prayed, the place was shaken where they were assembled together; and they were all filled with the Holy Ghost, and they spake the word of God with boldness."

Thus the soul winner's life should be a life of prayer. He should pray and pray for the power of God; then when God in mercy gives the power and souls are saved, he must expect that when another opportunity arises, he will need to pray again. Those who breathe out must breathe in again, if they would breathe out again.

A woman preacher said to me one time, "Brother Rice, I am praying that you will be filled with the Holy Ghost." I told her that I was glad she was praying for me, and that I pray more for the fullness of the Holy Spirit than for any other single thing. But I told her she might be disappointed when the fullness of the Spirit came upon me, and souls would be saved instead of my putting on some jabber in an "unknown tongue." Every Christian ought to pray daily for an enduement of power.

Paul reminded his people at Corinth that they were the epistle of Christ written "with the Spirit of the living God," and he could say, "But our sufficiency is of God: Who also hath made us able ministers of the new testament; not of the letter, but of the spirit: for the letter killeth, but the spirit giveth life" (II Cor. 3:5, 6).

"The letter killeth"! That means the letter of the Word of God itself is a deadening thing without the power of God! The Word of God is "the sword of the Spirit"; it is not my sword. It is like Goliath's sword, too heavy for me to handle. Oh, blessed Spirit of God, help the one who would win souls, and wield for him that mighty sword! The Spirit gives life, but the letter kills. Let every Christian remember that however much his knowledge of the Bible, it will not be effective or useful except as it is empowered by the blessed Holy Spirit.

IV. Will You Follow in the Train of All the Great Soul Winners Filled With the Holy Spirit?

You have seen how the great soul winners of the Bible were filled with the Holy Spirit. Read the biographies of the great men of God: Wesley, Spurgeon, Moody, Torrey, Charles G. Finney, J. Wilbur Chapman, Sam Jones, Bob Jones, Sr., Paul Rader. These all had a supernatural enduement. The marvels that God wrought through them were wrought through the Holy Spirit's using their minds, their voices, their handclasps, their tears, their pleadings.

Here is the time to get something settled in the heart of every reader. Will you now make a holy resolve that you will not go on without the power of the Holy Spirit? Will you now set out, under a holy contract with God, that you will not give up, that you will at any cost have the mighty power of God to help you win souls? God does not call everybody to preach to great crowds, but God wants everybody to speak to someone, to witness to someone, to win someone.

You will have to decide that if need be, you will be willing to be a fanatic. You will be willing to displease men in order to please God. You will be willing to put first things first, and lay aside incidental and secondary matters that you may seek and have the power of God, and that you may win souls.

It might well be that at this very point in this chapter, God means to change your entire life. I beg that today, with a holy resolution, you set out to seek and have the power of God on your soul-winning witness, and resolve that not only now, but again and again as a regular practice, you will seek the power of God for every day and that you will never be content with less than His holy anointing and enabling!

Remember that "be ye filled with the Spirit" is a command. Not to obey it is a sin. But you can be filled with the Holy Spirit. You can have the power of God for soul winning.

8. The Power of God's Word

"Being born again, not of corruptible seed, but of incorruptible, by the word of God, which liveth and abideth for ever."—I Pet. 1:23.

"The law of the Lord is perfect, converting the soul."—Ps. 19:7.

"For I am not ashamed of the gospel of Christ: for it is the power of God unto salvation to every one that believeth; to the Jew first, and also to the Greek."—Rom. 1:16.

ONCE A WOMAN CAME to this evangelist very earnestly saying, "I hope tonight you can tell some story that will touch my husband's heart and get him saved." But I told her she must pray that God would help me instead to have two other vital elements that led to the saving of souls: first, that the Word of God should be preached plainly; second, that it would be applied to the hearts of hearers by the Holy Spirit. I explained that an illustration, a story, is properly used to focus attention on a great Scripture truth and to emphasize that truth and make the truth appeal to the heart, but that it is the Word of God itself which must be used of the Spirit to work the miracle of regeneration.

We cannot emphasize too strongly this great truth: Saving souls is a supernatural, miraculous business. So the Apostle Paul was inspired to write his beloved people at Corinth, "And I, brethren, when I came to you, came not with excellency of speech or of wisdom, declaring unto you the testimony of God" (I Cor. 2:1)—not Paul's wisdom, but "the testimony of God," that is, the Word of God. Again he said, "And my speech and my preaching was not with enticing words of man's wisdom, but in demonstration of the Spirit and of power: That your faith should not stand in the wisdom of men, but in the power of God" (I Cor. 2:4, 5). In this same passage he further emphasizes that "we speak the wisdom of God. . . ." So Paul preached the Word of God in the power of God, and did not depend upon "enticing words of man's wisdom."

Oh, then, the soul winner must use this powerful weapon, this holy instrument, the Word of God, if he would win souls.

Consider the great soul winners, past and present, and you will find a certain unity and simplicity about them: they have the same message. And there is a remarkable likeness in the way they go at it. They depend on the Word of God and use the Word of God to bring men to repentance and faith. Some soul winners may not be great Bible scholars, but they are most ardent users of some simple Scriptures which make plain the Gospel, the way of salvation, through faith in a crucified Saviour!

I. The Word of God Is the Powerful Instrument of the Soul Winner

Yes, the tool, the message, the means by which the soul winner is used of God to do His wondrous work is the Word of God!

1. The Word of God Is a Fire, a Hammer.

The Prophet Jeremiah tells of some prophets "that prophesy lies in my name, saying, I have dreamed, I have dreamed"; then Jeremiah gives God's answer: "The prophet that hath a dream, let him tell a dream; and he that hath my word, let him speak my word faithfully. What is the chaff to the wheat? saith the Lord. Is not my word like as a fire?

saith the Lord; and like a hammer that breaketh the rock in pieces?" (Jer. 23:25, 28, 29).

What is a dream, or any opinion, or fancy of men, beside the Word of God? The dream is a lie, God says; but the Word of God is like a fire and like a hammer that breaks the rock in pieces. So the Lord says in the following verses that He is against the prophets that "steal my words every one from his neighbour" and "that use their tongues, and say, He saith." God is against those "that prophesy false dreams" and "cause my people to err by their lies, and by their lightness."

Remember that the truth we should preach is the truth of the Scripture, the Word of God; and all the efforts of a soul winner which do not strive to make plain this simple truth of the Gospel from the Word of God are lightness and fancy and dreams and lies! Oh, the Word of God itself is the powerful weapon of the soul winner against sin, the surgical instrument to work the marvelous operation. It is the fire for cold hearts, the hammer for hard hearts!

2. The Word Is a Sharp Sword.

What a striking description of the work of the Word of God is given in Hebrews 4:12: "For the word of God is quick, and powerful, and sharper than any twoedged sword, piercing even to the dividing asunder of soul and spirit, and of the joints and marrow, and is a discerner of the thoughts and intents of the heart."

Note that the Word of God is "quick," that is, alive. The Word of God is living, eternal, and partakes of many qualities of God Himself. It is full of power. It is sharper than any twoedged sword. The Word of God deals with matters of the soul, the life, the heart, the conscience. It brings into a man's consciousness the guilt and sinfulness and the purposes of his heart.

Oh, then, God's Word can do what human wisdom cannot do, and the soul winner must use the Word of God.

3. The Word of God Furnishes the Man of God.

Paul was inspired to write Timothy: "All scripture is given by inspiration of God, and is profitable for doctrine, for reproof, for correction, for instruction in righteousness: That the man of God may be perfect, throughly furnished unto all good works" (II Tim. 3:16, 17).

The man of God may be completely equipped, we are told, by the Scripture. It is inspired of God and profitable, and should be used for doctrine or teaching, for reproof and for correction, for instruction in righteousness.

Then the apostle charges, "Preach the word; be instant in season, out of season; reprove, rebuke, exhort with all longsuffering and doctrine." With doctrine? Yes, that is, with the teaching of the Word of God. So whether one preaches the Gospel to one person—as is certainly meant in the Great Commission command to "preach the gospel to every creature"—or whether he preaches to multitudes, the equipment, the instrument of the soul winner, is to be the blessed Word of God. It is to be used to make sinners conscious of their sins, to tell them of God's condemnation on sin, and of the Saviour who died for them, and that everlasting life is to be had by simply turning from sin and trusting Christ.

4. Thus the Word of God Is to Be Used to Cleanse Christians, to Convict and Save Sinners.

"Wherewithal shall a young man cleanse his way?" is the question in Psalm 119:9. The answer is, "By taking heed thereto according to thy word." In John 17:17 the Lord Jesus prayed for all of us Christians, "Sanctify them through thy truth: thy word is truth." Paul urged upon the elders at Ephesus, "I commend you to God, and to the word of his grace, which is able to build you up, and to give you an inheritance among all them which are sanctified" (Acts 20:32). So for his own heart and character and cleansing and Christian growth, the soul winner needs the Word of

God. What a blessed instrument it is, then, for him to use in God's work.

5. Throughout the Bible the Work of a Soul Winner Is Pictured As a Sower Going Forth to Sow Seed.

Jesus gave the parable of the sower who sowed, and some seed fell by the wayside and the birds got it. Some seed fell on stony places and sprouted, but did not take root in the ground. Some fell among thorns and grew, but brought no fruit to perfection. Some fell on good ground and brought an abundant harvest. Jesus explained, "Now the parable is this: The seed is the word of God" (Luke 8:11). Satan takes away the Word from the hearts of some when they hear it. Other hearts are stony hard, and while they are impressed and convicted, there is no genuine heart-turning to God, no new birth. Others are saved, but are hindered by worldly cares and attractions. Others make wonderfully fruitful Christians. But remember, "the seed is the word of God."

In the parable of the tares in Matthew 13, Jesus again speaks of the good seed as the Gospel, and when the seed sprouts and grows in the heart, the hearer trusts and is saved.

Surely it was this gospel seed-sowing that Isaiah pictured when he was inspired to write, "Blessed are ye that sow beside all waters, that send forth thither the feet of the ox and the ass" (Isa. 32:20). It is the sowing of the Word of God meant in Psalm 126:5, 6, "They that sow in tears shall reap in joy. He that goeth forth and weepeth, bearing precious seed, shall doubtless come again with rejoicing, bringing his sheaves with him." There is no soul winning without the Word. I believe this same seed-sowing is pictured in Ecclesiastes 11:1, 4 and 6:

"Cast thy bread upon the waters: for thou shalt find it after many days . . . He that observeth the wind shall not sow; and he that regardeth the clouds shall not reap . . . In the morning sow thy seed, and in the evening withhold not thine hand: for thou knowest not whether shall prosper, either this or that, or whether thy both shall be alike good."

Thus we find that the gospel soul winner does not simply persuade people, with human argument and reason, to be better, but he sows the wonderful, living seed of the Word of God, and when this seed is "mixed with faith" (Heb. 4:2) on the part of the hearer, then this living seed becomes "Christ in you, the hope of glory." One becomes regenerated, a miraculously born-again child of God.

II. The Saving Power of the Word of God

Several Scriptures speak of the regenerating power of the Word of God.

1. One Such Statement Is I Peter 1:23.

It says, "Being born again, not of corruptible seed, but of incorruptible, by the word of God, which liveth and abideth for ever."

Here we are told that the child of God has been born again by incorruptible seed, the living Word of God.

Sometimes in the night I have reached to the bedside table where there is always the Word of God, and have taken it in my arms joyfully, remembering that it is this blessed Word of God that was used to keep me out of Hell! I am born again by the Word of God! That does not leave out the miraculous work of the Holy Spirit, but the Spirit does not work in this matter without the Word.

2. In Psalm 19:7 Is a Remarkable Statement About the Word of God.

The heavens, the sun, and all the starry firmament are mentioned, but they are not perfect. They will pass away and be changed. But verse 7 says, "The law of the Lord is perfect, converting the soul." This same thought is expressed in the words of Jesus, "Heaven and earth shall pass away, but my words shall not pass away" (Matt. 24:35). So the perfect Word of God "converts the soul." The Word of God, then, is a living, divine thing. It is supernatural and miraculous, and it works the miracle of regeneration in the heart of one who hears it, and by faith receives it and the Saviour of whom it tells!

3. "Born of Water" Means Born of the Word.

Jesus said to Nicodemus, "Verily, verily, I say unto thee, Except a man be born of water and of the Spirit, he cannot enter into the kingdom of God" (John 3:5). I believe that here the Lord Jesus meant to refer to the two miraculous elements in the saving of souls. One is the Holy Spirit. The convert is "born of the Spirit." The other element, "born of water," seems to refer to the "washing of regeneration" of Titus 3:5, and to the "washing of water by the word" (Eph. 5:26) which happen when one is saved. It is not baptism which enters into the new birth. We are plainly told that one who believes in Christ is not condemned, that he already has everlasting life, that he has passed from death unto life (John 3:18, 36; John 5:24). Jesus told His disciples in John 15:3, "Now ye are clean through the word which I have spoken unto you." And in John 13:10 Jesus told them, "He that is washed needeth not save to wash his feet, but is clean every whit: and ye are clean. . . ."

Ephesians tells us that "Christ also loved the church, and gave himself for it; That he might sanctify and cleanse it with the washing of water by the word, That he might present it to himself a glorious church, not having spot, or wrinkle, or any such thing; but that it should be holy and without blemish" (Eph. 5:25-27). Here are pictured all the redeemed who will be assembled in Heaven. As soon as we trust Christ, we are washed in the sense of having a new nature. At the resurrection, with the adoption and perfection of our bodies, that cleansing work will be completed. But it is with "the washing of water by the word" that

Christ prepares those who become a part of that mystical body.

Oh, the soul winner must remember there is dynamite, there is a miracle of God, there is mighty saving power in the Word of God.

III. It Is the Preaching of the Gospel That Saves

We have spoken above of the saving power of the Word of God. It is part of the same truth to say that the Gospel saves, for the Gospel itself is the very heart of the Word of God and it is the saving part of the Word of God.

For example, the law is good and holy, but man, being sinful, cannot be saved by keeping commandments. Already he has broken God's commandments, he has come short, and the law can only bring more condemnation. But we are told, "For what the law could not do, in that it was weak through the flesh, God sending his own Son in the likeness of sinful flesh, and for sin, condemned sin in the flesh" (Rom. 8:3). The moral law is in the Bible and it ought to be preached, and it is used to arouse a conscience for sin. "The law was our schoolmaster to bring us unto Christ" (Gal. 3:24). But it takes more than law to save a soul; it takes the Gospel.

In India a few months ago a Mohammedan came to inquire of me about the Christian religion. When I spoke of Jesus, he said, "Oh, yes; he was a good prophet. There are several prophets." To that I replied, "Dear friend, a prophet will do you no good. You are a lost sinner, and you must have a Saviour or go to a Hell of torment forever."

And so I say here that all the good Word of God is important, but "the letter killeth" and the law is good only if it acts as a schoolmaster to bring us to Christ, to show our need of a Saviour, and to bring us to trust in His atoning death in our stead.

1. The Gospel, Not the Law, Saves.

So we need not be surprised that the Scripture says that the Gospel is the power of God unto salvation.

Paul was inspired to boast to those at Rome, "For I am not ashamed of the gospel of Christ: for it is the power of God unto salvation to every one that believeth; to the Jew first, and also to the Greek" (Rom. 1:16). The Gospel is the power of God unto salvation to those who believe!

In I Corinthians 15 the inspired apostle defines "the gospel which I preached unto you . . . by which also ye are saved. . . ." That saving Gospel was this: ". . . how that Christ died for our sins according to the scriptures; And that he was buried, and that he rose again the third day according to the scriptures." So the saving Gospel deals with the fact of our sins, the atoning death of Jesus for our sins, and then His resurrection as attested by infallible proofs; and to be saved one must mix that Gospel with faith, that is, he must put his trust in the Saviour who died for us sinners.

Elsewhere Paul equates preaching of the Gospel with "the preaching of the cross." He says, "For Christ sent me not to baptize, but to preach the gospel: not with wisdom of words, lest the cross of Christ should be made of none effect. For the preaching of the cross is to them that perish foolishness; but unto us which are saved it is the power of God" (I Cor. 1:17, 18). So later when Paul says, "For I determined not to know any thing among you, save Jesus Christ, and him crucified" (I Cor. 2:2), he simply meant that he would preach no other way of salvation but by Jesus Christ who died for our sins. That is the saving Gospel in brief.

2. This Saving Gospel, That Christ Died for Our Sins and Rose Again, and That People Are Saved Everlastingly by Putting Their Trust in Him, Is Sometimes Called "the Doctrine of Christ."

In II John 9 to 11 the inspired Word says:

"Whosoever transgresseth, and abideth not in the doctrine of Christ, hath not God. He that abideth in the doctrine of Christ, he hath both the Father and the Son. If there come any unto you, and bring not this doctrine, receive him not into your house, neither bid him God speed: For he that biddeth him God speed is partaker of his evil deeds."

You will note that one who "transgresseth, and abideth not in the doctrine of Christ, hath not God," that is, is not saved. On the other hand we are told, "He that abideth in the doctrine of Christ, he hath both the Father and the Son."

So the saving Gospel is wrapped up in Jesus Christ. Other doctrines, except those concerning the person and work of Jesus Christ, are not necessarily involved in salvation. But if Christ is the virgin-born Son of God, sent into this world to save sinners, and if in His deity He worked miracles, then died for our sins on the cross and rose again and ascended to Heaven, as the Scripture says, then He is the Saviour, and one who puts his confidence in that Saviour is saved.

One, then, might differ on lesser matters and be a Christian. One could be wrong on baptism, on some doctrine of the church, on some detail of the Second Coming or other lesser matters, but still be saved. But one who is essentially wrong on the doctrine of Christ is not saved. One who is wrong on Christ's virgin birth, deity, blood atonement, and resurrection, simply "hath not God." He has not been saved since he did not receive the Gospel, "mixed with faith." And one who thus does not abide in the doctrine of Christ is not to be received as a Christian; we are not to bid him "God speed." He is not a Christian.

Let us note, too, that the person of Christ and the doctrine of Christ in the Bible are inescapably connected. There is no Christ but the Christ of the Bible. There is no saving doctrine of Christ except the Bible doctrine about the person, life, atoning death, and resurrection of Jesus. One who does not believe the Bible doctrine about Christ does not have Christ and is not saved. The saving Gospel is involved in the Bible teaching about Christ and the fact that He died as God's atoning Lamb for us sinners.

So the soul winner must cling fast to the simple truth that Christ, God in the flesh, came and died for sinners to redeem us to God, and rose from the dead, and is now on the right hand of God interceding for us, and all who put their trust in Christ are saved.

3. It Is the PREACHING of the Gospel That Saves.

We are told in God's blessed Word, "For after that in the wisdom of God the world by wisdom knew not God, it pleased God by the foolishness of preaching to save them that believe" (I Cor. 1:21). This same passage says, "For the preaching of the cross is to them that perish foolishness; but unto us which are saved it is the power of God" (vs. 18). So people are saved not only by the Gospel, but by the preaching of the Gospel. I am glad when Gideons leave a Bible in a hotel room. I rejoice wherever Gospels of John are given out to the unsaved. But the simple truth is that in most cases God has planned that people should be saved, not simply by a sinner finding the Gospel for himself in the Bible, but by the Gospel's coming to a sinner through a Christian.

The poor lost sinner is "dead in trespasses and in sin." The god of this world has blinded him. We are told, "But the natural man receiveth not the things of the Spirit of God: for they are foolishness unto him: neither can he know them, because they are spiritually discerned" (I Cor. 2:14). So the Ethiopian eunuch, when Philip asked him, "Understandest thou what thou readest?" cried plaintively, "How can I, except some man should guide me?" (Acts 8:30, 31).

As the Ethiopian eunuch did not understand that sweet gospel passage in Isaiah 53 telling about the Saviour who would go like a lamb to the slaughter, and explaining that with His stripes we would be healed, and that on Him would be laid all our iniquity, so normally the poor sinner will not be saved except as somebody takes the Gospel to him.

If the Gospel comes to him warmed by the heart concern of the Christian, moistened with the tears of compassion, explained by the personal testimony of one who personally knows Christ, then the Spirit of God, working through the soul winner, can enlighten the mind of the sinner, bring him to conviction and to faith! It has pleased God "by the foolishness of preaching to save them that believe."

What translation of the Bible is best? I have twelve or fifteen translations, though all my memory work is in the King James Version of the Bible, and it is that which I read continually and from which I preach in the pulpit. But in truth, for a poor lost sinner the translation of the Scripture by a fervent Christian, brought to him with a loving heart, earnest entreaty and with Spirit-filled explanation, is the Gospel that saves!

We should remember that it is not simply the letter of the Scripture, but the spirit of the Scripture that saves. The letter kills. The barren Word of God, without any moving of the Spirit, without any enlightening of the darkened mind, does not save. I know preachers who quote Scriptures by the yard, but they do not know of any salvation except some kind which they think comes in the waters of baptism and by holding out faithful and by persistent good works. I have no doubt that millions have gone to Hell quoting Scripture, trying to obey rules, and trying to earn salvation by the law. No, the blessed Word of God does not save except as it is used by the Spirit of God. The Word of God is "the sword of the Spirit" (Eph. 6:17). And so when the blessed Holy Spirit comes upon the one who would win souls and helps him to wield the Spirit's sword, the Word of God, then sinners are convicted and saved.

Ah, the stumbling paraphrase of Scripture by an earnest, believing, Spirit-filled Christian is more effective in the heart of a sinner than the meticulous reading of the words, the letter only, of Scripture, by the most scholarly person. "It pleased God by the foolishness of preaching to save them that believe." The Word of God is to be carried by loving, believing hearts, accompanied with compassion and the divine wisdom of the Spirit. Oh, the soul winner must, in God's power, use the Word of God to win souls.

It is a blessed truth that the Holy Spirit works with the soul winner. Jesus said, "But the Comforter, which is the Holy Ghost, whom the Father will send in my name, he shall teach you all things, and bring all things to your remembrance, whatsoever I have said unto you" (John 14:26). And Jesus said of this same Comforter, ". . . he shall testify of me: And ye also shall bear witness, because ye have been with me from the beginning" (John 15:26, 27).

Some think that the Word of God alone saves sinners without a Christian witness or testimony, and they quote, "So shall my word be that goeth forth out of my mouth: it shall not return unto me void, but it shall accomplish that which I please, and it shall prosper in the thing whereto I sent it" (Isa. 55:11). But that Scripture, as I understand it, simply means that what God promises, He will fulfill; and what He prophesies will come to pass. It does not mean that the Word of God in the letter, without the power of the Holy Spirit, will work its miraculous saving work.

IV. The Soul Winner and His Bible

One can hardly overestimate the importance of the Word of God in the heart, life, and work of one who would win souls.

It is refreshing to consider the holy devotion which great soul winners have had for the Word of God and their reliance upon it. Liberalism, modernism, never begins with the Spurgeons, the Wesleys, the Moodys, the Torreys, the Sam Joneses, the Billy Sundays.

Years ago in Texas the question of evolution arose in a great university, my alma mater, and so there came a wide-spread discussion among our people as to whether the Word of God was verbally inspired or inspired in some lesser degree. Talking to a great evangelist, some prominent pastor asked, "Why make a to-do about it? If the Bible is inspired, isn't that enough, whether it is infallibly accurate, word for word, or not?"

The evangelist himself told me how he answered, and he was moved with emotion as he repeated it: "It matters to me. If I do not have the miracles of God day by day, I cannot have the great revivals. It matters to me when I face drunkards and harlots and infidels and every kind of worldling and sinner. I have to have an infallible Bible, the very Word of God, powerful, supernatural, inerrant, if I am to win souls. Some of you preachers can go on with your work without an infallible Bible. Some of you, if God were to die, could go on with your machinery, your budget, your organizations, for a year before you would know it! But I must have an infallible, supernatural Bible if I am to win souls!"

1. The Soul Winner Should Have the Word of God Burning in His Heart.

Jeremiah found it so. He had been in the stocks, punished for his warnings of destruction to come on Jerusalem. He cried out:

"O Lord, thou hast deceived me, and I was deceived: thou art stronger than I, and hast prevailed: I am in derision daily, every one mocketh me. For since I spake, I cried out, I cried violence and spoil; because the word of the Lord was made a reproach unto me, and a derision, daily. Then I said, I will not make mention of him, nor speak any more in his name. But his word was in mine heart as a burning fire shut up in my bones, and I was weary with forbearing, and I could not stay."—Jer. 20:7-9.

Derided, abused physically, placed in the stocks, put in a muddy dungeon, daily mocked and reproached for his testimony, Jeremiah fain would have held his peace, but he could not. "But his word was in mine heart as a burning fire shut up in my bones, and I was weary with forbearing, and I could not stay."

Oh, blessed is the soul winner to whom the Word of God has become such a living thing—burning in his heart, pressing always, so that whether he speaks to an individual or to a crowd, there is holy earnestness and divine fire in the words. Paul could well say, "Woe is unto me, if I preach not the gospel!" (I Cor. 9:16). And blessed is the soul winner who can say that there is such an urgency in his heart to get out the blessed Word of God that he dare not withhold his testimony, his pleading, with the Word of God.

2. The Soul Winner Should Be Jealous of His Gospel.

How the heart of Paul the apostle burned when he was inspired to write the first chapter of Galatians. He was moved to write about "our Lord Jesus Christ, who gave himself for our sins. . . ." And it was God speaking, not only Paul, when he wrote:

"I marvel that ye are so soon removed from him that called you into the grace of Christ unto another gospel: Which is not another; but there be some that trouble you, and would pervert the gospel of Christ. But though we, or an angel from heaven, preach any other gospel unto you than that which we have preached unto you, let him be accursed. As we said before, so say I now again, If any man preach any other gospel unto you than that ye have received, let him be accursed."—Gal. 1:6-9.

That Gospel Paul preached was "the gospel of Christ." To pervert it was a great sin, and God pronounced a curse on anyone, be it angel or the Apostle Paul himself or any one else, who should "preach any other gospel unto you."

The Gospel of Christ, then, is exclusive. Someone says, "We are all going to the same place; we are just traveling different routes." Well, if you are going to Heaven you can travel no other route but the simple gospel route of being saved from your sins by the blood of Jesus Christ who died for us and rose again. And that Gospel is the only one a soul winner can preach to win souls.

No wonder we are commanded that if one come and bring not this Gospel of Christ, we are to "receive him not into your house, neither bid him God speed: For he that biddeth him God speed is partaker of his evil deeds" (II John 10, 11).

3. The Word of God Is the Secret of Success for the Christian, and Eminently So for the Soul-Winning Christian.

In Psalm 1 we are told that the man is blessed who does not keep the company of sinners, of the ungodly, or the scornful! "But his delight is in the law of the Lord; and in his law doth he meditate day and night. And he shall be like a tree planted by the rivers of water, that bringeth forth his fruit in his season; his leaf also shall not wither; and whatsoever he doeth shall prosper" (vss. 1-3).

I hope that God in loving mercy will put in the heart of every reader a burning love for the Word, a holy sense of dependence upon the Word, and I hope that telling others the good news that Christ died to save sinners, that He is risen, that He is able to save to the uttermost, will be to you, the sweetest story ever told. I beg you, love the Word, meditate on the Word, enjoy the Word, and depend upon it, and use the Word of God in soul winning.

9. Direct Leading by the Holy Spirit

"For as many as are led by the Spirit of God, they are the sons of God."—Rom. 8:14.

"Now when they had gone throughout Phrygia and the region of Galatia, and were forbidden of the Holy Ghost to preach the word in Asia, After they were come to Mysia, they assayed to go into Bithynia: but the Spirit suffered them not. And they passing by Mysia came down to Troas. And a vision appeared to Paul in the night; There stood a man of Macedonia, and prayed him, saying, Come over into Macedonia, and help us. And after he had seen the vision, immediately we endeavored to go into Macedonia, assuredly gathering that the Lord had called us for to preach the gospel unto them."—Acts 16:6-10.

WINNING A SOUL to trust Christ as Saviour is a supernatural business. The message we bring to the sinner is given of God in the supernaturally inspired Bible. The change wrought when a sinner is born again and becomes a child of God, with a new nature, is miraculous. The power of the Holy Spirit is required in witnessing, for He alone can bring conviction, repentance, and the new birth.

Thus there is an absolute necessity for the wisdom of

God as well as the power of God in soul winning. Where shall I go? To whom shall I speak first? What shall I say? What is the secret of this man's need? Where is his conscience sensitive? What misconception hinders? What sin? So, to win souls one must have the leading of the Spirit of God.

It is true there are general instructions we already have in the Bible. We are commanded to win souls. We know, or can know, the Bible plan of salvation for every sinner. But which sinner is ready for the Gospel, which one is not? We have a whole arsenal of Bible truth in dealing with sinners, but only the Spirit of God knows which approach is best.

Note the difference in the way Jesus approached Nicodemus and the woman at the well at Sychar in John, chapters three and four, then the way He won the man born blind in chapter eight. See the varying way Philip won the Ethiopian eunuch in Acts 8, the way Paul dealt with Felix, the methods of Jesus with the woman taken in adultery, and with Zacchaeus. Yes, we need clear leading in individual cases, dealing personally with souls about salvation.

In public preaching the preacher has the Gospel, but he still needs to know which Scripture to use, how to outline it, what to stress, what illustrations to use, what appeal. He is called to preach—but where? The evangelist is to hold revival campaigns, but which invitation shall he accept, which reject?

I had a teacher, a greatly loved man of God, spiritual, a great preacher. However, he had a rule that he would never choose between engagements. The first invitation he got to preach somewhere, he accepted it, and the next, until his slate was filled. He never tried to decide between two invitations. The first one which came was accepted, if the date were open.

Thus he left to God or, I fear, to chance, that he should never be invited anywhere unless it was the will of God. I believe that he greatly limited his ministry. I think that every preacher ought to most prayerfully wait on God to know where to go, what to preach, what invitation to accept, and what invitation to reject. It is a mistake not to ask for and expect the direct leading of God's Spirit in doing the Lord's business.

And if that is true about preaching, it is equally true about dealing with individuals.

I. The Bible Clearly Teaches That Christians Are to Seek Clear Leading of the Will of God in Daily Life

To ask God for special leading in soul winning is only doing in particular what is everywhere commanded and taught in the Bible.

We are not only taught to ask for daily bread, to ask for deliverance from temptation, to ask for health in sickness, to ask that our needs be supplied. We are clearly taught that God's children have a right to ask Him for wisdom day by day and walk always in the light of God, knowing His will and thus receiving His blessing.

In James 1:5 God gives a sweet invitation, "If any of you lack wisdom, let him ask of God, that giveth to all men liberally, and upbraideth not; and it shall be given him."

David praised the Lord, his Shepherd, that "He leadeth me beside the still waters . . . He leadeth me in the paths of righteousness. . ." (Ps. 23:2, 3). He prayed, "Lead me in a plain path, because of mine enemies" (Ps. 27:11). And his petition was similar in Psalm 31:3 and Psalm 61:2 and Psalm 139:24.

Jesus pictured Himself as the Good Shepherd, and we His sheep. "And he calleth his own sheep by name, and leadeth them out" (John 10:3).

The children of Israel were led out of Egypt by a way they knew not, and always there went before them the pillar of cloud by day or fire by night. And when the cloud stopped, they camped under it. When it moved out, they followed. What a blessed object lesson of the leading of the Spirit of God to a Christian!

I knew a farmer in West Texas who prayed about his planting. Will there be enough rain for all this year to grow corn? And so, once every two or three years he would feel led of God to plant corn. His neighbors would scoff and say, "You cannot raise corn in this dry country." But that year the rainfall would be unusual; he would raise a good crop of corn. The next year he would pray and God would seem to move his heart not to plant corn; instead he would plant sorghum grains which grow with less rainfall. Meantime, some of his neighbors would say, "L. C. Wolfe grew corn! I will grow a crop this year." And that year it would be dry and the neighbors' crops would fail. The Christian farmer is wise to ask God for wisdom.

How often we read in the Scriptures that "David inquired of the Lord." And God revealed to him, in answer to his earnest inquiry, what he should do. When Ziklag, David's city, was destroyed, and his wild followers spoke of stoning their leader, "David enquired at the Lord, saying, Shall I pursue after this troop?" (the troup that had burned the city and stolen their wives and children and property). "And he answered him, Pursue: for thou shalt surely overtake them, and without fail recover all" (I Sam. 30:8). And so it was later in war with the Philistines, "David enquired of the Lord." And God said, "Thou shalt not go up; but fetch a compass behind them, and come upon them over against the mulberry trees. And let it be, when thou hearest the sound of a going in the tops of the mulberry trees, that then thou shalt bestir thyself: for then shall the Lord go out before thee, to smite the host of the Philistines" (II Sam. 5:23, 24).

And what clear instructions God gave Gideon.

Oh, how sad that Christians do not daily inquire of the Lord and have leading for His will in every thing! What blessings would be ours if we took the wisdom so freely offered from One who loves us.

In Romans 8:14 is an amazing Scripture. "For as many as are led by the Spirit of God, they are the sons of God." Elsewhere in the same chapter, Christians are identified as those that are "not in the flesh, but in the Spirit" (vs. 9). The Holy Spirit dwells in the body of every Christian. But here, in verse 14, the leading of the Spirit is regarded as an ever-present fact with every Christian. Oh, He who dwells within and makes your body His temple is always leading, whispering, pointing out the right way. How sad that Christians usually ignore, or do not listen; sometimes they are not even aware of the leading of the Spirit. But it could not be clearer than it is here, that every Christian can have, ought to have daily leading of the Spirit of God.

Now read the two verses following, Romans 8:15, 16: "For ye have not received the spirit of bondage again to fear; but ye have received the Spirit of adoption, whereby we cry, Abba, Father. The Spirit itself beareth witness with our spirit, that we are the children of God."

Here we have the great fact that should make us bold in appealing for guidance, for wisdom, for leadership every day. God is our Father! Those who are born of God have within them the Holy Spirit who leads us to say, "Abba, Father." And the term here, *Abba,* is the Aramaic term that a little child would call his papa, his daddy, and not the rather austere term *father.* And the little child has a right to say, "Daddy, where are you?" He has a right to say, "Daddy, which way shall I go?" And the Christian has a right to say, "O Heavenly Father, let me have my hand in yours and You lead me in a plain path and never let me get out of Thy will!"

And the blessed Holy Spirit of God in our hearts leads us to pray so, leads us to rely upon Him, and gives us the sweet assurance that as a father hears his children, so our Heavenly Father hears us and wants to give us the wisdom, the leading, the light on our pathway, which every Christian needs every day.

II. But the Bible Has Specific Teaching That a Christian Can Have Leadership About Soul Winning All the Time

Jesus, after laboring in Judea, ". . . left Judea, and departed again into Galilee. And he must needs go through Samaria" (John 4:3, 4). Now Galilee is perhaps eighty or a hundred miles north of Jerusalem where Jesus had been working. And the usual route between Jerusalem and Galilee would be to go down east to Jericho, and then follow the Jordan River up the valley, until near the Sea of Galilee. That would be the water-level route, the path most people traveled. But ah, that is not the route Jesus will go this time, for we are told, "He must needs go through Samaria."

Why must Jesus go through Samaria? I believe that there was a clear leading of the blessed Holy Spirit that a shabby, sinful, frustrated, lost woman would be at the well of Sychar, and to this poor, troubled, sinful woman He must speak and give salvation! We know that the dear Lord Jesus emptied Himself of the outward form of His glory, and that all His ministry was as a Spirit-filled man. Peter told Cornelius "how God anointed Jesus of Nazareth with the Holy Ghost and with power: who went about doing good, and healing all that were oppressed of the devil; for God was with him" (Acts 10:38). Jesus had the leading of the Holy Spirit.

I think that is how He knew where to send the disciples to find an ass' colt tied, and what answer to give those who would object and to lead the donkey colt away. I think that is how Jesus knew when to send the disciples to a man who would furnish an upper room for the twelve for the passover season and later for the pre-Pentecostal prayer meeting.

Jesus had a heart burning with compassion for poor lost sinners. He was in constant communion with God. No doubt the blessed Spirit of God moved His heart so that "He must needs go through Samaria," to win the sinful woman.

And we can have leadership the same way.

See how clearly and in detail God led Peter to go to the house of Cornelius miles away in Caesarea and there preach to this Gentile the Gospel, and see him and his household and a number of soldiers saved! Is not the God of Acts, chapter 10, the same God whom we too serve? And was Cornelius any more lost, or any more valuable to God than poor sinners who are around us?

How detailed and exact was the instruction the Spirit of God gave to Philip, the deacon-evangelist, in the case of the Ethiopian eunuch. In Acts 8:26 we are told: "And the angel of the Lord spake unto Philip, saying, Arise, and go toward the south unto the way that goeth down from Jerusalem unto Gaza, which is desert." Here the "angel" or the messenger of the Lord may simply be a term for the leading of the Holy Spirit. Or if the Holy Spirit appeared in some special angelic form, we do not know. But God's leading was specific.

Then in verse 29 we read further, "Then the Spirit said unto Philip, Go near, and join thyself to this chariot." The eunuch was reading Isaiah 53, and soon, beginning at the same Scripture, Philip won the man to trust the Lord Jesus and the new convert was baptized. "And when they were come up out of the water, the Spirit of the Lord caught away Philip, that the eunuch saw him no more. . . ." That was explicit, clear leading and instruction and guidance about soul winning.

We have a similar account in Acts 16, verses 6-10, as follows:

"Now when they had gone throughout Phrygia and the region of Galatia, and were forbidden of the Holy Ghost to preach the word in Asia, After they were come to Mysia,

they assayed to go into Bithynia: but the Spirit suffered
them not. And they passing by Mysia came down to Troas.
And a vision appeared to Paul in the night; There stood a
man of Macedonia, and prayed him, saying, Come over into
Macedonia, and help us. And after he had seen the vision,
immediately we endeavored to go into Macedonia, assuredly
gathering that the Lord had called us for to preach the gospel unto them."

Note that they "were forbidden of the Holy Ghost to
preach the word in Asia," that is, in Asia Minor. The Spirit
of God had other plans. "They assayed to go into Bithynia:
but the Spirit suffered them not."

No, God wanted Europe to hear the Gospel, so in the
night Paul saw a vision of a man in Macedonia saying,
"Come over into Macedonia, and help us." So they rightly
gathered that God planned for them to leave Asia Minor
and go into Macedonia and there preach the Gospel.

III. Some Remarkable Instances of the Spirit's Clear Leading of Soul Winners

In Dallas, Texas, when I was pastor of the Galilean
Baptist Church and God helped us all to win thousands of
souls, I remember one incident that illustrates well the leading of the Spirit of God.

One of my secretaries, Miss Viola Walden, who is still
with me, lived about six blocks from the church office. Regularly she would come down two blocks east on Center
Street to Beckley, then two blocks north on Beckley to Tenth
Street, and then east down Tenth Street a block and a half
to the church. But one morning she felt strangely led to go
directly north, crossing Jefferson and Tenth Street and
Ninth Street on to Eighth Street; then she turned east
on Eighth Street. In the summer morning a man was
mowing his lawn. He lived alone in a small garage-house
on the rear of the lot. As he stopped to mop his brow, he
spoke to her. She asked him where he attended church.

He did not attend church. Was he a Christian? No, he was not. But he knew he ought to be. So there on the sidewalk Miss Viola took her Testament from her purse, showed him Scriptures, and there he trusted Christ as his Saviour. She got his name and address and came happily to tell me at the office how she had been led to walk four blocks out of her way, but had won a soul to Christ.

A week later she came to the office with her eyes red from weeping. "What is the matter, Miss Viola?" I said.

In answer she laid the *Dallas Morning News* on my desk. The front-page headline: "Man Burned to Death in Eighth Street Fire." A gas stove left on, perhaps, caught a curtain, or in some other way the little building caught on fire. The man may have been overcome by the smoke. At any rate, before the fire company could put out the fire, he was burned to death. "Oh, what if I had not gone out of the way last week and so had been led to talk to him and get him to trust Christ?" the secretary said!

How often the dear Lord has led me clearly to a needy soul ready for the Gospel! Once I started to drive, with my wife and six girls, from Dallas to Chicago. All in the car and ready to start, we bowed our heads and prayed, first for journeying mercies, for safekeeping on the highways, then for leadership. "Lord, help me to find someone I can win to Christ on the way before I reach Chicago," I prayed.

We had a happy trip, as we usually did, with songs all the way from "Old MacDonald Had a Farm" to gospel songs. At Ardmore, Oklahoma, I missed a turn on the highway. The sky was overcast, there was no easy way to tell directions, and lo! I found myself fifty miles east, on the wrong road! I fumed a bit at myself—we had lost precious time on our trip of nearly a thousand miles. How could I have been so careless, I thought. And we had prayed so carefully for guidance!

Well, we stopped to get gasoline. The filling station attendant was a man of about forty. I asked him, "Are you a

Christian man? Have you ever been converted?"

"No, I am not a Christian," he answered. "But my wife is; she is one of the best Christians you ever saw! She has been talking to me. I know I ought to be saved." So I gladly showed him how to trust the Saviour. He asked the Lord Jesus to forgive and save him; he took my hand warmly as a token of his trust in Christ to give him everlasting life then and there, and said how happy his wife would be.

I paid the man, got in the car and drove away to get back to my proper highway. But at once there was a clamor of girlish voices behind me, "Daddy, don't you see? You asked God to lead you to a soul you could win today, so He brought you fifty miles to reach the man who was ready!" And indeed I doubt not that extra driving, when God took me in a way I knew not, to talk to a man whom God had prepared, will seem very sweet and wonderful when I meet that man again in Heaven!

You may not have the key to the heart of a soul of a sinner, but God does! Years ago I was in revival services at First Baptist Church, Hastings, Minnesota. It was a bright, brisk winter day, and the pastor told me he had some business on a farm out on a big island in the Mississippi River. Would I like to go along?

"Yes," I said. "Maybe there will be a chance to talk to someone about Jesus."

But the pastor said, "I'm afraid there will not be much opportunity. The farmer is a Catholic, a profane man. I have tried to talk to him, but he will not listen." However, I went for the ride.

While the pastor and the farmer attended to business in the front yard, I played with the children in the winter sun. We had a grand time, and when the farmer had finished with the preacher, I asked him, "How many children have you?"

"Only seven now," he said.

"Was there another one, then?" I asked.

"Oh, yes, the prettiest and smartest one of all! She was only three years old, but she fell in the river and drowned." His voice was hoarse with emotion.

"But you can see her again," I told him. "The little one has gone to Heaven, and you can get ready now and meet her there," I said.

"Oh, no, I cannot meet her, Preacher," he said. And when I insisted that he could, he turned half angry, and in tears, and said, "No, I cannot! You don't understand! She was not baptized! They wouldn't even let me bury her in the Catholic cemetery! She is gone!"

He thought that that little one, three years old, had gone to Hell because she was not sprinkled! I took my Bible, showed him how David's baby died too, but how David said, "I shall go to him, but he shall not return to me" (II Sam. 12:33). I showed him I Corinthians 15:22, "For as in Adam all die, even so in Christ shall all be made alive." All the baby lost by tainted nature, Christ had made up. No one goes to Hell for Adam's sin, but only for his own.

He was all attention. Then was I sure that a little baby, unbaptized, was taken straight to Jesus? Then he was as tender as a child! How eagerly he read the verses on salvation. How simply he prayed for forgiveness and trusted Christ to save him!

I have always felt that God's Spirit graciously led me to the one key that would open the man's heart! How else would it have happened so? God has the key! Ask Him.

Dr. Jack Hyles of Hammond, Indiana, tells how in a strange, cold, formal church where he was asked not to give a public invitation, he preached on the prodigal son. Always, he said, he was accustomed to calling the prodigal boy John and the elder brother Bill, as he told the moving story. But when he came to tell the prodigal's name, he strangely could not think of "John"—instead, he said, "We will call him Bill." Then when he came to the elder brother, he had already used the accustomed "Bill," so he stumbled momentarily, and said, "We'll call him 'Little Bud.' ' "

Near the close of that blessed story of the prodigal's return, a strange thing happened. A young man suddenly arose, left his seat, went to the back of the church down another aisle, went to an elder woman, and sobbing they came to the front of the church together. Then relatives from all over the church came to weep, and pray, and to hug the prodigal!

"How did you know?" asked the pastor. "How did you know?"

"How did I know what?" asked Dr. Hyles.

"How did you know that boy has been gone a year, and no one knew where he was till he came in the church today? How did you know his name was Bill? How did you know his brother is called 'Little Bud'? How did you know?"

The answer was that the blessed Spirit of God knew! Oh, to be always led by the Spirit who has the power, who knows all hearts, who holds all the keys.

IV. How to Have Clear Leading in Soul-Winning Efforts

Why is it we are so bumbling, so clumsy in soul-winning effort? Why walk in the dark when we can have light? Humbly I suggest some requirements if we would have the Spirit's guidance always.

First, let us ask for it. God can open the closed door. He can say "turn left here," or "speak to this man," or "don't make that trip today," or "sit on this seat in the airplane." Let us ask Him. "If any of you lack wisdom, let him ask of God, that giveth to all men liberally, and upbraideth not . . ." (Jas. 1:5). In this matter of clear guidance, of open doors, of the right contact, it is true as of other things, that "ye have not, because ye ask not" (Jas. 4:2).

The boldness, the miracle-working power of the Holy Spirit, the wisdom that will put the right words in one's mouth, that will lead one to come at the right time—these are from God. Oh, then if we are to do God's business, let us ask for His equipment! And that includes clear leading, day by day, and His direction and supervision whether we can always see it or not.

Second, if you would have the Holy Spirit clearly lead you, tell you what to do, then obey the divine command, "Quench not the Spirit" (I Thess. 5:19).

How sensitive is the tender Spirit of God! Unconverted people may insult Him, may refuse Him, may do Him despite and blaspheme Him till He comes no more to warn and convict and seek. God has promised, "My spirit shall not always strive with man" (Gen. 6:3). Sins against the Son of God may be forgiven, but there is a sin against the Holy Spirit Himself which has no forgiveness in this world or the world to come.

It is this sensitive Spirit of God who dwells within us. Where the greater love and the greater familiarity is, there one can be hurt the most. A loving wife could be hurt more by a husband's indifference and his slight than by a casual stranger. So the dear Spirit of God who lives in the body of a Christian, who is the comforter, the prayer helper, the appointed guide and teacher—oh, then when He speaks, hear Him. Do not argue against the way God's Spirit leads. Do not reason too much as to whether His plan will work. Make sure, dear Christian, if you are to have the leading of God's Spirit in soul winning, that you do not quench Him, argue with Him, disagree with Him, and disobey Him!

Some wonder why they do not have the leading of God, and then every time the Spirit of God whispers something they should do, they pour cold water on the plan of God. They put human reason up against supernatural leading.

Once in a college dormitory some of us who wanted to study were irritated by an idle talker who visited room after room during study hours, and took up the time of others who wanted to study. He was hard to discourage, but some of us found a way to do it! The door of the room was left slightly ajar. A ten-quart bucket of ice water was balanced on the top of the door. When Mr. Busybody came breaking in to disturb and chat with those who wanted to study, he was greeted with an icy deluge over his head! His enthusiasm for gossip was quenched for a time.

Oh, do not pour cold water of discouragement and argument and disagreement when God's Spirit leads.

In my boyhood I owned two horses. The sorrel horse Dick was a roughneck type, with mustang tendencies. The roan horse King was a gentleman, a horse of fine blood. It took a long time to break Dick, and he was never thoroughly surrendered. When I sold him after riding him five years, the buyer had to rope him to catch him, when I was not at home, and he bucked all over the place when he was saddled! When I rode him along the road and lifted a hand abruptly in greeting a passer-by, I needed to be careful that the reins were tight or there would be trouble. Once I walked home from church with a girl and led the sorrel horse. He stretched his long neck as far as he could and walked as if his feet were lead, and so I tugged and pulled and hauled until the girl begged me to get on the horse and ride him instead of leading him!

On the other hand, the roan horse King was my friend. He never had to be broken. He liked me. He would follow me to the kitchen door for a biscuit or a bit of sugar. I never needed a rope or halter to lead him, only a hand on his mane. He would guide or stop at the slightest touch of the rein, or be off at a gallop with a shift in my weight.

Ah, stubbornness is a bad thing in a horse you ride. Stubbornness must be a desperately evil thing to the sweet Holy Spirit who wants to guide you in soul winning. In Jesus' name, if you want God's leading and power, then do not quench the Spirit.

Again, the Scripture says, "And grieve not the holy Spirit of God . . ." (Eph. 4:30). But that command is connected. Before that we are commanded not to get angry and sin, not to give place to the Devil nor steal nor to let corrupt communications proceed out of our mouths. And following that we are commanded, "Let all bitterness, and wrath, and anger, and clamour, and evil speaking, be put away from you, with all malice: And be ye kind one to another, tenderhearted, forgiving one another, even as God for Christ's sake hath forgiven you" (Eph. 4:31, 32).

If the Holy Spirit may be quenched by our stubbornness, our insensitiveness, our self-will, oh, He may be grieved by our sin, our malice, our anger, our dirty talk, our bitterness of heart, our evil speaking! If you want the Spirit of God to speak to you, then make sure that He feels at home, ungrieved by sins hidden and coddled and excused in your own heart and life!

In conclusion, let me say that there are a thousand doors to be opened by the Holy Spirit, if we rely upon Him. Once I stepped out of a hotel room in Lima, Ohio, and felt led to speak to the maid who was making up the room next door. As she came into the hall to her cart I said, "Are you a Christian?"

She looked at me strangely, dropped her hands to her side, and said, "No, I am not, but I have been wanting to be for a long time." It was so simple and sweet to win her to the Lord. What if I had not listened to the Spirit's leading?

In Dallas, Texas, we were preparing for a great revival effort in the open air with a guest evangelist. With the building of the big platform, the building of a giant moving picture screen, the stringing of light wires, the hauling of seats and piano, the getting out of advertising materials from door to door, I was pressed without measure far into the night.

Yet that morning I had earnestly pleaded with the Lord that on this busy, busy Saturday He would open a door, that He would give me an opportunity to win some precious soul.

I was tied down about the Lord's business so that I

could not make a single visit. I could not set out to find a lost sinner. And as I came back rather sadly at nine o'clock at night to my home to eat a belated supper, wretchedly tired, I felt some sadness that some way my prayer had not been answered. I had found no lost soul I could win to Christ in the midst of the heavy, unavoidable duties! Suddenly the telephone rang. A young couple wanted to be married. All was in order; they were not divorced; they were not running away. He had had to work late on Saturday and they wanted no one but me to marry them. So they came to my home.

I took them aside when they came and found they were unsaved. Both the young bridegroom and the bride and, as I recall, a sister, were unconverted, and it was my great joy to win them all to Christ; then at eleven o'clock at night we had the marriage ceremony for a Christian young couple! God had opened a door in answer to prayer!

Oh, do not think you can be the soul winner God wants you to be without constantly beseeching Him for wisdom and guidance and open doors, and for the power of the Holy Spirit.

10. Heavenly Wisdom of the Soul Winner

"The fruit of the righteous is a tree of life; and he that winneth souls is wise."—Prov. 11:30.

THE ATHEIST FOOL thinks he is wise when he says there is no God (Ps. 14:1, Ps. 53:1). The liberal religionist, the modernist, the fool who is slow to believe all that the prophets have spoken in the Bible, thinks he is much wiser than the simple Bible believer (Luke 24:25-27). But holy Scripture tells us that these are fools. "For the wisdom of this world is foolishness with God" (I Cor. 3:19). We learn in the Bible that "the fear of the Lord is the beginning of wisdom" (Prov. 9:10). So we should not be surprised to go the next step and learn that the greatest spiritual wisdom is to win souls and so enter in with the love of God the Father who gave His Son, join in with the Saviour who came into the world to save sinners, and join in with the Holy Spirit who convicts the world of sin and righteousness and judgment, in winning men to love and serve the Saviour, in keeping people out of Hell! The soul winner is wise. The best Christian is the best soul winner, and the best wisdom is the wisdom of the soul winner!

So here in Proverbs 11:30 we find the gem of divine instruction, "The fruit of the righteous is a tree of life; and he that winneth souls is wise."

I. Soul Winning a Principal Emphasis of the Old Testament

One has read very carelessly the Old Testament who has not learned that the great hero of the law and the prophets and the Psalms is the Lord Jesus Christ, that He is the central theme, and that the salvation of sinners is everywhere joined to that theme by implication and often by direct statement.

1. The Theme of All the Prophets.

When Peter went to preach to Cornelius and his household, he seems to have given his theme at the start of the extended sermon he intended to preach. It was this: "To him [Jesus] give all the prophets witness, that through his name whosoever believeth in him shall receive remission of sins" (Acts 10:43). Later he reported to the brethren at Jerusalem, "And as I began to speak, the Holy Ghost fell on them, as on us at the beginning" (Acts 11:15), and he needed to speak no further. He had already given the key of all the Scriptures, and they who had so earnestly waited and prayed to know how to have peace with God and forgiveness of sins now knew it. It was through Christ and personal faith in Him. So Cornelius and his household were saved and filled with the Holy Spirit.

But here we have in divine revelation the truth that the theme of all the prophets, both Old Testament and New Testament, was Jesus, and that "whosoever believeth in him shall receive remission of sins" (Acts 10:43).

Christ is the seed of the woman promised to Adam and Eve. He is the prophet like unto Moses, promised to Israel. He is the suffering servant of Isaiah 50 and 53. He is the one crying out on the cross in Psalm 22. He is the child born, the Son given, of Isaiah 9:6 and 7. He is the virgin-born child of Isaiah 7:14. He is the seed promised Abraham. He is the Son of David who is promised to sit on David's throne. He is "the Lord our righteousness" in Jeremiah. He is the second David who will reign over both the houses of Israel, promised in Ezekiel.

Not only so, but Jesus is symbolized and pictured by object lessons throughout the Old Testament. He is the Passover Lamb. Yea, He is the scapegoat bearing blame which is not His. He is the mourning turtledove picturing the man of sorrows. He is the bullock, the burden-bearing Saviour. He is the white and stainless pigeon. Every bloody sacrifice, from Abel to the Passover Lamb killed the day Jesus was on the cross, pictured the atoning death of Jesus Christ.

The high priest anointed with oil pictured Jesus our High Priest filled with the Spirit. Young David, anointed to be king, pictured the Lord Jesus Christ anointed and filled with the Spirit to reign on David's throne one day. The golden candlestick, a lamp stand, pictured Christ the Light of the World, burning in the power of the Holy Spirit. The shewbread, twelve loaves placed fresh every Sabbath day in the tabernacle or temple, pictured Jesus the Bread of Life. The manna which fell in the wilderness is Christ also, the manna from Heaven.

The brazen serpent on a pole to whom the snake-bitten Israelites could look and be healed, is Jesus on the cross, as He Himself told Nicodemus.

Oh, the spiritual heart can find Jesus on nearly every page of the Old Testament. That is why the law was David's delight. Even before the law, Abraham saw Christ's day and was glad and believed on Him as we do. He saw in the offering of Isaac, the crucifixion; in the sparing of Isaac, the resurrection.

The furniture of the tabernacle was made of wood, to picture Christ's humanity, and covered with gold, to picture His deity. The pure white linen over the tabernacle pictured His sinless purity. The ram's skins dyed red pictured His atonement. The badgers' skins, dull and unattractive to the world, pictured Him as this outer world sees Him. And the blue curtains pictured Him as deity, a heavenly being.

The spiritually-minded reader sees a picture of Christ in the ark of Noah, Christ the refuge for sinners from the storms of judgment.

2. But Every Prophet of the Old Testament Also Taught Salvation Through Faith in Christ.

That is the inspired statement Peter gave Cornelius, "To him give all the prophets witness, that through his name whosoever believeth in him shall receive remission of sins" (Acts 10:43). In my book, *Twelve Tremendous Themes,* I have an extended chapter on "The Double Theme of All the Prophets," that is, Christ and salvation by faith.

We read that "Abraham believed God, and it was imputed unto him for righteousness" (Jas. 2:23 and Gen. 15:6). And "believe" here means just what it means throughout the book of John, and in Acts 13:38, 39, and in Acts 16:31. It meant personal faith in the Saviour, for Abraham knew about Christ revealed to him by the Holy Spirit and pictured in the sacrifices.

The great texts that were preached on by New Testament preachers were taken from the Old Testament. Jesus preached to Nicodemus from Numbers 21:5-9—the fiery serpents and the brazen snake on a pole. Surely it is as easy to preach a sermon on salvation by faith in Christ from Exodus, chapter 12, on the passover lamb and the blood on the door, as to preach from John 3:16. That wonderful Scripture on salvation, "For whosoever shall call upon the name of the Lord shall be saved," is quoted twice in the New Testament, but is quoted from the Old Testament in Joel 2:32. The great text that led Martin Luther to put his faith in Christ instead of depending on his works, "The just shall live by faith," is found in the Old Testament, in Habakkuk 2:4. And how often in the Psalms are we taught that blessed is the man who trusts in the Lord!

3. How Often Soul Winning Is Taught in the Old Testament.

When I first felt led to preach on and expound this text a week ago, I was surprised and pleased to find how much there is in the Old Testament on soul winning. Aside from the prophecies and types and object lessons about Christ and salvation in the Old Testament, God's Word there often speaks of soul winning.

And why should it not? Saving sinners from sin and Hell is the main activity of God. It is the dearest thing to His heart. It is the one thing Jesus came into the world to do, as Paul plainly tells us in I Timothy 1:15: "This is a faithful saying, and worthy of all acceptation, that Christ Jesus came into the world to save sinners . . . ." And Jesus Himself said: "For the Son of man is come to seek and to save that which was lost" (Luke 19:10). And He said: "I came not to call the righteous, but sinners to repentance" (Mark 2:17). It could not be clearer that the one thing dearest to God's heart, the one thing for which Christ died, the one thing the Great Commission was given for, the one thing the churches are left on earth for, is to win souls. Therefore, we should expect to find the theme of soul winning in the Old Testament.

Here in Proverbs 11:30 we find that ". . . he that winneth souls is wise."

In Psalm 51, in his heartbroken prayer of confession after his sin with Bath-sheba, David seems to be most concerned lest he should lose out in turning sinners to repentance and conversion. He said: "Cast me not away from thy presence; and take not thy holy spirit from me. Restore unto me the joy of thy salvation; and uphold me with thy free spirit. Then will I teach transgressors thy ways; and sinners shall be converted unto thee" (Ps. 51:11-13). With his backsliding forgiven and the Holy Spirit's power upon him, David promises, **"Then will I teach transgressors thy ways; and sinners shall be converted unto thee."**

In Joel 2:28-32 we have a preview of a whole New Testament age. Peter read that passage aloud to the people at Pentecost (Acts 2:14-25) and said, "This is that . . . ," that is, the prophecy of Joel was beginning to befulfilled. And what was that promise? "And it shall come to pass afterward, that I will pour out my spirit upon all flesh; and your sons and your daughters shall prophesy, your old men shall dream dreams, your young men shall see visions: And also upon the servants and upon the handmaids in those days will I pour out my spirit . . . And it shall come to pass, that whosoever shall call on the name of the Lord shall be delivered . . . ." And the word *delivered* in the New Testament is translated "saved."

Here in the Old Testament then is the basic teaching that the pouring out of the Holy Spirit is for witnessing or prophesying for Christ, and the result is to be souls saved. So God had in mind all the New Testament teaching and activity, and foretold it here in Joel. And the main thing with God then as in the New Testament times was that Christians should be filled with the Spirit and witness or prophesy for Christ and win souls. If Pentecost is a good example of soul winning, then soul winning is as clearly taught in the Old Testament as in the New.

Jesus gave the parable of the sower, of the seeds scattered far and wide. Some of the seed was wasted. It fell on the turn row and the birds got it. So Satan takes the Word of God out of some hearts. Some seed fell on stony ground, some among the thorns, but some fell on good ground and brought forth fruit abundantly. And we are told that "the seed is the word of God" (Luke 8:11).

But this theme occurs again and again in the Old Testament.

In Psalm 126, verses 5 and 6, the psalmist had pleaded for a revival. Israel had returned again to coldness and backsliding after the happy restoration from captivity. The Lord answered, "They that sow in tears shall reap in joy.

He that goeth forth and weepeth, bearing precious seed, shall doubtless come again with rejoicing ..." (Ps. 126:5, 6).

The sowing in tears here does not mean the simple physical planting of a crop, but the spreading of the Gospel. Even the best farmers do not normally weep as they plant the seed. But in the Lord's blessed work we weep over lost sinners; we plead with holy compassion. It was that sowing of the soul winner of which the psalmist was inspired to speak. In Isaiah 32:20 is this instruction for the soul winner as the seed sower is referred to again: "Blessed are ye that sow beside all waters, that send forth thither the feet of the ox and the ass." This world is spiritually a world of hills and valleys as was Palestine. Not on the stony hillside, but in the bit of alluvial soil and the river bottom and in the bend of a creek was a place for planting. So blessed is the Christian who is always looking for some fruitful soil where he may sow the gospel seed.

Three verses in Ecclesiastes 11 talk about spiritual sowing.

"Cast thy bread upon the waters: for thou shalt find it after many days" (vs. 1). Sometimes we must sow by faith and wait long for the reaping. "He that observeth the wind shall not sow; and he that regardeth the clouds shall not reap" (vs. 4). Oh then, soul winner, do not be discouraged. Do not regard the circumstances unduly. "In the morning sow thy seed, and in the evening withhold not thine hand: for thou knowest not whether shall prosper, either this or that, or whether they both shall be alike good" (vs. 6).

This is the same teaching as Jesus gave in the parable of the sower. Not every seed sown will bring a living plant. Not every seed will sprout immediately. Some blessed results will be manifest long later.

Last week a man reminded me that eighteen or twenty years ago I held a tent revival campaign in Brooklyn. One night a Catholic young man was saved. Last week that dear man of God brought me the good news that out of that family, the young man had now won thirty-five others from darkness to light. The reaping time does not always come at once. God does not always pay on Saturday night, but God always pays. We are to be instant both in season and out of season. We are to sow the seed where there is obviously good ground and we are also to sow it where there seems not much prospect of results. We are to sow in hard times and in good times.

You see, soul winning is taught in the Old Testament as clearly as in the New Testament.

And so in Proverbs 11:30 God reminds us that "the fruit of the righteous is a tree of life; and he that winneth souls is wise."

II. "The Fruit of the Righteous Is a Tree of Life"

This first part of our text is full of significance. The Christian is regarded as a fruit tree, and God stops not at the fruit, but says that the fruit of the Christian tree is another fruit-bearing tree.

1. The Devoted Christian Is Called a Fruit Tree.

In Psalm 1:1-3, the blessed man who avoids the fellowship of the wicked and who meditates day and night in the Word of God is promised, "And he shall be like a tree planted by the rivers of water, that bringeth forth his fruit in his season; his leaf also shall not wither; and whatsoever he doeth shall prosper."

This blessed Christian is planted by the rivers of water and the water here is the blessed Word of God. This Christian has his roots down in the soil by the river bank, and however arid the desert nearby, this tree always has plenty of water. We are in a semiarid earth, but the tree by the water course can always maintain its green leaves and its fruit.

In West Texas where I grew up, as in Palestine, there is not enough rainfall normally to grow big trees everywhere such as grow in Illinois, Indiana, Michigan, Kentucky, etc. Mesquite trees and chaparral bushes might be out on the prairie, but if looking across the prairies one could see a line of trees, big cottonwoods, elm trees, hackberry trees, and wild chinaberry trees, he would know that there was a water course. It might be dry much of the year, but at least some part of the year there was abundant moisture, and the trees could grow big and strong. So the Christian in a dry world may always keep his roots down in the richness and food of the Word of God.

But it is a fruit tree pictured here: he "bringeth forth his fruit in his season." It is true also that his leaves never wither. This Christian meditating day and night in the Word of God can be happy all the time. But it is significant that his success is in fruit bearing. Yes, the devoted Christian is to bear fruit, that is, to win souls.

The same picture is given in Jeremiah 17:7 and 8: "Blessed is the man that trusteth in the Lord, and whose hope the Lord is. For he shall be as a tree planted by the waters, and that spreadeth out her roots by the river, and shall not see when heat cometh, but her leaf shall be green; and shall not be careful in the year of drought, neither shall cease from yielding fruit."

This blessed man "that trusteth in the Lord, and whose hope the Lord is," is like a tree planted by the waters. So the drought will not harm this tree, nor the heat of summer, "neither shall [it] cease from yielding fruit." The Christian is pictured as a fruit tree.

When the children of Israel were about to go into the land of Canaan, they received the clear instructions to spare the fruit trees when they should besiege a city:

"When thou shalt besiege a city a long time, in making war against it to take it, thou shalt not destroy the trees thereof by forcing an axe against them: for thou mayest eat of them, and thou shalt not cut them down (for the tree of the field is man's life) to employ them in the siege:

Only the trees which thou knowest that they be not trees for meat, thou shalt destroy and cut them down; and thou shalt build bulwarks against the city that maketh war with thee, until it be subdued."—Deut. 29:19, 20.

But here is a parable, a spiritual lesson. It was the part of wisdom that the Israelites should not destroy the fruit trees which would add so much to their prosperity and welfare in the years to come. But surely God had in mind more than that. When the Lord made the rule, "Thou shalt not muzzle the mouth of the ox that treadeth out the corn," Paul tells us that God did not have in mind principally the oxen, but had in mind His preachers (I Cor. 9:7-12). And so here God surely had first in mind His spiritual fruit trees. Our beloved friend, Dr. H. A. Ironside, now with the Lord, published a good sermon on "God's Fruit Trees."

The fruit tree is a soul winner. God Himself has promised to take particular care of the soul winner. "Every branch in me that beareth fruit, he purgeth it, that it may bring forth more fruit," Jesus said (John 15:2). So all of us with loving care should seek the spiritual prosperity of a soul winner and should seek to protect his good name and his influence, seek to keep him from any sin or compromise that would hurt his soul winning, seek to restore him to fellowship when, with our mutual human frailty, he may be less than he ought to be.

The Christian then is a fruit tree.

2. But "the Fruit of the Righteous Is a Tree."

Will you notice that if the righteous is regarded as a coconut palm tree, the fruit he has is not simply a coconut, but the coconut planted and grown into a tree! If the Christian be the branch of a vine, then the fruit would not simply be a cluster of grapes, but other grapevines to grow from cuttings or from the grape seed. The fruit of a Christian then is to be not only a soul saved, but another soul winner.

In Isaiah 61:1-3, we have prophecy about the coming of the Saviour and what He would do in preaching the Gospel to the meek, in binding up the brokenhearted, bringing liberty to the captives, and comforting the mourning. And then after all these blessings that Jesus would give in salvation, the passage ends, ". . . That they might be called trees of righteousness, the planting of the Lord, that he might be glorified." In verse 6 it is promised, "But ye shall be named the Priests of the Lord: men shall call you the Ministers of our God."

Oh, God intended not only that the poor sinner should hear the Gospel, that his tears should be wiped away, his sorrows of heart cured, the binding and slavery of sin's chain broken, but that those who are saved should be trees of righteousness, priests of the Lord, ministers of God, that is, soul winners!

Is not that the clear teaching of the Saviour in the Great Commission as given in Matthew 28:19 and 20? There we are commanded to go into all the world and teach or make disciples in all nations. We are to baptize converts and get them committed, sold out, and publicly lined up for Christ in the appointed way, by baptism. Then we are commanded, "Teaching them [the new converts] to observe all things whatsoever I have commanded you." That is, we are to teach the new converts that they, too, are to go into all the world and make disciples. They, too, are to preach the Gospel to every creature and get the converts baptized and then teach the converts to win souls. That Scripture is teaching that your work is not done when you win a soul. You should get him baptized, get him committed, get him publicly lined up for God, get him to be a real disciple. You should also teach him to observe everything that Christ taught the New Testament Christians, that is, to take the Gospel to all the world.

The Lord Jesus is saying here that the fruit of a Chris-

tian is not only a new convert, but a new convert who is
taught to win souls!

So the fruit of the righteous is a tree—not just a coconut, but another coconut palm tree bearing coconuts. And
the fruit of a Christian is another Christian who is a soul
winner.

And this tree is a tree of life. We are not now discuss-
ing the blessed truth of the joy that God gives in children
and grandchildren. We are talking about the blessedness of
winning souls, giving people eternal life and getting the
new converts to give others the gift of life, too, through
faith in Christ as Saviour.

III. The Wisdom of the Soul Winner

The wisdom of the soul winner is far beyond all human
wisdom. The soul winner deals with eternal values, gives
eternal blessings, has eternal rewards. His work abides
forever. The soul winner helps bring to consummation the
plan of God, the joy of Jesus Christ. The soul winner thus
for himself attains the highest level of devotion and of understanding of the Scriptures and of fellowship with God.
And the soul winner reaps eternal rewards.

*1. The Soul Winner Is in An Eternal Business With Eter-
nal Values.*

Jesus told of the rich man whose ground brought forth
plentifully. He built bigger barns. He congratulated himself,
"Soul, thou hast much goods laid up for many years; take
thine ease, eat, drink, and be merry." But God said to him,
"Thou fool, this night thy soul shall be required of thee:
then whose shall those things be, which thou hast provided?" And Jesus said, "So is he that layeth up treasure
for himself, and is not rich toward God" (Luke 12:16-21).
Hay in the barn, grain in the granary, potatoes in the cellar,
hams in the smokehouse, money in the bank—these after
all are a poor kind of riches. They are soon gone.

In a great American city a rich lumberman built for his wife a dream home. I have gone through the building. I slept in one of the beautiful bedrooms with tapestry on the walls instead of wallpaper. The floor was beautiful hardwood parquet. The doors were three-inch-thick solid mahogany from Honduras. The hardware on the doors, the hinges and door knobs, were of solid silver. The whole great mansion was built of the most expensive glazed brick. The man who lived in the servant's quarters told me these quarters were a seven-room mansion. The great home itself had a private elevator because the lumberman's wife, whom he loved so dearly, had heart trouble and he was afraid for her to climb the stairs. Everything that money could buy and love could lavish was put on that beautiful home. It occupied one half a block of very expensive ground in a city of a half million.

Yet this great property that cost a quarter of a million dollars to build, besides the very expensive half-block of ground on which it was built, was sold to a Bible institute for $30,000. And how did this come about? The rich lumberman's wife died. His daughter ran off and married a drunken profligate. The old man was left desolate and alone in the palace he had built. Every stairway, every room haunted him with memories. He moved out of that house and took a small apartment. He told his real estate agent, "Sell the place! Don't wait! I never want to see it again. Get rid of it!" So it was sold to a Bible institute for $30,000.

So passing and so failing are all the wealth and values of this life and this world!

But he that winneth souls is dealing with eternal destinies. One who helps a young couple to be happy for a time in a new home does well. One who gives a child a toy and makes him happy feels repaid, perhaps, with shouts and laughter. But the simple truth is that all the gains of this world are only temporary and fleeting.

In view of the disappointments, the failures, and the

waning happiness of this world, how important it is to win
a soul. There is frustration everywhere. As I speak to great
crowds and as they intently listen and do not think to look
pretty, their faces assume the grim lines that come naturally from a grim, sad struggle in their hearts. More people
buy sleeping pills and take tranquilizer tablets; more people
go to mental institutions and to psychiatrists; more people
have nervous breakdowns, because this world is a disap-
pointing world.

Youth starts out with the attitude, "We'll soon conquer
the world," but it isn't long until there is a grim struggle to
make ends meet and to make the home go and to keep up
with the Joneses. Day by day there is the struggle, the wear
on nerves, the ulcers of the stomach, the complaint of conscience, the new standards that everybody has to face.
After awhile one finds that some old men are bitter, some
are grim, some are defeated and quit. Always this world is
a world of unhappiness, a world of struggle.

Think of all the homes that start out so happily; then one
out of every three ends in divorce. There is one divorce suit
for every three marriages in America now. Think of all the
hopes when new businesses are started, but so many of them
fail. It is a sad business, this world's frustrations.

If a person wants to help somebody, it can't be done with
a little money now or a job or a bit of education or comfort
in sickness. There are only temporary alleviations of the
trouble. But to get a soul right with God, which gives him
peace in his heart and a home in Heaven for eternity—
what an eternal investment!

In view of the complaining, of the sadness, the failures
in business, the breakdown in health, the divided homes,
the broken friendships—in view of the failures and disappointments and the unhappiness of this world, in Jesus'
name we ought to win souls. It is so much wiser to make an
investment for eternity!

I saw children playing on the beach in the wet sand.

They built fortresses and castles and tunnels. But in a few hours the waves of the rising tide had lapped them all down to smooth sand again. So he who builds on the popularity or the wealth or the fleeting joys of this world is not wise. No, the true wisdom is to build for the eternal world. Souls who are won will last when the stars grow cold, will enjoy the presence of God when earth's triumphs seem futile and transitory and unimportant. One who wins souls deals with eternal values. He keeps people from Hell, he populates Heaven, he makes for eternal righteousness and eternal blessedness. Oh, how wise is the soul winner!

A wonderful truth is here, that people who are wise take the long look, and the soul winner is the wise person who looks to eternal blessedness, eternal issues, and eternal rewards. A number of cases in the Bible illustrate this.

Consider Jacob and Esau. Many would suppose that Jacob was not as good a man as Esau. Esau was a dutiful son, I suppose, and greatly loved by his father Isaac, but Esau didn't care about being the head of a promised nation in the future, and being an ancestor of the Lord Jesus who was to come, and helping God fulfill a world-wide plan. Jacob did. Esau would rather have a bowl of chili now than to have the eternal blessings of heading a nation and being the ancestor of the Lord Jesus. That is why the Bible calls him "that profane person, Esau." He was not wise. He took the short look and asked for immediate comforts instead of eternal rewards.

Another illustration of a man who took the long look is Abraham. He left his father's house and country and Ur of the Chaldees, and came to Palestine. And all the rest of his days this man who grew up in riches lived in a tent and had his meals cooked over a campfire. The Scripture tells us that he looked for a city that hath foundations, whose builder and maker is God. All of these, the Bible said—Abraham, Isaac, and Jacob—dwelt in tabernacles, that is, in tents, because they had not yet received the promises; but someday they will. They took the long look and were willing to wait for the reward.

On the other hand, Lot pitched his tent toward Sodom. He wanted a nice home now, and cultured companions for his children. He wanted the money and the fame and the good standing that would come among worldly men. Lot took the short look, and the ruin that followed in Sodom came because he was not wise.

2. The Worth of a Soul and the Fact of Hell Make It Wise to Win Souls.

Now, it is wise to win souls. I call your attention to several great truths which illustrate that. One of them is the worth of a soul. Oh, how much is it worth to keep a soul from going to eternal torment forever? The Lord Jesus said on this matter, "What shall it profit a man, if he shall gain the whole world, and lose his own soul? Or what shall a man give in exchange for his soul?" (Mark 8:36, 37). What matter the banks, the railroads, the airlines, the stocks and bonds, the coal mines, the real estate, if a poor soul goes to Hell? In view of the worth, the eternal worth of the precious soul, then how much is it worth to win souls? It is wise to save a soul.

I grew up in the cattle country in West Texas. We raised mules and fine-blooded horses. One winter we kept about forty-four mule colts in the home pasture, and we drove them up each day and fed them after they were taken away from their mothers. One day as I drove these mules across the dam of the little creek and through the pasture up to the house, a mule colt jumped into the creek above the dam and bogged down in the mud and water and couldn't get out. He struggled, and I stood on the bank and shouted and whipped my big Stetson hat on my thigh, but he couldn't get out. After awhile, in two feet of water and two feet of mud, I suppose, the mule got cold and gave up. When his big head went under the water, I went into the cold water and helped straighten him up. He shook the water out of his ears as I got his feet under him, got him by the tail and lifted and shouted and struggled as he struggled. He pulled those long legs out of the mud and got out; then he ambled crookedly toward the house. I was nearly frozen in that January weather. But I had saved a fifty dollar mule colt. Yet how much greater is the worth of an immortal soul!

Consider also the fact of Hell. It is the most concrete and terrible fact in this universe, that men without God go into eternal torment, that unconverted, unrepentent men are away from God and peace forever in a place the Bible calls Hell.

If you are a Bible Christian, then you will know the Bible has much to say about Hell; that the wicked shall be cast into Hell with all the nations that forget God. If you claim to love and follow the Saviour, you must know that the dear Lord Jesus said that Hell is a place where the worm dies not and the fire is not quenched. He said the smoke of their torment ascendeth up forever and that people in Hell have no rest day nor night. The Lord lifted the lid off Hell and told about a man who these two thousand years or more has been crying for a drop of water to cool his tongue, a man tormented in flame and tormented by memory of what could have been and might have been, had he not missed his opportunity.

I say, the Lord is one who warns us of the fact of Hell. And in view of the torment of the damned and the awful ruin that awaits the eternal perdition of those who go without God, how important it is to win souls! I do not wonder that Proverbs 11:30 says, "The fruit of the righteous is a tree of life; and he that winneth souls is wise"—how wise in view of the eternal torment of the damned!

3. Christ's Sufferings Show How Much It Is Worth to Save a Soul.

Then, how shall we measure what it is worth to win a

soul? Well, what did Jesus pay? Consider the sufferings of Christ. The dear Lord Jesus, who emptied Himself of His glory and laid aside the garments of majesty white as the light and His face shining as the sun, took on Himself the form of a servant and became obedient to death, even the death of the cross. Consider the dear Lord Jesus. He was born in direst poverty in a manger, laid in a stable, with no room in the Inn. He grew up in a carpenter's shop and lived among the poorest of the poor peasants in Galilee and Nazareth. The Lord was thirty homesick years away from Heaven and the angels and the gold streets and the gates of pearl and the effulgent smile of the Heavenly Father. Thirty years was He in poverty and misunderstanding; then came three and a half years of ministry to men who would not come, years of disappointment, enmity, hate, and spite.

Then with His face set toward the cross came a traitor's kiss and a mocking trial. Stripped naked, beaten with a Roman scourge, nailed to a cross, and for hours hanging naked there between two thieves and even the Father turning His face away, He died. When you consider the sufferings of the dear Lord Jesus, and all of it to keep sinners out of Hell, all of it in order to keep people from the ruin of sin and bring them into peace with God—in view of what Jesus paid to save souls, it must be wise to win them. Anyone who would be like Jesus, anyone who would accept divine wisdom and would accept God's own evaluation of eternal things will, then, in Jesus' name, win souls on account of how He valued them. Oh, he that winneth souls is wise.

4. The Glories of Heaven to Which We Win People Show How Wise Is the Winner of Souls.

Consider also the glories of Heaven. I mention elsewhere that there are wonderful rewards here and now for soul winning. One of the sweetest is that day by day one can walk in fellowship with God. You know it is wonderful to be a partner with Jesus Christ in keeping sinners out of Hell.

I remember how I won my first soul as a fifteen-year-old boy. In that West Texas cowtown I turned to a fifteen-year-old boy beside me and got him to admit he was a sinner and to call on the Lord Jesus for mercy and to put his trust in Christ and then later to claim Him openly. Oh, the soul winner's joy! I was conscious of the Lord's presence and the sweet influence of the Holy Spirit in my life. Then day by day I learned the joy of answered prayer.

Then another earthly blessing is the gratitude of those who are saved. But the joy and blessings here are nothing compared to those of Heaven.

The soul winner is not counted so wise here. The man who makes the money, who gets elected to office, the man who has the big pull, is the smart one now, men think. Even in Christian circles, the soul winner is not worth nearly as much in the sight of men as the money raiser or the man who boosts the program. He is going to get farther among men than the man who keeps harlots and drunkards out of Hell and gets men to repent and turn to God. I say, the evangelist and the soul winner may not rate so high here but, bless God, one day he will. That may be one reason why the Lord Jesus said so often that many of the first shall be last and the last first.

Daniel 12:3 says, "And they that be wise shall shine as the brightness of the firmament; and they that turn many to righteousness as the stars for ever and ever." What a wonderful thing to keep people out of Hell! Earthly fame flees away. Wealth slips from palsied fingers on the deathbed or perhaps in a day or a night of disaster before death. Families are broken up, friends forsake, and loved ones die and leave you. Oh, everything earthly is fleeting, but the fame and blessings of the soul winner are eternal. We can thank God for that.

"He that winneth souls is wise"!

11. You Can Always Win Souls

"And Jesus went about all the cities and villages, teaching in their synagogues, and preaching the gospel of the kingdom, and healing every sickness and every disease among the people. But when he saw the multitudes, he was moved with compassion on them, because they fainted, and were scattered abroad, as sheep having no shepherd. Then saith he unto his disciples, The harvest truly is plenteous, but the labourers are few; Pray ye therefore the Lord of the harvest, that he will send forth labourers into his harvest."—Matt. 9:35-38.

"After these things the Lord appointed other seventy also, and sent them two and two before his face into every city and place, whither he himself would come. Therefore said he unto them, The harvest truly is great, but the labourers are few: pray ye therefore the Lord of the harvest, that he would send forth labourers into his harvest. Go your ways: behold, I send you forth as lambs among wolves."—Luke 10:1-3.

"Say not ye, There are yet four months, and then cometh harvest? behold, I say unto you, Lift up your eyes, and look on the fields; for they are white already to harvest."—John 4:35.

THE LAKE of human life near you is full of fish, and fish are always biting! There are always souls who can be won. The harvest is always great, always plenteous, always white. In nearly forty years of ministry as an evangelist and six years of active personal soul winning before I was a preacher, I have found that there are always sinners who can be won to Christ. I cannot win everybody, but I can win somebody.

Nearly everywhere I go somebody says, "Don't you find that it is getting harder to win souls, harder to have revivals?" Or people ask, "Don't you find that it is harder to have revivals in the North than in the South?" And in nearly every place I go to preach, people tell me, usually including the pastor or pastors, "We have a very peculiar and difficult situation here." When my dear friend, Bennie Hedstrom, leading the Christian Business Men's Committee in Chicago, which he founded, invited me to come to Chicago for noonday evangelistic services in a theatre down in the Loop, broadcast over a powerful radio station, he told me, "You'll find it harder here. You cannot win souls here as you can down South. Don't be disappointed if we do not have the same results." But bless God, we did have the same kind of results, most wonderful cases of salvation.

When I went to Canada in a revival effort, a pastor told me, "You won't have the kind of results here that you had in Chicago. We are Britishers. We are conservative. We do not move as quickly here as people do down in the States." I told him that yes, we had that kind of people down South where I grew up, too, only we called them backsliders. Then, thank God, I remember with what joy the distinguished pastor called me back to his study one night after we had had some fifteen adults come to Christ. He had his arms around a gray-headed man, and could hardly talk for weeping, and he said, "I have been praying for this man for twenty years and now, Brother Rice, here he comes!"

The plain, simple truth is that the soul winner's harvest is white. There are always souls who can be won.

I. God's Word Plainly Guarantees That There Always Will Be Souls Available Who May Be Won

It is remarkable that three times in the New Testament, on different occasions, Jesus said almost the same thing.

And to the twelve, when He was moved with compassion over the great multitudes about Him like sheep having no shepherd, He said, "The harvest truly is plenteous, but the labourers are few; Pray ye therefore the Lord of the harvest, that he will send forth labourers into his harvest" (Matt. 9:37, 38). The harvest was plentiful then.

Later, since the twelve could not enter all the open doors, could not reach all the places needing the Gospel, Jesus sent other seventy also. They were nobodies. We do not know the name of a one of them. Evidently they were new converts, not mature sheep, but "lambs," which Jesus sent, "among wolves." And He said unto them, "The harvest truly is great, but the labourers are few: pray ye therefore the Lord of the harvest, that he would send forth labourers into his harvest" (Luke 10:2). Oh, He did not have mature, well-trained Christians, so He sent new converts because the harvest was so great.

Again, as Jesus talked to His disciples at the town of Sychar in Samaria, after He had won a Samaritan woman and she had gone running to town to tell the men, "Come, see a man, which told me all things that ever I did: is not this the Christ?" and while the townspeople were coming out to meet this wonderful Saviour, Jesus said to His disciples: "Say not ye, There are yet four months, and then cometh harvest? behold, I say unto you, Lift up your eyes, and look on the fields; for they are white already to harvest" (John 4:35).

We have no cases where Jesus ever indicated the harvest was over as far as a community or individual workers are concerned. There are no kinds of people where some cannot be won. There are no ages in church history when the Gospel loses its power, or when sinners cannot be brought to trust the Saviour.

That is indicated by the great promise of Psalm 126:5, 6: "They that sow in tears shall reap in joy. He that goeth forth and weepeth, bearing precious seed, shall doubtless come again with rejoicing, bringing his sheaves with him." Here is a positive promise: Those who sow in tears shall reap in joy. Here is a clear-cut guarantee: One who goes forth with weeping, bearing the precious seed of the Gospel, is certain to come back with sheaves. We are not promised that we will catch every fish in the lake, but we are promised that we can catch a mess of fish. We are not promised that every effort will win a soul, but some of our efforts will if we keep on trying.

In the Great Commission, Jesus plainly implies that there are always some who can be won. He said, ". . . Go ye into all the world, and preach the gospel to every creature. He that believeth and is baptized shall be saved; but he that believeth not shall be damned" (Mark 16:15, 16). There are some who will believe when the Gospel is preached in power, when any community is covered with personal soul-winning effort in the power of God. Jesus stated the Great Commission again in Acts 1:8, "But ye shall receive power, after that the Holy Ghost is come upon you: and ye shall be witnesses unto me both in Jerusalem, and in all Judea, and in Samaria, and unto the uttermost part of the earth." The implication here is that when the Holy Spirit comes on us there will be the power of God to change hearts and save souls in our witnessing. And then the Great Commission is given in Matthew 28:19, 20. Jesus finished with the plain statement, "And, lo, I am with you alway, even unto the end of the world." Surely we ought to understand this to mean that Christ's presence will give some measure of power and success in witnessing.

In the parable of the sower in Matthew 13:3-8, the Lord Jesus outlines the difficulties and the blessings of a soul winner. Some of the precious seed falls by the wayside and is eaten by the fowls of the air. That represents the gospel word taken out of the hearts of sinners by Satan so that they are not saved.

And some seed, we are told, falls upon stony places— hardened hearts who may make some resolutions but who have no work of grace in the heart and are not truly born again. When persecution or trouble comes, they fall away from their profession.

And we are told that some seed falls among thorns and although the seed sprouts and grows, it brings no fruit to perfection. Every soul winner is sad over some he wins to Christ who never do much as Christians. They do not leave off all the ways of the world. They are not fruitful Christians.

But, thank God, we are told, "Other fell into good ground, and brought forth fruit, some an hundredfold, some sixtyfold, some thirtyfold."

Here we have the four kinds of ground upon which the gospel seed falls. The song says,

> Going forth with weeping, sowing for the Master,
> Tho' the loss sustained our spirit often grieves;
> When our weeping's over, He will bid us welcome,
> We shall come rejoicing, bringing in the sheaves.

Oh, we cannot win everybody, but we can win somebody! The birds of the air get some seed, and some seed falls on stony ground, but some seed falls on good ground and brings forth fruit, if we keep on sowing and if we keep on going after sinners with the Gospel!

It is the unanimous teaching of the Scriptures that always there are people who can be won to Christ, that the harvest is always white. Brother, there is **great fishing!** The fish are biting!

II. A Study of God's Dealing in Great Times of Declension and Sin Shows That Souls Always Can Be Won to Christ

The time of greatest backsliding and spiritual decline in Israel was, I suppose, a little before the captivity of Israel, when Ahab was king and even more wicked Jezebel was queen. Then most of the prophets of God were killed and a few were hid by fifties in a cave and fed on bread and water. Four hundred and fifty prophets of Baal, idol prophets, ate at the king's table. Only one man of God stood true, and Ahab hoped and earnestly tried to kill that one man, Elijah. But when Elijah called Israel to Mount Carmel and gave the challenge that if Baal could answer by fire from Heaven, all should serve Baal, but if God should answer by miraculous fire in answer to prayer, all should serve God, the people assented, and God wonderfully showed His power. The four hundred and fifty prophets of Baal were killed. The people fell on their faces and cried, "The Lord, he is the God." And in God's mercy the captivity was postponed a season.

Oh, if one could win souls in the days of Ahab and Jezebel, in the days when idols were put in the temple of God and the prophets were killed, and the people liked it so, he can win souls today.

We remember that Jonah went to wicked Nineveh and preached. Strangely enough, in that heathen city the king himself was convicted and called on the people to put on sackcloth and ashes and fast and pray. God heard, and a multitude turned to God. They were really converted, too, for Jesus said, "The men of Nineveh shall rise in judgment with this generation, and shall condemn it: because they repented at the preaching of Jonas; and, behold, a greater than Jonas is here" (Matt. 12:41). Those men were saved and will be in Heaven and will bear witness at the last judgment against others who are not saved. If God could use Jonah to win souls in Nineveh, He can use you to win souls in the most difficult situation.

The early days of the apostles in Jerusalem, after Christ was crucified, give us an amazing story of victory. The nation had rebelled against Christ's teaching. The Pharisees and others had conspired to have Him killed, and the mob went along with their leaders. So they hated and rejected Jesus and nailed Him to a cross and mocked Him while He died. Judas Iscariot, one of the twelve, sold his Master for thirty pieces of silver. Peter, the best preacher and the best Christian in the world, cursed and swore, denied the Saviour publicly, then quit the ministry. What a forbidding situation in which to try to win souls! The people were Gospel-hardened; the wicked men who killed the Saviour would like to have killed His disciples. Yet the disciples waited in the upper room until the power of the Holy Spirit came upon them, and they went out and won three thousand souls in a day, and other thousands in the days that followed, multitudes both of men and women! If they could win souls in Gospel-hardened Jerusalem, we can win souls anywhere.

Jesus found the harvest white in Samaria among those half-breed false religionists.

Centuries since Pentecost, when the church was licentious, worldly, unbelieving, its ministers largely unconverted deists, in England John Wesley set new converts to winning souls and changed the moral and spiritual face of England and saved England from a French Revolution. In dissolute, profane, lawless New York State in pioneer times, Charles G. Finney set out to preach the Gospel in power and won thousands.

God guarantees that the harvest will always be white, that there will always be souls to win, that the Gospel is the power of God unto salvation. And the history of the Gospel proves it is so.

III. God Has Infinite Resources for the Soul Winner Which Make It Always Possible to Win Souls

Paul was inspired to write, "The weapons of our warfare are not carnal, but mighty through God to the pulling down of strong holds" (II Cor. 10:4). The man who has enough dynamite, and has big enough power shovels, and sufficient power to run them, and the authority to get the supplies he needs—that man can move mountains. Thank God, His resources, freely available, always provided, make it so the soul winner can always win.

First, there is the Word of God. Paul said, "I am not ashamed of the gospel of Christ: for it is the power of God unto salvation to every one that believeth" (Rom. 1:16). Oh, there is power in the Word of God!

God said to Jeremiah, "Is not my word like as a fire? . . . and like a hammer that breaketh the rock in pieces?" (Jer. 23:29). The Word of God has soul-saving power and it is sharper than a two-edged sword. The Word of God has a part in every soul saved, "Being born again, not of corruptible seed, but of incorruptible, by the word of God, which liveth and abideth for ever" (I Pet. 1:23), and "The law of the Lord is perfect, converting the soul . . ." (Ps. 19:7).

Oh, this blessed Word of God! If Jesus Christ were here today to preach, He would have nothing better to preach than the Bible which we have. When He was here He preached out of the Old Testament all the time. One who has the Bible has an infallible element in soul winning.

There is the grace of God, His loving mercy for sinners, His brooding, compassionate heart that will never be satisfied until the last sinner has a most urgent invitation to be saved. I beg you, go look in your Bible again! If John 3:16 is still there, then you can still win souls! Does God still "so love the world" as He did when He gave His only begotten Son? If God had it to do over again, would He give Heaven's fairest and best, and the dearest of His heart, His Son, to keep people out of Hell? If God's loving grace, freely offered sinners, is a fact, then, thank God, that is a resource always available for soul winning.

But one answers back and complains that there is sin everywhere, there is the darkness of unbelief and liberalism. There is the flaunting of God's laws, the profaning of God's names, the secular-minded indifference to spiritual matters. Oh, this is a sinful world! We are a sinful, fallen race of men. The human heart is wicked beyond description. In fact, we are told by divine inspiration, "The heart is deceitful above all things, and desperately wicked: who can know it?" (Jer. 17:9). Ah yes! But God knew all that ahead of time. Then we are given the triumphant, glad statement that "where sin abounded, grace did much more abound" (Rom. 5:20). The love of God, the grace of God, the pity of God, the compassion of God, the unceasing love of the Father and of the Son and of the Holy Spirit for lost men, make it so the soul winner can always win souls. There are so many factors stacked in favor of the soul winner!

Then, a weapon too largely ignored, a resource so little used, is the fullness of the Spirit of God! There is the anointing of the Holy Ghost! There is the breath of Heaven which may come on the heart and mind and words of the soul winner. The Holy Spirit finds no cases too hard. The Holy Spirit can convict the hardest hearts. I have seen it up and down this country. I saw it in India when hundreds turned to Christ last January. Not occasionally, but regularly in my major campaigns, I have seen drunkards, harlots, infidels, Catholics, Jews, hardened sinners, self-satisfied religionists, won to Christ and salvation. Too often we chip away with our own hustle, our own brains, our own personality, when we could have the dynamite of God set off in the hearts of sinners. If we would only wait upon God for the fullness of the Spirit, to speak when we speak, to witness where we witness! The Word of God may seem powerless in my hands alone. "The letter killeth," but the sword of the Spirit is not powerless when God the Spirit wields it.

Oh, then, there are resources which make it so a Christian can always win souls. Let us make sure we use these resources.

God answers prayer. As long as the promises of God are true, I can have clear leading where to go, to whom I should speak, and what to say. As long as God answers prayer, He can make circumstances fit in with my soul-winning testimony.

Since God answers prayer, He could bring Philip and the Ethiopian eunuch together, and have the eunuch reading Isaiah 53.

Since God answers prayer, Paul could have Elymas the sorcerer stricken blind when he hindered the winning of Sergius Paulus, and so could bring the hesitant sinner to saving faith (Acts 13:6-12).

Since God answers prayer, there are doors that can be opened, contacts with the right persons that can be made. When Paul and Silas prayed, they shook the jail doors open and broke the bonds and shook the jailer not only out of his bunk but out of his complacency to beg, "Sirs, what must I do to be saved?" (Acts 16:30).

I say, there are divine resources which make it so the harvest is always available, so sinners can always be won.

IV. The Nature of Mankind in This World Is Such That There Are Always New Opportunities for Soul Winning

There was a great increase in marriages and in war babies following World War II. Now everywhere in America new high schools are being built, and the colleges are getting ready for a great upsurge in college attendance. The increase in population means that business leaders plan to have more steel mills, build more automobiles, open more stores. Every one of that new crop of babies, millions of children and young people, need to be won to Christ. Always, year after year, there are thousands upon thousands of boys and girls coming to the ages of accountability.

I rejoice greatly that my six daughters and my six sons-in-law are all saved. But I have twenty grandchildren. Seven of them have professed faith in Christ. That means that thirteen of them in the next few years are to be won. I know that there is a new crop of souls to be won.

The secular world talks about the "population explosion," and scientists urge birth control measures. Well, for the soul winner, that "population explosion" simply means millions more people need the Gospel and are available to win.

Then on every hand the bereavements, the disappointments, the heartaches, the failures inevitable among a sinful race tend to prepare people for the Gospel. Communists take advantage of every great unrest, every clash between races or governments. Well, surely with all the unrest, all the blessings and plagues, there are movements of God's Spirit to prepare people to be saved.

In Fort Worth, Texas, a five-year-old girl died after a short illness. The brokenhearted father could not be consoled. But, oh, how his heart opened to the blessed truth that the Lord Jesus may come at any time and that he could be ready to meet his little girl again. He had lain and sobbed on the bed. Suddenly he sat upright and said to me vehemently, "I wish He would come today!" Every sore heart means that much hearing for the Gospel.

In Dallas, Texas, I was called to a home. A man had gone out on a drunk. His angry wife called me. Two children sat awed and silent at the tragedy in the home. The woman nagged, "I don't believe he loves me. He says he does, but he doesn't act like it." The man with his face in his hands wept like a child. He told me, "My boss says if I go on one more binge, I am fired. He can't put up with that anymore. My wife says that she can't live like this. She will go home to her mother. Oh, Brother Rice, if there were only some way I could get hold of myself and leave off this drink and be the man I want to be!" That tragedy was the door to paradise! That heartbreak was the occasion of heartease and joy in Jesus Christ. How sweet it was for us all to kneel together in that room, and there he trusted Jesus Christ.

In Shamrock, Texas, a young woman, daughter of a prominent family, had threatened to commit suicide. I asked her friend to bring her to my home, and she came. She told me, "I wish I were dead. I have tried everything. There is nothing in life fit to live for." She had been sent abroad by a doting father and had visited the art capitols of the world. She had had college and mink coats and travel. She had had music. She was a member of the country club set. She had tried all the pleasures of the world. She said, "For a little time I fool myself and think I can be happy again, then when I am home after a party, I wish I were dead. I would kill myself but for the grief of my father and mother."

I told her how she could have peace and find life sweet and blessed every day. She looked at me in disbelief; then with trembling lips she asked me, "Please tell me how!"

I said, "Kneel here by your chair and tell Jesus Christ what you have told me. Tell Him you have tried all the world has to give and it brings only heartache and frustration and dissatisfaction. Tell Him that your heart is empty and hungry and sad and you want peace and forgiveness. Tell Him you will trust Him now."

We knelt together and I prayed. Her tears made a six-inch spot on the carpet as she prayed and sobbed. Then she trusted the Saviour and rose up with glad joy in her face and went out to a life of peace and happiness.

I am saying that the frustrations and troubles and emergencies and bereavements of this world make it so there are always hearts open to the Gospel.

Two young people came to be married with stars in their eyes. Their love was sweet and beautiful. Because the bride's heart was so tender as she thought of a home of her own

with the man she loved so well, she was grateful and glad
and thankful to God, and it was easy to win her to Christ.

A strong young man wept by the casket of his mother.
She was such a good woman and she loved him so. He was
overwhelmed at the thought of his loss. In a few moments
he put his trust in his mother's God. I have seen several
hundred people saved either at funerals or beside the casket
in their own homes or beside the open grave.

I knew one who was saved and rejoiced and clapped her
hands when I preached to women in a jail in Fort Worth.
She praised God aloud, "Thank God I got in jail! I wouldn't
go to church, wouldn't listen to the radio. But I got in jail
and I thought I would rot. I couldn't see anybody, had nothing to read, nobody to talk to. So for a change I came to the
chapel for the service. Thank God I got in jail and God kept
me out of Hell!"

You needn't tell me there is nobody to win. As long as
sin abounds, grace will much more abound. The more trouble and heartache there is in the world, the more people
there are who can be won to Christ. The brokenhearted
mother who lost her baby, the man who played the fool and
broke up his home, the man who wasted his opportunities
and failed in business, the wild young people who found that
Satan's apples all have worms and that the end of that
mirth is heaviness—all these are good opportunities for the
Gospel.

One night in North Texas we found a car overturned by
the highway. That night I won two of those young people to
Christ in a midnight prayer meeting.

Do you think no one has a fear of death? Do you think
no one has a moving of conscience? Do you think no poor
wayward girl ever wishes she were pure again, and longs to
have forgiveness and cleansing? A secular writer writing
about work in the penitentiaries tells how the newcomers to
the penitentiary often cry out in the night, "O Lord, I'm
sorry!" One prisoner told me sadly how his father had

mortgaged the farm, how his mother's hair had grown snow white and she wept most of the time. He was eager to find peace and forgiveness. I am saying that human nature and this world being what they are, there are always hearts ready for the gospel message, ready to be saved.

V. Do Not Be Discouraged by Disappointments and Rebuffs: There Are Still Souls That Can Be Won

I remember one dear Christian woman who heard a sermon on soul winning and decided that she would earnestly try to win someone to Christ. The first person she approached brushed the matter aside and did not turn to Christ. She told me she was so disappointed that in the two or three years since that time she had never tried again to win a soul! It is said, "Faint heart ne'er won fair lady." And it is weak and sinful to give up soul winning because of a little difficulty or disappointment.

In Luke 14:15-24, Jesus gives a wonderful picture of a soul winner at work. He told the parable of a man who made a great supper and bade many and sent his servant at suppertime to say to them that were bidden, "Come; for all things are now ready." And we are told that "they all with one consent began to make excuse." One had bought a piece of ground and must needs go and see it at suppertime. Another had bought five yoke of oxen and now he must set out to prove these oxen. Another had married a wife, and without saying, "Have me excused," simply said, "Therefore, I cannot come." It is obvious that all those were excuses, not reasons. If a man had already bought the ground, it would be there tomorrow. If he had already bought the oxen, suppertime is not the best time to prove them. A man who has married a wife would normally want to take his lovely bride out to a supper. And Jesus intended these excuses and rebuffs to indicate the treatment that a soul winner is to expect.

That servant went back and reported to his lord, who

said to him, "Go out quickly into the streets and lanes of the city, and bring in hither the poor, and the maimed, and the halt, and the blind." And the servant did so. If he could not get one class, he would get another. If he could not get those who were first invited to come, he would invite others. I am so glad that the poor and the halt and the lame and the blind are dear to God and welcome.

But still there was room! So the master commanded his servant, "Go out into the highways and hedges, and compel them to come in, that my house may be filled." And the servant did so and the supper was furnished with guests.

How many rebuffs! How much disappointment! He could not get everybody, but he could get somebody. And so can you! Do not be discouraged. You know ahead of time that not everybody is going to be saved.

Do you think that the vacuum cleaner salesman going from door to door makes a sale at every house? Does an automobile company sell to everyone who looks at a car? Do you think that every voter a candidate shakes hands with votes for that candidate? Does every boy who asks a girl for a date get to marry that girl? When a fisherman goes fishing, does he get a fish for every bait he puts on the hook? It is foolish to suppose that immediately and easily everybody we approach will turn to Christ. That is not what God promises. But He does promise that there are those we can win and that we ought to do it.

Yesterday morning I started out in an Iowa town, where I am engaged in revival services, going from business house to business house. I suppose I talked to twenty people. There were Catholics, Methodists, Disciples, Congregationalists, nominal Christians of every kind, and some openly making no pretense of religion. Some were kindly but reserved. Some brushed me off. Some made excuses. But one business man, in his forties, as we talked with him in the furniture department of a big store, turned to Christ. Twice people brushed by us in the aisles, and once we had to move to another part to finish our conversation and prayer, but the man asked the Lord to forgive him and he trusted Christ as Saviour.

In a recent twelve-month period, Dr. Jack Hyles won 250 people to Christ. But he told me that it took nine and a half interviews with as many people for each soul that he won in the year's time. Sometimes he would win three people in succession, one after the other. One time he earnestly pleaded with forty different people before he won one to Christ!

Oh, do not give up so easily! The harvest is white! The fish are biting! There are always souls you can win.

In this matter of soul winning, the Lord pronounces a blessing on the persistent worker: "Blessed are ye that sow beside all waters, that send forth thither the feet of the ox and the ass" (Isa. 32:20). And in Ecclesiastes, chapter 11, are three verses with important counsel for the soul winner. Verse 1 says, "Cast thy bread upon the waters: for thou shalt find it after many days." Some who are not won today you can win later by repeated efforts.

Again in verse 4 we are told, "He that observeth the wind shall not sow; and he that regardeth the clouds shall not reap." It is a mistake to pick only the easy cases, to talk to only those you know are already interested. Oh, many a time an earnest word of entreaty, then scriptural help, will win a soul in the most unlikely time and place.

Again in verse 6 we are told, "In the morning sow thy seed, and in the evening withhold not thine hand: for thou knowest not whether shall prosper, either this or that, or whether they both shall be alike good."

Suppose you talk to a sinner and he does not turn to Christ: is your work in vain? Ah, no! If a man goes to Hell, by all means let him go warned. If a man will not be saved, then get the blood off your own garment. Take the responsibility for his lost soul off of yourself! So abundant sowing will bring more fruitful reaping. Some seed will fall by the wayside, and Satan will take the Gospel out of somebody's heart who will not be saved. Some people will make a profession who are not truly saved. But do not be discouraged; keep on sowing.

Remember the sweet injunction of Galatians 6:9, "And let us not be weary in well doing: for in due season we shall reap, if we faint not." Oh, then, do not be discouraged. "Faint not." Keep on praying, keep on weeping, keep on talking to sinners, keep on using the Word of God! And, oh, as certain as God's Word is true, the sower who goes weeping, bearing precious seed, will doubtless come again with rejoicing, bringing his sheaves with him.

VI. The Sin of Not Trying: Hungry Hearts No One Seeks to Win

The sad truth is that most of our difficulties about soul winning are in ourselves, not in the lost people around us. Sadly I have found, as has every other soul winner, that if he does right, he must make himself go when his old carnal nature finds a thousand excuses for not going! In long years as an evangelist, I have found it easier to win a lost soul than to get a Christian to go win souls. Since Satan is against soul winning, he constantly raises objections, biases and excuses to keep a Christian from doing what God says do, that is, take the Gospel to every creature.

On every hand I find that good Christian people put on the brakes about soul winning. We are constantly told, "Do not go until you have clear leading to go," or someone thinks that you cannot win Jews or that you cannot win Catholics. Or there is no use to go to this man because he is a drunkard, or that man is a scoffer who does not believe the Bible and you couldn't win him. The most honest and sincere Christian in the world must constantly check his own motives and rebuke his own unbelief in order to do the will of God about soul winning.

Everywhere I have found there are hungry hearts for the Gospel where Christians do not suspect it. In one church the pastor told Dr. Jack Hyles that there were no prospects, and he could not expect to see people saved in that church. That same evening Dr. Hyles went early and got acquainted with all the choir, and he found five lost people in the choir whom he personally won to Christ that night and led them to make open profession of faith! Oh, God forgive us for our blindness about the white harvest fields!

Some years ago in revival services in the "Tent Evangel" in Brooklyn, New York, my daughter Grace (now Mrs. Allan MacMullen) was pianist in the tent campaign, and each afternoon she had a meeting for children at the tent. My, how they came—from all the apartments in that densely populated section. Grace found that nearly all the children were of Jewish and Catholic families. She was somewhat surprised that they came. She thought surely that if she came out boldly pressing the claims of Jesus Christ and urging these children to turn to Christ and be saved, their parents would immediately stop them from coming to the services.

So, for the first few days she taught them choruses and told Bible stories about Noah and Daniel and David and Goliath. But her concern grew more and more for these youngsters, many of them twelve and fourteen years old, who flocked about her to learn the songs and hear the Bible stories. So at last, with much trepidation, she gave them a lesson on sin and salvation from John, chapter 3, showing how all needed to be born again, how all were guilty sinners and needed new hearts, and that Christ died on the cross to pay for our sins and now one who would trust in Him could get forgiveness and salvation and everlasting life. Then timidly she put the question to perhaps a hundred children, "How many here are conscious that you are a guilty sinner, your heart is bad, you need forgiveness, you need to be born again, and you want me to pray now that God will forgive your sins and save your soul? Will you hold up your hand?"

One brilliant Jewish boy was the most outspoken leader among the children. He learned each song first. He asked the most questions. He was the most enthusiastic listener. Immediately he put up his hand, "I sure know I am a sinner," he said with deep seriousness. "I want you to pray for God to forgive me and save me." Then many, many others lifted their hands too in that solemn period.

So she asked them all to bow their heads and simply and humbly she prayed that God would help them put their trust in Christ then and there and receive forgiveness and new hearts. When the prayer was over she said, "How many here are ready to trust Christ as Saviour and claim Him openly and give him your heart forever?" Immediately the Jewish boy leaped to His feet. Then others followed. And I suppose there were twenty or more that day who trusted Christ and claimed Him openly.

She went over the Scriptures again very carefully to make sure they understood that they honestly turned from sin in their hearts, that they now depended on Christ for forgiveness and salvation, and would set out to live for Him.

After that was over, this Jewish boy eagerly held up his hand. He wanted to speak and this is what he said, "Say, Miss Grace, that is the most important thing that anybody could settle in the whole world, isn't it? To think of having your sins forgiven, and knowing that you are God's child and to go to Heaven forever! Why, isn't it strange that none of us thought of that before, and we have been having services all week!"

My daughter felt greatly rebuked in her heart for her unbelief. That twelve-year-old boy saw immediately that the most important thing anybody in the world could do was to get his sins forgiven, to be born of God, to make sure of eternal happiness. How strange that we are so earth-minded that we are not thinking of that all the time!

Last year in Bombay, India, we had between two and three hundred people saved, I judge, in a fifteen-day campaign in a high school auditorium. Most were adult men. There were many women and a good many teen-agers and a few children. The preaching, with an interpreter, was as plain as I could make it. And yet, naturally, the careful dealing in the inquiry room with all those who came to trust Christ as Saviour required a great deal of time, and often an hour or more of instruction was given to these who came to claim the Saviour. I believe that the work was very thorough.

Meantime, since I could not talk to most of the people except through an interpreter, I would wait until the inquiry work was done so I could ride back to the apartment across town where I was a guest, or I would deal with the groups that were brought to me.

One night as I stood outside the high school auditorium waiting for those who would take me home, a woman brought me a young couple, a man and a woman. "These two want to be saved," she said. She meant that they wanted to be saved then and there. So I talked to them, sentence by sentence, as she translated. Yes, they knew they were sinners. Yes, they understood that Christ died for our sins and they must rely on Him and depend upon Him as their own Saviour. Step by step I led them until they were ready to bow their heads in prayer and ask for forgiveness and salvation, and then trust the Saviour.

Then there was some talk among these Hindu people and the woman led a boy to me and said, "He wants to be saved, too." Many people in India are very small. I suppose that there are millions of Indian men who weigh less than a hundred pounds, not over five feet tall, so the children are small, too, compared to American standards. The little fellow who looked eagerly up into my face with his brown face and dark intelligent eyes did not look to be over six or seven years old. I said a few words which were translated and told him that yes, he too must trust the Saviour. Then I dropped the matter. I was so anxious to do thorough, solid work, I felt the language barrier a hindrance, and he was so small. We talked about spiritual matters as I waited. This woman and all the people with her waited, too. Then after awhile she said to me, "Don't forget this boy. He wants to be saved now."

I asked the child's age and was surprised to find he was ten years old. I found he had long known he was a sinner and wanted to be saved there and then. I gladly showed him the way of salvation as the woman interpreted for us, and he was saved. But I would have let the boy go home unsaved if the woman had not pressed the matter.

Of course, if the boy had been only six or seven, he might still have been taught to trust the Saviour, but I thought that a boy that young, with an utterly heathen background, might not know what I was talking about.

Oh, I know there are millions with hungry hearts whom we could win if we only looked for them.

In Roosevelt, Oklahoma, in a big tent revival campaign, one night during the invitation fifteen or twenty people came to accept Christ as Saviour. They were lined up in front and people came to shake hands with them over their glad decision. A young woman pressed through the crowd and came to me and asked, "Will you come to see my mother?" I said, "Yes, I will be glad to see your mother, but what about you? Are you saved?" She answered that she was not, but that her mother was desperately sick and about to die, and wanted to be saved. Would I come to see the mother?

She told me that her mother lived in the farm home five miles west, the first white house beyond the Davis school house, as I recall. I was to come. The girl went away.

The next day I was called to a nearby town to an all-day meeting. I won one boy to Christ and came back for the evening service in the big tent. The next morning came and as we had the daytime service under the tent someone came and called the pastor outside. When the service was over he told me that the visitor had asked him to prepare for the funeral of the woman we had hoped to see. I waited one day too late to see her. Now she was gone!

Oh, there are souls to win. They are all about us. Many are hungry-hearted. Many who do not consciously know that they are in such danger, yet could be won to Christ. Many who are not concerned could become concerned if we went with the sword of the Spirit and the dynamite of the Holy Spirit to warn them, and plead with them, and instruct them with the Word of God.

The harvest is always great, the fields are white, the laborers are few.

It is still true, as the Bible so clearly promises, "They that sow in tears shall reap in joy. He that goeth forth and weepeth, bearing precious seed, shall doubtless come again with rejoicing, bringing his sheaves with him" (Ps. 126:5, 6).

12. Special Plans and Occasions

"One of the two which heard John speak, and followed him, was Andrew, Simon Peter's brother. He first findeth his own brother Simon, and saith unto him, We have found the Messias, which is, being interpreted, the Christ."—John 1:40, 41.

"And Levi made him a great feast in his own house: and there was a great company of publicans and of others that sat down with them."—Luke 5:29.

"There cometh a woman of Samaria to draw water: Jesus saith unto her, Give me to drink."—John 4:7.

THE THREE Scriptures quoted above indicate that Jesus used varying plans and occasions for soul winning. Andrew brought Peter to Jesus, just as Philip brought his friend Nathanael to Jesus, and Jesus did the rest that was necessary. Levi, after he was converted, made a great feast for his fellow tax collectors and had Jesus present to talk to them. Jesus started a conversation with the woman at the well of Samaria and asked her for a drink and so led her to be saved. Thus the one who is always soul-conscious, always looking for a way to talk to someone about the Saviour, will find a thousand ways to make a contact and to find an open door and show himself a friend.

1. Use the closest human ties.

Set out to win those you love the best, those you ought to be best able to influence for God, those near you. Jesus told the apostles "that repentance and remission of sins should be preached in his name among all nations, *beginning at Jerusalem*" (Luke 24:47). They were to begin where they were.

When the maniac of Gadara was saved, and the demons were cast out, and he was clothed in his right mind, he wanted to travel with Jesus, "Howbeit Jesus suffered him not, but saith unto him, Go home to thy friends, and tell them how great things the Lord hath done for thee, and hath had compassion on thee" (Mark 5:19). He was to go to his own friends. Or as Jesus told him in Luke 8:39, "Return to thine own house, and shew how great things God hath done unto thee."

Andrew was saved and "he first findeth his own brother Simon," told him that he, Andrew, had found the Saviour, "and he brought him to Jesus." That is a simple and sweet statement.

The jailer was encouraged by Paul and Silas in Acts 16 that his own family could be saved the same night, and they were and they were baptized and "rejoiced, believing in God with all his house" (vs. 34). Fathers and mothers should win their children, brothers should win their brothers and sisters. I had the sweet joy of winning the girl who was to marry my brother Joe, and the joy of winning my wife's sister-in-law. Family ties should be used with much prayer and kindness and concern to win those near us and dear to us.

2. One of the simplest and best steps that most people can make toward getting lost people saved is to get them to attend church with them.

In Hammond, Indiana, a Catholic man who had been saved in my services at the Pine Street Presbyterian Church, after earnest entreaty, got the man who worked next to him in the mill to come with him in his car. The man was saved that night. In the Galilee Baptist Church in Chicago our revival services overran the little auditorium and we moved out into a park auditorium for the closing Sunday night. In the closing service in that crowded auditorium a number were saved and we had the benediction. But before we could stir, here came others to be saved. So we sang invitation songs again and encouraged others to take Christ. Again, we started to leave, but there was a commotion in the back of the auditorium and I heard a woman's voice as she cried out with holy enthusiasm, "Here he comes, Brother Rice! Here he comes! Oh, I prayed so hard. We went by and got him in our car. And now here he comes, thank God!"

One of the best ways to get your friends saved is to tell them that you would like for them to be saved, and tell them of some preacher who is interesting and who preaches earnestly to sinners; arrange to go together in the same car and sit together to hear the preacher. Then at the invitation time it is a simple thing to quietly whisper, "I hope you will go and take Christ as Saviour. If you want to go, I will go to the preacher or the inquiry room with you."

3. I believe in personal soul-winning effort, quietly and wisely done by good Christians during the public invitation to accept Christ, both in services with an evangelist and in the regular evangelistic services of a good Bible-believing church.

I know that there ought not to be disorder, and all the workers should listen carefully so as not to cause confusion and to stay under the control of the preacher who directs the service. Those who do not make an effort to win souls outside the public services probably should not do much in the public service. There ought not to be argument or confusion. But courteously and gently, a Christian could suggest, "Wouldn't you like to go tonight and take Christ as your Saviour? I will be glad to walk with you down the aisle if you are ready to take Christ."

4. Take your unsaved friend or loved one to meet the preacher.

Sometimes when one is on friendly terms with an unsaved man or woman, he may get them to come with him to church services. And then he may suggest later, "I want you to meet our pastor," and in his presence you can say to the pastor, "This is Mr._____. He is a good friend of mine. We work together at such and such a place (or we live side by side, for example). Although I believe he is not a Christian, I hope he will be." That is no more than a good friend ought to say about his unsaved friend, and his spiritual pastor or evangelist surely should take the hint that here is the chance to speak to one about his soul.

Sometimes it is better to be direct. If there are problems you cannot solve for your unsaved friend, why not say, "Let's go now and see the pastor and get this settled." In Spearman, Texas, a man brought his French Catholic war bride to the home where I was staying so that I could win her to Christ. At Highland Park Baptist Church in Chattanooga, Tennessee, after I had preached on soul winning, a twelve-year-old boy on three or four successive nights brought a boy friend to meet me as I came into the auditorium for the evening service. He would say, "Brother Rice, this is Jim _____. He is twelve years old. He wants to be saved. I have been talking to him." Or it was Bill, ten years old, on another night.

5. Tracts and other Christian literature may be used definitely to win souls.

I am sorry to say that I think tracts are often used as an excuse for *not* winning souls. Some people are ardent tract distributors but never take time to seek out a lost one, use the Scripture to show him his lost condition and his need for the Saviour, and bring him to trust in Christ and make public profession. In that case, giving out tracts is simply a substitute for doing the main thing.

I believe just to walk down the street, slap a man on the back and say, "Jesus saves!" is not enough to turn him to Christ. For the same reason, I believe that to give him a short tract that does not expound any Scripture and does not show his sinful need of a Saviour is not adequate. I believe in giving out tracts, but I cannot have any enthusiasm for giving out tracts when I have no evidence that they ever result in anyone's being saved. And I think the casual, careless giving out of tracts that are short, are not specially well written, sometimes on cheap and shabby paper, tracts that have not been proven by actual experience as soul-winning tracts, is not effective. And even the very best tracts, if used carelessly without prayer, without personal testimony, generally have little effect. On the other hand, tracts that give a very clear scriptural truth in good language, well written, and accompanied by an earnest plea that one turn to Christ as Saviour, do help win thousands.

I suppose about fifteen million copies of my little twenty-four-page booklet, *"What Must I Do to Be Saved?"* have been distributed in almost thirty languages. We have been very careful in the way it has been distributed. We give a single copy to anyone who asks for it. We will furnish free copies to those who give them out, only if they sign a solemn pledge with every supply they ask for, that the booklet will be given only to those who promise to read it, or to those who take it of their own choice from a tract rack or table. We have always said that if anybody wants to stand on the street corner and hand them out by the thousands without any personal conversation or effort to win the people to Christ, he should pay for them himself, since we do not find that method as profitable.

But of those gotten out carefully and with strict in-

structions as we have given, so that in many, many cases
those who receive this tract have promised faithfully to
read it through and in some cases the tract has been accompanied by an earnest word of exhortation—thus we
have averaged about one reported conversion for every
thousand of the booklets gotten out.

Dr. Ford Porter's little tract, *God's Simple Plan of Salvation,* has resulted in many people being saved. It is not
as extended a treatment as the booklet *"What Must I Do
to Be Saved?"* but is very scriptural and explicit.

I suggest that you take this little booklet, *"What Must I
Do to Be Saved?"* and show it to a friend. Call attention
to the fact that it is printed in almost thirty languages
and has been very popular and that God has used it to save
many souls. Show him the decision form on page twenty-
three; tell him that after he reads this booklet, you hope
he will be ready to make that decision and then sign his
name to it. And tell him that you will be praying for him,
that you want to see him after an hour, or tomorrow morning, and you hope that he will then ask any questions about
what he does not understand, and that he will be ready to
take Christ as his own Saviour. Then faithfully follow it up.
Thus many have been saved.

Again and again mothers have read this booklet to their
children, and in the home have had these children to take
Christ as Saviour and say so, and then they have signed
their names to the decision form and copied it in a little
letter and sent it to me.

A young Christian had determined to win souls. He
was deeply stirred at the conference on revival and soul
winning at Lake Louise, Toccoa, Georgia, some years ago.
That afternoon, determined to win a soul, he took the
booklet, *"What Must I Do to Be Saved?"* and stopped at
a roadside fruit stand. He stammered and didn't know
quite what to say. So he went back to his car, got a copy
of this booklet, and read it through aloud to the man who

kept the fruit stand. The man was happily saved. I believe in tracts when they are accompanied with earnest entreaty and personal testimony, and when they are not used simply as an excuse for failing to make the soul-winning effort we should make.

Certain literature is particularly suited for people with certain backgrounds or in certain situations. The beautiful gift book *Bible Facts About Heaven* has been greatly used of God to win people who are bereaved or people who are old and sick. The first six months or so after this little book was first published, we had letters from some two hundred people who wrote to tell me they had found Christ as Saviour through it. Some pastors regularly give this book to homes where death has come.

My pamphlet *Sermon From a Catholic Bible,* as preached in the Chicago Arena in a city-wide campaign some years ago, has been greatly used to win Catholics. In every case there should be an earnest and friendly effort to be a blessing, and the literature should be simply a part of the effort.

In South Texas a rich young playboy who lost a quarter of a million dollars of his father's money in a few short months, went to hear an evangelist. He was convicted, but seemed not to be sure, not to know exactly how to take Christ as Saviour. The evangelist gave him the booklet *"What Must I Do to Be Saved?"* He read it through, and the next day came to claim Christ as Saviour. His questions were all answered and the Scriptures convinced him. My pamphlet *Religious But Lost* has been used of God in dealing with church people who are unconverted. God has used it to save many.

6. Special dinners are often used to win lost people.

When Jesus passed by and saw Levi sitting at the receipt of customs (collecting taxes), He said, "Follow me," and Levi did follow Him. He is later called Matthew and wrote the Gospel according to Matthew. But he immedi-

ately prepared a great dinner and brought his tax collecting companions and friends to the dinner and had Jesus
there. I am sure he had in mind that they should meet the
Saviour and learn to love and trust Him.

So a father-son banquet or a mother-daughter banquet
makes an occasion for a mother to bring her unsaved daughter and have a good meal and sweet fellowship, an interesting program, and hear someone give the Gospel plainly.
Or a "two-by-two" banquet may be had with a special guest
speaker and it may be required that everyone who attends
must have with him someone else who does not attend
church or who is not saved. One can have an attractive
evening with good music and nice food and sweet fellowship, and then a speaker can earnestly present the claims
of Jesus Christ while the guests sit informally around the
table. Thus many have been saved.

The woman who was a sinner knelt at Jesus' feet as He
reclined on a couch at dinner with Simon the Pharisee. With
her tears dripping on His feet, she kissed His feet and
wiped them with the hair of her head and Jesus turned and
forgave and saved her. The informality and fellowship of
a dinner hour make it a good time to talk about the Lord
Jesus.

Sometimes a church can have a dinner for all the graduating seniors of the high school, or for all the young men
and women who have just reached voting age, or for young
men about to go into the armed service, for example, and
use the dinner properly as a soul-winning occasion.

7. *Weddings often make a good background for soul
winning.*

At a wedding rehearsal a few weeks ago, when people
came from out of state, it was my joy to win to Christ a
thirteen-year-old girl and a twelve-year-old boy. They were
relatives of the bridegroom; they were thrilled at taking
part in the wedding and so they were open to happy fellow-

ship and naturally they respected the man who would preside at the wedding ceremony.

In Fort Worth, Texas, a young man came to ask me if I would perform the marriage ceremony for him and a lovely Sunday School teacher in the church. He loved Miss Clark very much: that one could see. I asked him plainly if he were worthy to be the husband of such a good Christian woman. I told him that he ought not to marry a Christian woman and then make her miserable with an ungodly home. There in the pastor's study he gladly trusted Christ as his Saviour. Strangely enough, in three months he became sick and died. The approaching wedding had been the best key to winning him to Christ.

In my home at Dallas, Texas, a young couple came to be married and I won both the bride and groom to Christ. Their hearts were very tender. They had high hopes. They wanted God to bless their marriage. In Shamrock, Texas, a young man drove from Oklahoma and brought his bride and her family, and there I had the joy of winning her to Christ. She wanted a good home, and her heart was touched with the blessing God was giving her. It was a good time to win her. Oh, the weddings and wedding rehearsals and wedding dinners and wedding showers are merry occasions. But the hearts of the principals are very tender at such times and it is a good time to win them to Christ.

8. Funerals are a great opportunity to win people to Christ.

By God's grace and mercy I have been able to win hundreds of people to Christ in connection with the death of their loved ones. The pastor is welcome at the hospital, whether it is visiting hours or not. When death comes, even the worldly and ungodly relatives feel that it is proper to dignify the occasion by the services of a minister. The minister is expected to bring comfort and help. Oh, there is no help for a broken heart like the peace which Jesus gives in salvation! The pastor usually may see the bereaved ones in the home before the funeral. After he has conducted the funeral service, usually the general crowd is left out and the pastor and relatives are together as the casket is viewed for the last time by the loved ones. At the cemetery often there is time for a few words and an earnest exhortation. Then after the funeral, relatives ought not to get away without an earnest plea that they turn to Christ. The pastor who goes among them and shakes hands and says a word of consolation here and gives a verse of Scripture there ought never to make that simply a formal routine. Oh, what a good time it is to talk about Jesus Christ!

Things must be done reverently, orderly, and with proper respect, of course, for the feelings of the people involved. But it is a sacred time and the preacher is foolish and cowardly who does not try to use it to say a good word for Jesus Christ and to urge people to trust Him. And it is far better in a funeral sermon to talk about Jesus than to talk about the virtues of the man or woman who is gone.

9. New babies offer a wonderful opportunity to talk about the Lord.

In a South Texas town where I was engaged in revival services, I talked for an hour or two with a man, a hardened sinner. I could not bring him to trust in Christ. He was not a Christian, but his leaning was toward a sect that makes much of baptismal regeneration. He was not ready to be saved. He was not ready to give up his sins. I could not win him to Christ.

However, some days later I heard that God had given his family a new baby. I felt clear leading in my heart and I said to my wife, "I believe God has given me that man today!"

I went and knocked at his door. When he came to the door, I said to him, "I hear that you have a new baby. Isn't that wonderful!"

Yes, he had a new baby and he was very proud.

"And I hear that it is a boy baby you have," I said, with a smile. "Then you must be a better man than I am, for I have a houseful of girls but no boys!"

"Yes," he said proudly, "he is a boy and he weighs over eight pounds! I wanted a boy and that is what I got!"

"Well, could I see this fine boy of yours?" I said.

He was glad to take me to the bedroom where his wife lay with the little one wrapped in a blanket beside her. "Wife," he said, "Brother Rice wants to see our new baby. You see, his babies are all girls. He doesn't have a boy like we have."

The wife was eager and glad to show her baby. She unwrapped and unwrapped the blue blanket with the rabbits on it from around the little one. And soon his wrinkled face, his bald head, and his red skin were visible. The mother shyly said, "Others may not think he is so pretty, but I think he is beautiful."

"Yes," I said, "and he has an immortal soul; he is made in the image of God. He will spend eternity somewhere. Yes, a baby is wonderful!" Then I said to the mother, "Now would you like for me to pray for the baby?"

"Oh, that would be sweet! Yes, please do," she said.

Then I asked, "Shall I pray for him to be like his dad and never go to church, and take God's name in vain, and not be converted, and after awhile perhaps die and go to Hell? Or shall I pray for him to be converted and be a child of God and live right and go to Heaven?"

"Oh my!" she said. And she seemed stricken at the thought. "Yes, I want him to be a Christian. He must be a good man. Pray for him to be a Christian and serve God and go to Heaven," she said.

"All right, I will," I said. "But wait! Who is going to teach this boy to be a Christian. Are you a Christian?"

Again she said, "Oh my!" She said, "I never thought of

that. Why, I don't know how to raise a boy to be a Christian. You had better pray for me!"

I told her that the only way she could be a good mother and win her boy to Christ was to be saved herself, and so I would pray that God would help her to trust Jesus now and be born again. Her eyes were filled with tears and she hugged the little one to her heart. I turned to the father. He was sitting very soberly in a cane-bottom chair. I said, "Are you a Christian?" Of course I knew that he was not and he soon said plainly that he was not.

"Then what are you doing with that motto on the wall, 'Christ is the head of this house, the Unseen Guest at every meal, the Silent Listener to every conversation?' A home where you never pray, you never read the Bible, you do not go to church, you take God's name in vain—there is not a single Christian in the house and you say, 'Christ is the Head of this house.' "

He was startled and then greatly abashed. He said, "Well, please, Brother Rice, don't think I meant to be sacrilegious. That sounds awful. I didn't think how it would look. I just saw that motto and thought my wife would like it and I brought it home and put it over the door. We will take it down. No, we are not fit to have that motto in our house with nobody here saved."

"But wait," I said. "Why not just ask the Lord Jesus to come into your heart, too, as He comes into the heart of your wife, and make both of you Christians and help you win the boy and let Christ really be the head of this house? What do you say?"

"Yes, please pray for me, too," he said. "I ought to be a Christian."

So I prayed and the woman hugged to her heart that little bundle of life. The man's tears dripped between his fingers and Jesus Christ came into both hearts and into that home. Oh, a new baby gives a wonderful chance to win somebody to Christ.

See that the new baby is enrolled in the cradle roll of your Sunday School and that somebody calls regularly in the home to see how the little one is. Take time to talk to the mother and pray with her and get her saved. Talk to the proud father about his opportunity and responsibility.

10. Business contacts make a wonderful opportunity to win souls.

When the insurance man tries to sell you insurance, tell him that you will listen to him talk and then you want to talk to him about the matter of his soul and salvation. To the vacuum cleaner salesman and the Fuller Brush man at the door, you can talk about Christ. Read with them some Scriptures. The paper boy, the milkman, the postman, the garbage collector—take time to make friends. Sometimes ask them in for a cup of coffee or ask them to try a slice of your new cake. Ask them about their families. And payday, when people come to collect bills, is a good time to talk to them about the Lord. Be courteous, be fair, and oh, may the breath of Heaven be upon you in every business contact.

My friend, Mr. Fred Hawkins, owns a feed mill at Springfield, Missouri. He was won to Christ because a man who bought feed for his dairy cows from the mill would always buy just enough feed for one day, and that day he would bring his Testament and show Fred Hawkins some Scripture and urge him to be saved. Every weekday for three months that customer came and would buy one day's cow feed and would talk about the Lord until at last Fred Hawkins got so concerned that he arose at five o'clock in the morning, went down to the mill and knelt on the concrete floor in the basement and asked God to give him the new heart that his friend had been showing him about in the New Testament! Business contacts are a good time to talk about Jesus.

I need not remind you that Daily Vacation Bible School,

the Sunday School class, the opening exercises of Sunday
School departments, the young people's meeting, the child
evangelism class, the men's brotherhood are all good times
to be on the lookout to bring someone to the services who
is unsaved and see that he is won to Christ.

In Dallas, Texas, one night the Galilean Baptist Church
was considering plans for a new building and the building
fund. After prayer meeting I asked that all the businessmen of the church meet me, the pastor, for counsel as we
planned and prayed about the meeting. I suggested that
every man present might stay, whether he was a member
of the church or not.

After we had discussed the building fund plans, I asked
if anyone had anything else to say. One man arose, his
face deeply contorted with emotion, and with tears he said,
"My wife was saved three weeks ago. I have been coming
to this church ever since, hoping that someone would talk
to me about the Lord and tell me how to be saved. Here
these men go on with their business and they are interested in that and they can't take time to tell a sinner how
to be saved!"

The Christian men present were shocked and shamed.
I let that sinner go on and tell his story. He was doing better
preaching than I could do, preaching that backed up all that
I had been saying about personal soul winning. Then when
he had said his say and began to sob, I took the Bible and
showed him how to be saved. Yes, people can be saved at
a building fund committee meeting, provided always we
seek the leading of the Spirit of God and are always soul-
conscious, and always on the lookout for the dear lost sheep
for whom the Saviour died.

13. How to Do It: Practical Help

"And the lord said unto the servant, Go out into the highways and hedges, and compel them to come in, that my house may be filled."—Luke 14:23.

MANY PEOPLE would like to win souls, but they have no practical knowledge of how to go about it. In a city-wide revival campaign one pastor who co-operated in the meeting, who believed the Bible and seemed in real sympathy with the preaching and objectives, wanted to win souls. But when I suggested that he go into the inquiry room to take the Bible and make clear to people how they could be sure they were saved, he shrank from it and plainly said he would not know how to go about it. So that he could have some part in the salvation of sinners, I had him stand by me, and when converts came forward, he led them to the inquiry room and came back for more. But it was pitiful to see a preacher who had no practical understanding of how to deal with people in soul winning.

On another occasion I was in a revival service in a large Canadian church. A good many people came forward to take Christ as Saviour and I dealt with each one briefly as they came to take my hand at the pulpit. But then these new converts and the wayward Christians who were rededicating their lives went into an inquiry room for further instruction, and the assistant pastor was sent by the pastor into the inquiry room to make certain that these converts had really trusted Christ and knew their sins were forgiven. A little later when I went into the inquiry room to help and to check up, I found the assistant pastor, a college graduate and seminary graduate, going into great detail in a theological discussion on the fall of man, Adam and Eve in the Garden of Eden, while the bewildered converts sat patiently listening to his harangue. He was a good man. He was fundamental in doctrine. But he knew nothing about how to deal with souls.

Here I want to make some practical suggestions about the soul winner's person, personality, and plans for showing lost sinners that they need to be saved, showing them how to be saved, and getting them to claim the Saviour.

I. The Preliminaries of Soul Winning

We make here some brief suggestions that have proved helpful as people plan to win souls.

1. Pray earnestly before you go.

Pray for God to guide you where to go and what to say. Pray particularly for the power of the Holy Spirit upon you. Remember, soul winning is a supernatural business and no one can do it without supernatural help.

2. When going among strangers, and from house to house particularly, it is often wise to go two by two.

It was so when the Lord Jesus sent the apostles and the seventy. One paralytic man was "borne of four" to the Saviour. Usually, in dealing with one particular person, one person should do the talking while the other tries to see that there is no interruption. Sometimes he will play with the children or answer the doorbell or telephone. The fact that he is there will give courage and moral support to the worker who is speaking and will add weight to his testimony. Perhaps in the next visit the silent partner should take over. But to interrupt and both try to speak at the same time generally leads to a discussion and sometimes to argument that is not helpful. One person should do the talking, as a general rule.

3. Dr. Jack Hyles, in the little book, HOW TO BOOST YOUR CHURCH ATTENDANCE, says: "Be clean and neat."

If a person is going to be a soul winner he must not be offensive to the people with whom he talks. It is a definite asset for a soul winner to be careful to bathe often, to avoid body odor. Teeth should be brushed, and breath should be tested. Carry mints in your pockets or some good flavored chewing gum which will help keep the breath from being offensive. One of the most damaging things in soul winning is the effect of halitosis. By all means, a soul winner should watch this carefully. The soul winner should also be neatly dressed. A lady should be dressed conservatively, and I think it is best for a man to at least wear a shirt with a tie."

A good salesman tries to avoid baggy pants, dandruff, or an unshaven face. The soul winner ought to look like a respectable, trustworthy lady or gentleman.

4. The soul winner should always have his New Testament with him.

Of course, the personal soul winner would expect to use the Bible, but a large and cumbersome Bible may frighten the people at whose door you stand. A New Testament in your pocket is unobtrusive, readily available, and usually all you will need in winning a soul. Generally it will be best to hold the Bible so that the one with whom you deal can read it easily. Point your finger to the verse as you read it to him, or sometimes you may ask him to read it. But Christians should avoid trying to make a big show of being religious. You do not come to appear like a preacher but as a Christian friend to do the man a favor. Sometimes the Scriptures you want to use may be available in a tract, but it will be more impressive if you show the one with whom you deal the verses in the New Testament.

5. Be pleasant, considerate, courteous.

Don't be bossy. This is simply another way of saying that there ought to be a genuine, warm love in your heart for sinners, a compassion, a sympathetic understanding of people, and a liking for people. I have known people to try to win souls who did not even shake hands, who did not say even a pleasant "good morning." Sometimes people try to win a soul when they do not even know the man's full name, whether he is married, whether he has any children, where he works. I think that I was able to win a Catholic woman in Norfolk, Virginia, largely because I was attracted to her little three-year-old girl and made friends with the little one and took her in my arms. In Texas I won a hardened sinner because I came to see his new baby and was interested in the baby. One must love sinners and show it, be interested in what they are interested in. An Orthodox Jewish man kept me for two hours when he found that I talked with real interest to him about the Passover, about the dietary laws of Leviticus, about the offerings and priesthood of the New Testament and the meaning of circumcision.

Sometimes because of company or a date or pressing duty, the one on whom you call cannot spend much time with you. Be kind. You might ask, "Could I come back to see you this afternoon?" or "If you like, I will call another time."

6. Stay on the main track.

You come to talk to people about sin and the Saviour. I know one man who went out on visitation hoping to win souls, and he argued with a man for nearly an hour about the tobacco habit. Someone intended to call on some Catholics in an effort to win them to Christ, and asked me for literature proving that the mass was wrong, that the popes were not all good men, and literature to show that the papal infallibility was a false doctrine! When I talk to a Catholic, I never start out to show that Protestants are right and Catholics are wrong. Instead, when I speak to a man about his soul and he says, "Well, I am a Roman Catholic," I frequently say, "Yes, and it happens that I am a Baptist. But I know that many, many Baptists are not good Christians and I am sure you know some Catholics who are not good Christians." I suppose every Catholic will assent to that.

Then I sometimes say, "Well, it is clear, then, that to be a member of a church, whether my church or your church or any other church, is not enough unless one is right with God in his heart." And every sensible person surely would agree to that. I have never had it challenged. Then I say, "Well, the important thing is whether or not you know your sins are forgiven, whether you have come to Christ and trusted Him personally and have assurance that He is your own personal Saviour."

The simple truth is that one may be a Catholic and be saved (I fear that most Roman Catholics are not, but that is not the point). The important thing is not to deal with the differences between Catholics and Protesants, and not to show anybody that their convictions and rearing and traditions are wrong; the important thing is to bring every sinner to face the fact that he is a sinner who needs forgiveness, and to show him that Christ is ready to save him.

I never say, "You are a sinner." Instead I say, "Of course, you know that we are all poor sinners, and Christ died to save sinners like you and me." In the first place, it is true that I needed the same Saviour as others do. It is also the courteous and considerate way to state the matter.

Somebody says, "How shall I deal with a Jew?" Deal with him like a sinner; you and he both need the same Saviour, and so with loving and considerate heart you can tell him that you know the way one can have his sins forgiven and have peace in heart, and you would like, if he will allow you, to show him from the Scriptures how he can know. Stay on the main line. Don't argue about eternal security, about holiness, about the Second Coming, or worldly amusements, or habits. Don't argue over denominational differences. Keep the conversation on the simple plane that all of us, therefore including the friend to whom you are speaking, are sinners and need the Saviour, and show him that by the Scriptures. Stay on the main track.

7. The soul winner should largely control the conversation.

Dr. Jack Hyles suggests that if the person with whom you are dealing brings in some other subject, asks questions as to where Cain got his wife or why God allows war or why there are so many denominations or about hypocrites in the church, you say something like this: "That is a good question. Remind me after a little bit and I will try to answer it, but first, let me tell you this . . . ." An unsaved woman who talked to D. L. Moody insisted that she saw no harm in the theater and the dance. D. L. Moody wisely said, "I promise to answer that to your satisfaction if you will first trust Christ as your Saviour." After she trusted Christ, she found the problem already solved in her heart.

You are dealing with the most important subject in the world. You should have planned ahead of time some simple steps. I beg you, try to control the conversation and lead through the matter of the guilt of sin, the free salvation paid for by Jesus Christ, and the fact that this salvation may be had at once by personal faith in Christ. Then press for a decision.

II. Simple Steps in Winning a Soul Using
John, Chapter Three

It is easy to show the plan of salvation. One simple, easy way to win a soul to Christ is by using certain verses in John, chapter 3. The book of John is specially written to show people how to be saved. John 20:30, 31 says: "And many other signs truly did Jesus in the presence of his disciples, which are not written in this book: But these are written, that ye might believe that Jesus is the Christ, the Son of God; and that believing ye might have life through his name." So there are more verses on the plan of salvation in the book of John than in any other book in the Bible. But one need not use many Scriptures nor go all through the Bible in winning a soul. In most cases a few verses near each other are sufficient. Do not make a hard job of showing that people are sinners, that they need to be saved, that Christ died for them, that one who trusts Christ will have everlasting life. Sometimes, indeed, the one you seek to win knows the essentials and simply needs to be urged to the decision to trust Christ here and now.

In John, chapter 3, Jesus showed Nicodemus, a religious, moral man, that he was lost and needed to be saved, and showed him how to be saved. I suggest that you now look at John, chapter 3, and learn to use these simple steps in winning a soul.

1. Read verses 1 to 3.

"There was a man of the Pharisees, named Nicodemus, a ruler of the Jews: The same came to Jesus by night, and said unto him, Rabbi, we know that thou art a teacher come from God: for no man can do these miracles that thou doest, except God be with him. Jesus answered and said unto him, Verily, verily, I say unto thee, Except a man be born again, he cannot see the kingdom of God."

Now I would call attention to the fact that this man was

a good moral man, one of the religious leaders and rulers of the Jews, evidently a member of the Sanhedrin. He is called a Pharisee, and Pharisees were the strictest religious sect among the Jews. And to this man, moral and religious and upright, Jesus plainly said, "Ye must be born again."

2. Now it is well to call attention to the insistant warning Jesus gives, that being born again, born from above, is an absolute necessity.

Verse 3 says, ". . . Verily, verily, I say unto thee, Except a man be born again, he cannot see the kingdom of God." This refers not just to Nicodemus; no person can see the kingdom of God without being born again.

In verse 5 Jesus said, ". . . Except a man be born of water and of the Spirit, he cannot enter into the kingdom of God." The water here evidently pictures the Word of God. "Born of the Spirit" means that the change must be worked in the heart by the Holy Spirit after one hears the Word.

In verse 7 Jesus said, "Marvel not that I said unto thee, Ye must be born again." Jesus did not say that one merely *ought* to be born again, or that it would be wise for him to be born again. He said, "Ye *must* be born again."

3. Then call attention to verse 6: "That which is born of the flesh is flesh; and that which is born of the Spirit is spirit."

You might say to the sinner, "Perhaps you had a wonderfully good mother, as I did, and a good father by human standards. But our parents were human and frail and imperfect, and so we were born the same way. The reason we need to be born again is because we were born with a fallen nature in the first place, and so any fleshly birth then still means we must be born again to ever see God in peace."

It is well here for you to stress that we are all sinners. Get the sinner to admit that he is not perfect, that he has fallen short in God's sight, that often when he means to do well, he does not do right, that when he makes resolutions, he sometimes breaks them. Do not leave the impression, "I am good and you are bad." No, make sure that you take the sympathetic, honest position that we are all sinners alike and need forgiveness alike, and that unless we come to get a new heart, there is no hope of Heaven.

4. Now, if the thing is not clear, it might be well to call attention to verse 8: "The wind bloweth where it listeth, and thou hearest the sound thereof, but canst not tell whence it cometh, and whither it goeth: so is every one that is born of the Spirit."

How will one feel when he is born again? The Bible does not say. It is God who works the miracle of the new birth, and we do not need to understand it, but should simply turn the matter over to God to do for us what we cannot do for ourselves.

5. And now you are ready for verses 14 and 15.

Jesus reminded Nicodemus that when the Israelites complained at God, fiery serpents came among the people and bit the people and much people died. But God told Moses to put a brazen snake on a pole and whoever looked to that brass snake would be healed. So Jesus told Nicodemus: "And as Moses lifted up the serpent in the wilderness, even so must the Son of man be lifted up: That whosoever believeth in him should not perish, but have eternal life."

That snake on a pole pictured Jesus bearing our sins on the cross. Those people looked at the brass snake and believed that God would heal them by looking, and so they were healed.

6. Now follow with John 3:16: "For God so loved the world, that he gave his only begotten Son, that whosoever believeth in him should not perish, but have everlasting life."

Now the soul winner can say, "Here God tells you ex-

pressly how to be born again. Do you admit that you are
a sinner, that you need a new heart, that you want forgiveness? And you can see that God loves you. He gave
His Son to die for you and for me and the whole world.
Now 'whosoever,' anyone in the world—you, me, anybody—
that believes in Christ or depends upon Christ or relies upon
Christ for forgiveness and salvation will not perish, will
not go to Hell, will not be lost forever, but he shall have
'everlasting life.' "

You might illustrate faith by showing how a sick person relies upon the doctor and turns the case over to the
doctor. Believing good things about the doctor does not do
one any good unless he turns his case over to the doctor and
risks him.

One who has a lot of money and feels insecure about
it takes it to the bank and deposits it. He trusts his money
with the bank for safekeeping. He relies upon the bank
because the bank has promised to keep it safely for him
and is able to do it. Just so one needs to turn himself over
to Jesus Christ, relying on Him, depending upon Him
for salvation. One who trusts in Christ or relies upon Christ
for salvation has everlasting life, according to the plain
promise here.

7. *Now I would go over that again with the sinner.* "*Do
you understand that you are a sinner?*"

Doubtless he will say yes.

"Do you believe that Christ died for your sins and mine
on the cross, and wants to save you?"

Doubtless he will say yes, that he understands that.

Next, "Do you see, then, that if you rely upon Jesus
Christ and turn your case over to Him, depending on Him
to forgive you and give you everlasting life as He promised,
that is all you are to do to obtain salvation?"

Then you might say, "Then let us bow our heads and I
will whisper a prayer and ask the Lord Jesus to forgive

you and save you now." And then you may pray, and ask him if he will.

After you pray a very simple, short prayer, then you might suggest words of suitable prayer for him. You might say, "Can you honestly repeat the words of this prayer as I give them to you? 'Lord, I confess that I am a poor sinner who needs saving.' " Let him repeat that.

"I believe, Lord Jesus, that You died on the cross to pay for our sins and that You are willing to save me." And have him repeat that.

"Lord Jesus, I ask You now to forgive my sins and save me." And have him repeat that.

"Lord, the best I know I trust You now to forgive my sins; I give You my heart forever." Then ask him if he can repeat that.

I do not believe one must pray aloud in order to be saved. Sometimes a timid person will pray silently. One is saved when he turns to the Lord and trusts the Lord. But sometimes the matter is much clearer in the mind of a sinner and the transaction is remembered as a definite transaction if he can express his faith in the words of a prayer. Besides, if he asks the Lord to forgive, then he always has extra promises like Romans 10:13, "For whosoever shall call upon the name of the Lord shall be saved," as an evidence that he has really been saved.

8. Once the person has asked Christ to forgive him and save him, I suggest that there be some open demonstration of his decision.

I would say, "Now you have asked Jesus Christ to forgive your sins and save you. If you are ready to turn your case over to Him, ready to rely on Him to forgive your sins and save you as He promised to do, will you now take my hand and let this handshake be a sign between you and me and God that you now trust Christ as your own personal

Saviour and give Him your heart forever? Will you do that?"

If the sinner has been honest thus far, in most cases he will be ready to make that open profession of his faith in Christ.

If a loved one is present who is already a Christian or if another worker is present, it is good for him to shake hands also with them. Sometimes if it is a child who has been saved and the mother or father is present, I might say, "Isn't that wonderful! Now you have trusted Christ as your Saviour. If you are glad and you want your mother to be glad with you, come and put your arms around Mother's neck as a sign that you have taken Christ as your Saviour."

Sometimes it is well to say, "The pastor is nearby; suppose we go and tell him that you have trusted Christ as your Saviour." Or it may be the mother or father or a wife or husband. At any rate, it is good for the one who has trusted Christ to commit himself as openly as possible. There is a special blessing for those who confess Christ openly, and assurance and joy often wait upon that public confession of Christ.

9. Now before you leave the person, there is one more thing that is important. The new convert ought to be assured by the Word of God that he now has everlasting life.

So, often I turn to verse 18 in the same chapter of John and have the one who has now trusted Christ look on and read with me: "He that believeth on him is not condemned . . . ."

Now you can say to the one who has trusted Christ, "Here we see that one who has trusted in Christ and relied on Him is not condemned, is not lost, is not going to Hell. Have you trusted Christ?"

Usually he will say yes.

"Then, since you have believed on Him and relied upon Him, are you condemned?"

And he can say, on the authority of the Scriptures, "No, I am not condemned anymore!"

Then show him John 3:36: "He that believeth on the Son hath everlasting life." And again you may ask him, "Have you now trusted Christ or believed on Christ as your Saviour the best you know how, relying on Him to forgive you?"

And he, of course, can answer yes.

"Then what does the Bible say that you now have?"

Have him look on the verse with you. Have him see for himself and then he can say, "The Bible says I have everlasting life!"

And then you can say, "Now the way to know that you are saved is not because you feel a certain way, but because the Bible says that when you trust Christ you have everlasting life.

You may put step nine before having the new convert go to tell others that he has trusted Christ, if that seems wise.

This plan is simple; all the Scriptures are found in one chapter in the Bible, and God has helped me to win hundreds of souls from this chapter.

And sometimes people are so ready that just on John 3:16 alone the matter of salvation can be made so clear that they can trust Christ at once.

III. How to Win a Soul to Christ With a Few Verses in the Book of Romans

Dr. Jack Hyles has used this plan and taught it to hundreds of others so that thousands have been won to Christ through using the Scriptures here suggested. I believe that it may make Christ's substitutionary death for our sins clearer than using some other steps. I found this method particularly useful in India among heathen people who know almost nothing about the Christian religion. And here, in a few moments, you can use a few Scriptures that make clear the whole matter of man's sin, man's condemnation, Christ's substitutionary death, and being justified by faith.

First, Dr. Hyles says, "Make a map in your New Testament." Start with Romans 3:10 and on the margin by it in pencil, write 3:23, so that you have before you the next verse to turn to. By Romans 3:23, write 5:12 in the margin. Then by Romans 5:12, write 6:23. Then by Romans 6:23, write 5:8. Then in the margin by Romans 5:8, write 10:9-13.

In starting to talk to the lost person about salvation, you might say, "The book of Romans has much to say about sin and salvation, and just a few verses here will make the whole matter clear as to why you need to be saved and how to be saved."

Now you are ready to go through the Scriptures in order as you have them, stepping from one to another, following the map you have marked in your New Testament or Bible.

1. Have the one with whom you are dealing look at Romans 3:10.

It is better to have him read it aloud if he will. "As it is written, There is none righteous, no, not one." It is fair to ask him then, "Is there anyone really righteous in God's sight?" Then you might say, "Then I must admit that I am not righteous, because 'there is none righteous, no, not one.' " Then you might explain, "Of course, men are relatively good men or bad men in the sight of other men and by human standards, but in the sight of God who sees the heart, we are all sinners alike; there is none righteous. Now may I ask you then, according to the Scripture, are you righteous in God's sight?"

The person will see that he cannot honestly claim to be righteous in view of that verse.

2. Now the next step in your Testament is Romans 3:23. Have him read it with you or read it aloud: "For all have sinned, and come short of the glory of God." And then you can say, "Of course, I must admit that I, too, have sinned. So has everybody else sinned. Now, looking at this verse, don't you think that you, too, would have to say that you have sinned the same as everybody else has, and that you have come short of the glory of God?" An honest inquirer, of course, will have to say, "Yes, I have sinned, too."

3. The next step is Romans 5:12: "Wherefore, as by one man sin entered into the world, and death by sin; and so death passed upon all men, for that all have sinned."

Now is the time to make clear that sin came into the world when Adam and Eve sinned in the Garden of Eden, and since that time everybody else is sinful, "So death passed upon all men, for that all have sinned." You can show the inquirer that that is why people die. And you can show him also that because of our sins, eternal death in the lake of fire is the proper judgment for all of us poor sinners. Sentence is already passed, the sentence of death on all men. I think there you might ask him, "Do you see then why all of us by nature are lost and need to be saved?" If he understands the Scripture, he will see that.

4. The next step is Romans 6:23: "For the wages of sin is death; but the gift of God is eternal life through Jesus Christ our Lord."

Now you can show that "the wages of sin is death"; that is, the normal result of our sins is eternal death. That is wages we have earned. That is strict justice. It is what we ought to get.

But you can show him that "the gift of God is eternal life." Everyone who goes to Heaven must get salvation as a free gift. We do not deserve it. You can show him that all who go to Hell are simply getting what they deserve; they are getting the wages of sin. All who go to Heaven have to go as a gift of God through Jesus Christ.

5. The next step is Romans 5:8: "But God commendeth his love toward us, in that, while we were yet sinners, Christ died for us."

Here is a wonderful truth. As the sinner reads this Scripture, call his attention to the fact that because of His love for us, "while we were yet sinners, Christ died for us." Somebody had to die for sin. Either I must die for my own sins or someone else who is worthy and sinless must die for me. So because of His great love, Jesus Christ died in my place and died in the sinner's place.

So you might say to the sinner, "Do you see that here is a debt you deserve to pay, but Jesus has paid it for you?" You may show him that on the cross the Father turned His face away and Jesus suffered all the agonies of a lost soul. God counted Jesus a sinner and let Him suffer like a criminal, so that He could forgive my sins and count me righteous for Jesus' sake. Thus you can show the sinner that Christ's love made it so his sins were all paid for and now he can accept that free salvation if he will. It is already bought and paid for.

6. The next step is Romans 10:9: "That if thou shalt confess with thy mouth the Lord Jesus, and shalt believe in thine heart that God hath raised him from the dead, thou shalt be saved."

Now that Christ has died in the sinner's place and paid the sinner's debt, then all that is left is for the sinner to claim what Christ offers him. Jesus says, "I have redeemed you. I have paid the debt of sin. Will you take the forgiveness and salvation I have purchased for you by My suffering?" And the poor sinner can either say yes or no. He can accept it or reject it. If one believes in his heart that God raised Jesus from the dead, that means he believes that Jesus is the Son of God, the perfect, sinless sacrifice, and since He is raised from the dead, that proves He is able to save us. Now if one claims with his mouth this Saviour, believing that He is God's own Son, the atoning Saviour, he "shalt be saved."

Then show verse 10, "For with the heart man believeth unto righteousness; and with the mouth confession is made unto salvation." It is in the heart where faith is, and the outward confession is simply an expression of what happened when the heart decided to trust in Jesus.

Then you may dwell for a moment on verse 11: "For the scripture saith, Whosoever believeth on him shall not be ashamed." One who trusts in Christ will never be left embarrassed and disappointed. When one trusts in Christ, He saves him.

Now verse 13 will be clear: "For whosoever shall call upon the name of the Lord shall be saved." Why not then have this convert bow his head and tell the Lord, "Lord, I ask You now to forgive me. I now believe that You do forgive me. I trust You to be my Saviour. I want to live for You beginning today."

Then you may show from verse 13 that he who has honestly called on the Lord is saved, and he can know it because the Bible says so.

IV. Shorter Methods to Win Souls With Single Well-Known Passages of Scripture

The above two plans of using the third chapter of John and of using the Scripture verses in Romans to win a soul are thorough, and often that much attention and Scripture is needed. On the other hand, many people are ready to be saved in a shorter time. The main thing is that the worker have a heart that is warm and led by the Spirit of God so that he does not do shallow, superficial work. The sinner should know that he is a sinner who needs forgiveness. He should know that Christ alone can save, and he should definitely trust Christ as Saviour, and then he should be taught to claim the Saviour openly and to know that his sins are forgiven. But the Bible is full of the plan of salvation.

1. When I was a university student, one summer I won sixty-six people using Isaiah 55:6 and 7.

"Seek ye the Lord while he may be found, call ye upon him while he is near: Let the wicked forsake his way, and the unrighteous man his thoughts: and let him return unto the Lord, and he will have mercy upon him; and to our God, for he will abundantly pardon." You will note that these verses indicate an urgency to settle the matter at once since tomorrow He may not be near. Then verse 7 stresses the fact of sin, the need for an honest repentance, a heart turning away from sin and turning to Christ. The unrighteous man is to give up his own thoughts or plans about how to be saved and take what God says. And then there is the sweet promise that if he returns to the Lord, He will have mercy on him and will abundantly pardon. There is very sweetly and simply the plan of salvation.

2. Isaiah 53:6 also states the Gospel very simply.

All we like sheep have gone astray; we have turned every one to his own way; and the Lord hath laid on him the iniquity of us all." It says that all of us have sinned and are lost. It says that the heart of sin is our self-will, our wanting our own way. It says that Jesus Christ has borne all of our sins.

An English preacher had preached in one of the outlying towns and then rushed to the railway station to catch the train back to London. One man deeply convicted of his sins followed the preacher to the station and there said, "I want to get saved. Please tell me how." The last train for London for the night was about to leave. Heavy duties made it imperative for the preacher to go. So he said to the earnest inquirer, "Do you have a Bible?"

"Yes," said the lost man, "but I do not know where to read."

"Turn to Isaiah 53:6. Have you got it?"

"Yes, Isaiah 53:6."

"Then," said the preacher, "come in at the first 'all' and come out at the last 'all' and you will be saved." And he stepped on to the departing train.

What a strange way to be saved, the lost man thought. But he went home, opened his Bible, and discovered that the first word in the verse is "all"—"All we like sheep have gone astray." "Well, I can come in there, for I have gone astray; I am a sinner," the sinner said to himself.

But then his instructions were to "come out at the last 'all.'" And the last word of the verse is "all"—"The Lord hath laid on him [on Jesus] the iniquity of us all." Then the sinner thought, "And I am one of those whose iniquities were laid on Jesus. My sins are paid for! Well, I will come out there, and so I will be saved!"

3. Many a sinner has been saved by the simple Gospel in Numbers 21:5-9.

There is the clear illustration that all are sinners, and the death that comes by sin is illustrated by the fiery serpents. There is the clear picture of Jesus on the cross being counted the serpent, a sinner. And there is the illustration of faith so that every poisoned person who looked at the brazen snake on a pole was healed. So a sinner may be taught to look and live.

4. Thousands have been won to Christ by John 5:24.

"Verily, verily, I say unto you, He that heareth my word, and believeth on him that sent me, hath everlasting life, and shall not come into condemnation; but is passed from death unto life." "He that heareth my word. . . ." You can say to the sinner, "You have heard it many times and you are hearing it now, are you not, as we read this?" Of course the sinner will agree to that.

"And believeth on him that sent me . . . ." So you can

say to the sinner, "Do you believe that God loved the world and gave His Son to save sinners? Then are you willing to risk that God and that Saviour today, and turn your case over to Them and rely upon Them?" Then you can show the plain statement that one who thus believes and trusts "hath everlasting life, and shall not come into condemnation; but is passed from death unto life." And that is a wonderful promise for assurance and certainty.

5. Many have been saved by the story of the publican and the Pharisee who went up into the temple to pray (Luke 18:10-14).

The Pharisee, self-righteous, self-satisfied, was never saved. The poor publican who confessed his sinfulness and asked for mercy was saved and went down to his house justified. And so you might well ask the sinner to bow his head and make this prayer his prayer. You can teach him to pray, "God, be merciful to me a sinner, and save me for Jesus' sake." And then when he has prayed that prayer, you can ask him if he will here and now trust the Lord Jesus to do what He said He would do, and to manifest it either by taking your hand solemnly, or by going with you to tell the pastor or a friend, or by going forward in a public meeting.

Whatever Scriptures you use, there are two or three things that must be involved. The sinner must know that he is a sinner, and wants to turn from sin and be forgiven. Then the sinner must know that God has promised to save those who trust in Christ, and he must be brought to personally trust Christ as his own Saviour.

V. Certain Devices Are Helpful in Soul Winning

In the case of the woman at Samaria in John, chapter 4, the Lord Jesus suggested, "Go, call thy husband." Thus He was led of the Spirit of God to bring out the fact that she had been married five times and was living in sin with a man to whom she was not married.

In the case of the paralytic man borne of four given in Mark 2 and in the other Gospels, Jesus first said, "Son, thy sins be forgiven thee," and then as an evidence and assurance of forgiveness of sins He healed the man's body.

He evidently used the shame or public disgrace to win the woman taken in adultery to whom He said, "Neither do I condemn thee: go, and sin no more" (John 8:11). The spiritually-minded soul winner will find different devices to help illustrate the Gospel and to cause people to see that they are sinners and need salvation, and to give assurance of salvation when they trust the Saviour.

1. It is often wise to get the sinner to pray.

We know, of course, that when the heart turns to Christ and trusts Him, one is saved, whether he consciously prays or not. But both public confession and prayer are used as the outward form or demonstration of faith. So "with the heart man believeth unto righteousness; and with the mouth confession is made unto salvation," we read in Romans 10:10. The confession does not save, but it is a demonstration of saving faith. Likewise we are told in the same passage, verse 13, "For whosoever shall call upon the name of the Lord shall be saved." But the following verse plainly says, "How then shall they call on him in whom they have not believed? . . ." So when one calls on the Lord for mercy any forgiveness, he will be saved, because in his heart he has already believed that there is such a Saviour, that Jesus does save people who call upon Him. An honest heart calling upon Christ for mercy and forgiveness and salvation is a believing heart.

Thus it is a little simpler and easier for many people to take a definite step of faith when they call upon the Lord for forgiveness. The dying thief prayed and was saved (Luke 23:39-43). The publican in the temple prayed and was saved (Luke 18:13,14). Three times in the Bible, in Joel 2:32, in Acts 2:21, and in Romans 10:13, we are told that "whosoever shall call upon the name of the Lord shall be saved." Thus the one who calls in connection with his faith is likely to have more assurance. He has something clear-cut that he can remember. He can honestly say to himself, "The best I knew, I called on Jesus to save me and trusted Him to do it."

Even when one is in a crowd, or when the sinner is timid and may not like to pray aloud, you can say, "God knows what is in your heart now, does He not? If you in your heart ask Him to forgive you and want Him to save you now, He will know it, will He not?" Of course, every sensible sinner will know that that is true. "Then," you may say, "I will whisper a prayer softly as we stand here together and I will ask Jesus to come into your heart, forgive your sin, and save you this moment. Now as I pray, will you down in your heart say, 'Yes, Lord Jesus, I admit I am a sinner, I want You to forgive me. Please save me now.'" It is wise to try to see that there is a definite transaction in a choice of the will, a holy decision to trust Christ and claim Him, when the sinner turns to Christ.

2. For a similar reason it is important that there should be some way for the sinner to make his decision known.

Years ago in a great tabernacle service in Tulsa, Oklahoma, I preached on "The Banquet Invitation," the great supper to which many were bidden and many made excuses. I said, "Who here tonight will say, 'Brother Rice, I want to be at that great supper. Please tell the Lord Jesus that I accept His invitation and thank Him. If He will have me, I will be His and will be at that great supper'?" I asked the question more or less as a rhetorical question to bring decision in the mind. But a young man who had just gotten home from the Navy and was heartsick over sin jumped to his feet and said, "I will, Brother Rice! I will!"

I most often use the simple device of saying to the sinner, "If you are ready to take Christ as your own Saviour, relying on Him to forgive you and give you everlasting life, then let me suggest the way you can show it. As a sign between you and your friend here and God and me, would you be willing to shake hands with me, meaning, 'Lord Jesus, here and now I take You to be my own personal Saviour'? If you will, grip my hand." And as I indicated before, it is wise to get the convert to tell someone else.

3. Sometimes it is wise to use an object lesson to make clear that our sins are all laid on Jesus.

Sometimes you may select a weight, a stone, a book, and say, "Let this represent your sins. Now you hold this weight in your hands. Now all your sins are on you. Now suppose we put this weight over in the hands of this other man. Let him represent Jesus Christ. The Bible tells us that Christ has borne our sins. Jesus suffered in our place. He was the substitute for us. Now your sins are all laid on Jesus. Then they are not charged to you but charged to Jesus. Jesus died for them, and you are not to be judged for these sins anymore!"

Or you can illustrate the matter this way. A man has been sick, out of work, and cannot pay his grocery bills, and they have mounted up until he is in disgrace. But a friend who loves him goes to the store and pays the bill. All the grocery bills are marked paid and turned over to him. Thus the poor man does not owe that debt anymore.

4. It is important to give assurance of salvation.

When I was saved, no one showed me the Scriptures so I would know that I had everlasting life. I asked my father if I could join the church and he implied that I was not old enough, that I had not been saved, and he took the matter no further. Years later I asked another preacher to pray for me and he said, "All right, I will, John, and

you pray for yourself." But the matter could have been settled in five minutes with the Word of God. After three miserable years I was reading through the Gospel of John and
came to John 3:36: "He that believeth on the Son hath everlasting life . . . ." I said to myself, "Well, that is the only
thing I know for sure that I did when I went forward to
take Jesus." I saw that when I trusted Jesus, I got the whole
thing settled. And I am not conscious that I have ever had
a moment's doubt since that time that my sins are forgiven,
that I am saved.

VI. It Is Important to Follow Up the New Convert, Leading to Public Profession of Faith, Baptism, and Church Membership

A few weeks ago my daughter was delivered at the hospital of a lovely baby boy, and the eight-pound, two-ounce
boy was named for his proud grandfather, John Robert
Rice, II. (His father is also a Rice.) But his parents did not
leave the baby at the hospital! They brought him home and
began elaborate care of the little fellow—feeding, bathing,
changing diapers. So when you have a soul born, do not
leave the lamb for the wolves; do not leave the new convert
without assurance of salvation and without leading him in
the road for success and happiness in the Christian life. In
the Great Commission the Lord Jesus said that when souls
are saved, then we are to baptize them, "teaching them to
observe all things whatsoever I have commanded you."

*1. First, arrange if possible for a public profession of
faith.*

I would explain simply that one who is on the Lord's
side ought to say so. He has been all this time before without Christ and on Satan's side, and now he should make
known publicly his grand decision and the transaction by
which he is made now a child of God. I would teach the new
convert Matthew 10:32: "Whosoever therefore shall con-

fess me before men, him will I confess also before by Father which is in heaven." There is special joy in claiming Christ openly. And I would explain that that simply means that his decision ought to be made known in some simple way. The most logical way is for you to arrange to pick him up in your car or to meet him at some church service where he will be given an opportunity to come forward and let it be known that he is taking Christ as Saviour. You make the plans to take him to some such good Bible-preaching church. Sit by him in the services. Walk forward with him and tell the preacher, "My friend here has trusted Christ and wants you to know it and wants you to tell the people that he has been saved."

2. The new convert should be taught to be baptized.

Jesus made much of this. It is in the Great Commission as expressed in Matthew 28:19 and 20, and in Mark 16:16. It was the universal practice of New Testament Christians that as soon as one was saved, he was taught to be baptized, often "the same hour of the night," as with the Philippian jailer and his family.

And of course the young convert should be taught to attend some Bible-believing church where he will learn the Word of God and will find usefulness and fellowship. And he should be taught to start out to read his Bible through, reading daily, and to have a secret time of prayer every day and to get into soul-winning activities.

14. Earthly Blessings of the Soul Winner

"The fruit of the righteous is a tree of life; and he that winneth souls is wise."—Prov. 11:30.

"And he that reapeth receiveth wages, and gathereth fruit unto life eternal: that both he that soweth and he that reapeth may rejoice together."—John 4:36.

"Blessed are ye that sow beside all waters, that send forth thither the feet of the ox and the ass."—Isa. 32:20.

"How beautiful upon the mountains are the feet of him that bringeth good tidings, that publisheth peace; that bringeth good tidings of good, that publisheth salvation; that saith unto Zion, Thy God reigneth!"—Isa. 52:7.

"And if thou draw out thy soul to the hungry, and satisfy the afflicted soul; then shall thy light rise in obscurity, and thy darkness be as the noon day."—Isa. 58:10.

THE CHRISTIAN who wins souls has special blessings which other Christians, who do not win souls, never have. The Christian who does not obey Christ's commands to win souls is not as good a Christian, does not have as many promises, does not have as much joy, does not have as many answers to prayer, does not know Christ as well, as one whose life is centered on soul winning.

To be a Bible scholar is not as good as being a soul winner.

To be separated from worldly habits, amusements, and company is not as good as being a soul winner.

To be a defender of the faith is not as good as being a soul winner.

To be a martyr, to suffer persecution and death for your convictions, is not as good as being a soul winner.

No, there are special blessings of God for soul winners which are not given, in like degree, to anyone who does not win souls. I do not mean, of course, that the soul winner should not live a clean life, should not be devoted to and know his Bible, should not defend the faith, should not suffer persecution for Christ. Of course he should. The truth is that these virtues find their best examples and their highest development in soul winners. That is part of the blessing God gives those who obey His blessed command to take the Gospel to every creature.

But other Christian virtues and values are all secondary to the one great end of keeping souls, for whom Christ died, out of Hell. So the soul winner is the best Christian, has the best promises, has the most happiness here, the greatest rewards hereafter.

So there are special blessings exclusively for the soul winner.

I. The Soul Winner Is the Best Christian

Soul winners are still imperfect, frail, failing mortals, as are all Christians. Some soul winners are better than other soul winners. But it is still true that a soul winner is a better Christian than the Christian who does not win souls. If "the Son of man is come to seek and to save that which was lost" (Luke 19:10), and if "Christ Jesus came into the world to save sinners" (I Tim. 1:15), then those who work to do the same thing Jesus came for please Him better than those who do not. If the greatest good one can do for a person is to keep him out of Hell, give him everlasting life, make him God's child and give him a blessed eternity with God, then the soul winner does more good than anyone not a soul winner can possibly do.

In the book, *The Ruin of a Christian*, I have a chapter on "The Seven-Fold Sin of Not Winning Souls," and I want to name those sins again here.

1. The Sin of Disobedience to the Main Command of Jesus Christ.

The Great Commission of Christ in Matthew 28:19, 20, says, "Go ye therefore, and teach all nations, baptizing them in the name of the Father, and of the Son, and of the Holy Ghost: Teaching them to observe all things whatsoever I have commanded you: and, lo, I am with you alway, even unto the end of the world. Amen." So every convert is to be baptized and then taught to observe all things Christ commanded the apostles. New converts, then, were given the great commission to win souls. This is the Great Commission, the main command for every Christian. Not to obey it is grievous sin.

2. The Sin of Lack of Love for Jesus Christ.

Jesus said:

"If ye love me keep my commandments."

"He that hath my commandments, and keepeth them, he it is that loveth me . . . ."

"If a man love me, he will keep my words . . ."—John 14:15, 21, 23.

Clearly, then, one who does not obey the one main command of Christ to get the Gospel to every creature, to make disciples, lacks love for Christ. It is not head trouble, it is heart trouble, that keeps a Christian from obeying Christ and winning souls.

3. The Sin of Not Following Jesus.

In Matthew 4:19 Jesus said: "Follow me, and I will make you fishers of men." In Mark 1:17, He said it again, "Come ye after me, and I will make you to become fishers of men."

Then it is clear: one who follows Jesus will be a soul winner, but one who does not win souls is not truly following Jesus in the sense of that Scripture.

4. The Sin of Not Abiding in Christ.

Jesus said to His disciples and to us, in John 15:5, ". . . He that abideth in me, and I in him, the same bringeth forth much fruit: for without me ye can do nothing." Here Jesus speaks not of *being* but of *doing*. He speaks *not* of the "fruit of the Spirit" named in Galatians 5:22, 23, but of the fruit of a Christian, that is, making more Christians.

A tree may be *beautiful,* but beauty is not fruit. The nature of a tree is one thing; the fruit of a tree is another. Beauty, fragrance, size, and color in a fruit tree are like the Christian graces wrought in a Christian by the Spirit. But peaches or apples or oranges are the fruit of the trees, and the fruit of a Christian is the spiritual reproduction of himself. The fruit of a vine is grapes, the fruit of a cow is a calf, the "fruit of the womb" in the Bible is a child; so the fruit of a Christian is another Christian. One who abides in Christ brings forth much fruit. One who does not win souls, then, does not abide in Christ.

5. The Sin of Dishonesty in a Sacred Trust.

Paul was inspired to write, "I am debtor both to the Greeks, and to the Barbarians; both to the wise, and to the unwise. So, as much as in me is, I am ready to preach the gospel to you that are at Rome also" (Rom. 1:14, 15). Paul was in debt for a salvation beyond price. He could pay the debt only as he preached it to others. Those who hear the Gospel and do not tell it are dishonest, crooked. They do not pay an honest debt. To the servant who hid the money given him to use for the master's profit, and who brought no increase, the master said, "Thou wicked and slothful servant . . ." (Matt. 25:26). To take and not give, to owe and not pay is dishonest. So then is the Christian who does not win souls.

6. The Folly of a Shortsighted Fool.

"He that winneth souls is wise," says Proverbs 11:30.

"And they that be wise shall shine as the brightness of the firmament; and they that turn many to righteousness as the stars for ever and ever," says Daniel 12:3. The soul winner is wise, with blessed eternal rewards, and the shortsighted Christian who does not win souls is not wise, but is a fool, God says.

7. The Sin of Spiritual Manslaughter, Soul Murder.

See the warning given Ezekiel.

"Son of man, I have made thee a watchman unto the house of Israel: therefore hear the word at my mouth, and give them warning from me. When I say unto the wicked, Thou shalt surely die; and thou givest him not warning, nor speakest to warn the wicked from his wicked way, to save his life; the same wicked man shall die in his iniquity; but his blood will I require at thine hand."—Ezek. 3:17, 18.

As Ezekiel was a watchman who must give an account and be blood guilty if his negligence let people die in their sins, so is every Christian accountable. The Christian who lets loved ones and neighbors die unwarned has blood on his hands and will face Christ to give account at the judgment seat of Christ!

The soul winner is the better Christian than any one guilty before God for all the sins above. There are special blessings for the soul winner.

II. The Soul Winner Has Special Nearness and Fellowship With Christ

Surely every Christian longs to be consciously near the Saviour, longs to know daily, hourly fellowship with Christ. That fellowship, in Heaven, will be complete. But the soul winner, here and now, has a degree of the joy, the leading, the boldness, the peace, the comfort, the assurance of that fellowship which other Christians cannot have. Consider here some sweet scriptural truths.

1. Christ Promised the Soul Winner, "Lo, I Am With You Alway."

Yes, in Matthew 28:19, 20, Jesus said, "Go ye therefore, and teach all nations, baptizing them in the name of the Father, and of the Son, and of the Holy Ghost: Teaching them to observe all things whatsoever I have commanded you: and, lo, I am with you alway, even unto the end of the world. Amen." It is true that in some sense Christ is always with everybody, saint and sinner. But this promise would be no promise, if it meant no more than that. No, this promise is conditional. Jesus said, "Go ye therefore, and teach [or disciple] all nations . . . and, lo, I am with you alway, even unto the end of the world." Those who go and win souls have the promise. The intimate fellowship, the conscious nearness with fellowship, protection, and success implied are promised only to soul winners.

This coincides with the teaching of Jesus, ". . . He that abideth in me, and I in him, the same bringeth forth much fruit: for without me ye can do nothing" (John 15:5). Abiding in Christ and fruit bearing go together. The intimacy of abiding in Christ is shared only by soul winners. Those who enter into Christ's compassion and burden and labor to win the lost are thus specially blessed beyond other Christians.

2. The Obedient Christian, a Soul Winner, Has Special Love and Manifestation From Christ.

We reminded ourselves above that the main command of Christ is the Great Commission, the command to win souls. But Jesus said in John 14:21, "He that hath my commandments, and keepeth them, he it is that loveth me: and he that loveth me shall be loved of my Father, and I will love him, and will manifest myself to him." To the one who obeys and wins souls Jesus says that that proves his love, and promises, "And I will love him, and will manifest myself to him."

Paul gave up much "to win Christ," or be used, and also "that I may know him, and the power of his resurrection, and the fellowship of his sufferings, being made conformable unto his death" (Phil. 3:10). He wanted to share Christ's heart burden for lost people, to suffer the persecution of a soul winner, and so to "know Christ" in a way other Christians not soul winners could not "know Him."

3. The Soul Winner Is a Witness for Christ.

Jesus was speaking about the soul winning that should come at Pentecost, and other soul winning after that pattern, when He said in Acts 1:8: "But ye shall receive power, after that the Holy Ghost is come upon you: and ye shall be witnesses unto me both in Jerusalem, and in all Judea, and in Samaria, and unto the uttermost part of the earth." A personal witness for Christ has a special nearness.

When Jesus rose from the dead He appeared to the disciples:

"Then said Jesus to them again, Peace be unto you: as my Father hath sent me, even so send I you. And when he had said this, he breathed on them, and saith unto them, Receive ye the Holy Ghost" (John 20:21, 22). Already He had showed His hands and side and said, "Peace be unto you" (vss. 19, 20), that is, the peace of salvation by the cross. But now He offers another step and degree of peace, the peace of those who are sent by Jesus as He was sent by the Father, those who have received the Holy Spirit to live within, implying what later happened at Pentecost, that they would seek and have soul-winning power. So the soul winner has an intimate fellowship with Jesus, sent by Him, specially loved by Him, special peace given by the Lord Jesus.

III. The Soul Winner Is Promised Special Cleansing for More Fruit Bearing

In John 15:2 Jesus promised the fruit-bearing Christian, the soul-winning Christian, "Every branch in me . . . that beareth fruit, he purgeth it, that it may bring forth more fruit."

So the Christian who wins souls has special help in living right, because he is a soul winner. In his case God is honored more by helping the soul winner live a clean life. In his case it is true, as with David, "He leadeth me in the paths of righteousness for his name's sake" (Ps. 23:3). The Lord commanded Israel in taking Palestine that in attacking a city they must not cut down fruit trees (Deut. 20:19, 20). As fruit trees are dear to men, soul winners, God's fruit trees, are dear to God.

The soul winner can quit the tobacco habit easier than a Christian not a soul winner. A soul winner sees more quickly what is wrong with the unequal yoke of the lodges than other Christians. Soul winners are often protected from temptations when other Christians might sin.

God's ministers sometimes feel that they should first teach Christians the Bible and Christian living and later hope they will win souls, but they do not make as good Christians of young converts as the pastors and evangelists make who teach people to win souls as the main Christian duty. For God Himself presses on the soul winner to be clean. He "purgeth it that it may bring forth more fruit." All over America some Bible teachers and pastors teach Christians a code of conduct without soul winning, and make Pharisees, "don'ters."

But when God's Spirit puts the inward urge in a Christian that he must "by all means save some," there is a real striving for spiritual holiness, a consecration of life and talents that rules cannot make.

Everywhere I go as an evangelist, I find pastors shocked, grieved, troubled, and struggling because of the drift of their people away from clean, holy living, their entanglements in the world's amusements and pleasures and aims. Even in the most fundamental churches I find the young people going continually away from the standards the church has set in many, many cases. But I find that trouble among churches fundamentally sound in doctrine is far more prevalent where there is not a strong soul-winning program in the church. In those great churches over America (and I am acquainted with many of them) where the whole program of the church is centered about soul winning, I find there is a holy enthusiasm for Christian living. Christians who earnestly labor at soul winning feel they are citizens of a heavenly country, that they are not supposed to be like the people of this world. They are trying to snatch people from the fire, and they tend to hate the garments spotted by the flesh.

I have been bombarded with thousands of letters from Christians, particularly young Christians, asking, "What is wrong with dancing? What is wrong with moderate drinking? And why not join in with other moral, good people in lodges and secret orders?" But I have found in literally hundreds of cases that Christians who set out to win souls decide for themselves, from an inner compulsion by the Spirit of God, that this or that worldly thing is not for them the way of happiness and the way of blessing. God Himself is pledged to help to purge and cleanse the life of a Christian to win souls! Oh, there are blessings a soul winner has beyond those of any other Christian.

IV. The Fullest Blessing of the Holy Spirit Is Given
Only to Soul-Winning Christians

We know, of course, that every Christian has been partaker of some of the ministries of the Holy Spirit. He was convicted by the Holy Spirit (John 16:7-11). Every Christian is "born of the Spirit" (John 3:5) for every Christian, in some varying measure, the Holy Spirit is the comforter, the teacher, the prayer helper (John 14:16; Rom. 8:26, 27). This comforter, the Holy Spirit, abides in the body of every Christian (I Cor. 6:19, 20; Rom. 8:9).

But we remember that after Jesus breathed on the apostles on the day of His resurrection from the dead (John 20:19-22), He commanded them to "tarry ye in the city of Jerusalem, until ye be endued with power from on high" (Luke 24:49). And He promised, "But ye shall receive power, after that the Holy Ghost is come upon you: and ye shall be witnesses unto me both in Jerusalem, and in all Judea, and in Samaria, and unto the uttermost part of the earth" (Acts 1:8).

It is clear that there is a special power and enduement for soul winning which is intended. And when the day of Pentecost was come, "they were all filled with the Holy Ghost" (Acts 2:4) for soul winning, and three thousand were saved. Again, "And they were all filled with the Holy Ghost" (Acts 4:31), and they witnessed with great power and won many souls. We are told of John the Baptist that "he shall be filled with the Holy Ghost, even from his mother's womb. And many of the children of Israel shall he turn to the Lord their God" (Luke 1:15, 16). We are told of Barnabas, "He was a good man, and full of the Holy Ghost and of faith: and much people was added unto the Lord" (Acts 11:24). It is abundantly clear from these and many other Scriptures that the fullness of the Spirit is only for soul winning, and comes only to those who are committed to winning souls.

Various groups seek what they call the fullness of the

Spirit in order to have the old carnal nature destroyed, or in order to have help in their problems, and daily joy. But these have all missed the point. They do not see what God has promised and what is involved in the fullness of the Spirit. The fullness of the Spirit is simply an enduement of power from on high for witnessing and winning souls. Anyone who claims to be filled with the Spirit and does not win souls is not using the term with its Bible meaning, and he does not have what Christians in Bible times had when they were filled with the Spirit. The fullness of the Spirit is given for witnessing for Christ.

And I think it is only fair and proper to add that those who are filled with the Spirit for soul winning are more under the control and blessing of the Holy Spirit in other matters. The soul winner is more apt to have the leading of the Spirit. He is more apt to have the comfort of the Spirit. He is more likely to understand the Holy Spirit's interpretation of the Scriptures.

The fullness of the Spirit is given for soul-winning power, according to the clear statements of the Scriptures, and that blessing other Christians do not have. But I think surely the other ministries of the Holy Spirit are also more sought and enjoyed by those who are filled with the Spirit.

V. Soul Winners Can Understand the Bible Better Than Other Christians

There is a clear relationship between a spiritual understanding of the Word of God and God's power in soul winning.

1. God's Special Interest in the Soul Winner Means That the Soul Winner Can Have More Divine Help in Studying and Preaching the Word of God.

Jesus pledged that "every branch in me that beareth ... fruit, he purgeth it, that it may bring forth more fruit" (John 15:2). There is special care of the soul winner in protecting him from evil influence. God cares for His fruit trees more than for other trees.

David used this argument with God, that if God would cleanse him and keep him near Him, and "restore unto me the joy of thy salvation; and uphold me with thy free spirit. Then will I teach transgressors thy ways; and sinners shall be converted unto thee" (Ps. 51:12, 13). That prayer is inspired, and is recorded by the Holy Spirit for us. So it was a Spirit-inspired bargain. We are taught then to expect God to give us Christian joy, to uphold us by His Spirit, and otherwise help us on the condition that we will teach transgressors His ways and have sinners converted. Surely that would involve help in understanding the Word of God.

It is a blessed thing how God has kept major soul winners away from disastrous heresies.

For example, Charles Spurgeon grew up with a post-millennial viewpoint that the world was getting better, and that the Gospel would soon conquer the whole world. But in truth there is a premillennial flavor all through Spurgeon's preaching. His viewpoint was that Christians were citizens of another world, that Jesus might come at any moment. Reared a Congregationalist, he was shown by an Anglican teacher that baptism should be for believers only and was made a Baptist! Spurgeon, in a day when theologians thought that one must be a strict Calvinist or an Arminian, was nominally a Calvinist and said so repeatedly. But he preached for forty years with unceasing power to the multitudes that "whosoever will" might come and be saved, and that Christ died for all. The doctrinal background which would have led him astray was counteracted by the mighty power of the Holy Spirit in his soul-winning ministry. His soul winning made Spurgeon different from the hyper-Calvinists of today with their teaching of limited atonement and man's total inability to repent.

Note the premillennial, fundamental flavor of the teaching of John Wesley and D. L. Moody and R. A. Torrey and

Billy Sunday. See how John and Charles Wesley, ardent Arminians, yet wrote some of the greatest hymns on salvation by grace without works and stressed the new birth.

I am acquainted with most of the greatest soul-winning pastors in America. Is it not striking that the greatest soul-winning churches are all pastored by premillennial, fundamental Bible preachers, although, as in the case of Southern Baptists, and American Baptists, most of their denominational leaders and their seminaries are amillennial, and believe in some limited inspiration and not verbal inspiration of the Bible? The churches that baptize from three hundred to fifteen hundred new converts each year in America are all pastored by openly avowed premillennial, fundamental pastors. You see, the Holy Spirit helps protect from disastrous errors in doctrine those Christians who win souls.

2. Soul Winners Must Use the Bible More Than Others.

Every soul winner uses the Bible: "For I am not ashamed of the gospel of Christ: for it is the power of God unto salvation to every one that believeth . . ." (Rom. 1:16). It is by the Word of God that people are saved, "Being born again, not of corruptible seed, but of incorruptible, by the Word of God, which liveth and abideth for ever" (I Pet. 1:23). We are told "the law of the Lord [the Bible] is perfect, converting the soul . . ." (Ps. 19:7).

Everyone who teaches real soul winning—R. A. Torrey, William Evans, Will Houghton, Billy Sunday, the Bible institutes—all teach how to use the Word of God in soul winning.

Thus it is not surprising that the soul winner learns to rely on the Bible more; he loves it more, and the Holy Spirit helps him more as he reads it and uses it.

Two great Presbyterian Bible teachers were Warfield of Princeton and R. A. Torrey. Warfield was a theologian and not primarily a soul winner. Torrey was both Bible teacher and soul winner, but his whole life was primarily given up to soul winning and training soul winners. But Warfield was hyper-Calvinist, a postmillennialist, and believed in covenant theoolgy, while R. A. Torrey, the great soul winner, was blessedly preserved from these three great heresies. And these two men are probably the best representatives of the two kinds, the Bible teacher-theologian on the one hand and the soul winner on the other.

If you compare the two great Southern Baptist seminary heads, John A. Broadus and L. R. Scarborough or Mullins and Scarborough, you will find that the man who is not much of a soul winner is postmillennial in theology, believes in a limited kind of inspiration, and has other flaws in doctrine which, by God's mercy, the great soul winner Scarborough escaped.

Or compare Torrey and Gray, both of them under the mighty influence of D. L. Moody, both associated with Moody Bible Institute. Gray was a great Bible teacher with very little soul-winning activity or results. He was a noble, good man. But he fell in with the Plymouth Brethren theology; the baptism of the Spirit to him meant simply a technical or dispensational matter. But with Torrey, as with D. L. Moody and Charles G. Finney and other great soul winners, the baptism of the Spirit was synonymous with the fullness of the Spirit for soul-winning power. So it turns out that between these two great Bible teachers, both noble men of God of the Moody tradition, it seems to me that one is far safer to follow R. A. Torrey, the soul winner, than James M. Gray, the Bible teacher, just as one is safer to follow L. R. Scarborough, the premillennialist, rather than his great teacher and patron, B. H. Carroll, the postmillennialist. The soul winner has help in understanding the Bible and has the safeguarding and protection of the Spirit in major matters of doctrine that one will not have except as he gives himself wholly to the main business of soul winning.

3. The Soul Winner Best Understands the Compassionate Heart of God for Sinners and So Is More in Tune With Divine Revelation and the Scriptures.

Surely no one could question that Christ came into the world to save sinners. The central theme of all the prophets, as Peter was inspired to tell Cornelius, is, "To him give all the prophets witness, that through his name whosoever believeth in him shall receive remission of sins" (Acts 10:43). Then surely, no one can understand the heart of God like the one who thinks with God about sinners, who weeps with God over sinners, who loves sinners with some of God's own love, and who toils and weeps and is persecuted in this blessed soul-winning work, along with the toils and tears and persecution which Jesus received.

Oh, God could hardly have revealed through anyone else—some cold-hearted Bible student who did not win souls—all those wonderful things He revealed through the Apostle Paul in some fourteen books of the New Testament. How can the head understand the things of God when the heart does not enter into the purposes of God in the Bible? You know, the soul winner is on the main track. He is going in the same direction with God. He has the special help of the Spirit of God. In a special sense he abides in Christ. Then surely a soul winner can understand the Bible better than if he were not a soul winner. One of the tremendous blessings God gives the soul winner is not only to know the Bible better, but to delight in it and use it effectively.

VI. The Soul Winner Has Joys Above Other Joys of Earth

Does it seem that we are claiming a tremendous lot for the soul winner? Indeed we are. And I think I can prove from the Bible, as I know from experience also, that the joy of the soul winner exceeds any other Christian joy.

1. Special Joy Is Promised to the Soul Winner.

In Psalm 126:5 and 6 are these two blessed promises about the soul winner's joy: "They that sow in tears shall reap in joy. He that goeth forth and weepeth, bearing precious seed, shall doubtless come again with rejoicing, bringing his sheaves with him."

Jesus said, "I say unto you, that likewise joy shall be in heaven over one sinner that repenteth, more than over ninety and nine just persons, which need no repentance" (Luke 15:7). And again He said: "Likewise, I say unto you, there is joy in the presence of the angels of God over one sinner that repenteth" (Luke 15:10).

Jesus said that in Heaven there is greater joy over one sinner who repents than over ninety-nine just persons that need no repentance. Does not Jesus here say that the joy over a soul saved is superior to other human joys? Here one Christian has a happy marriage. Another Christian graduates from college. Still another Christian, in answer to prayer, is raised up from a sick bed. Let every one of the ninety-nine "just persons which need no repentance" have some wonderful thing to happen to them: It is still true that what happens when a sinner gets saved, is born of God, kept out of Hell forever, destined for Heaven, now the possessor of everlasting life—that is better than all that could happen to the ninety-nine Christians already saved. There is no blessing like salvation. Jesus told the seventy who returned with joy, after their triumphant journey, "Notwithstanding in this rejoice not, that the spirits are subject unto you; but rather rejoice, because your names are written in heaven" (Luke 10:20).

Then we who rejoice over a soul saved have greater joy than others. And we who have part in God's wonderful saving work have a part in the greatest work in the world and have part in the greatest joy.

All Heaven rings with gladness when a soul is saved.

And some of the bells ring sweetly in the heart of the soul winner, too.

In Toronto, after I had preached one night to a tremendous crowd and some fifteen adults had come weeping to trust Christ as Saviour and had gone into the inquiry room for further instruction, I stepped out of the pulpit as the great crowd filling the building filed out so that hundreds of others could come in for a second service. A man stepped up to me to ask, "Brother Rice, have you been baptized with the Holy Ghost?"

I told him that by God's loving mercy I had some measure of the breath of Heaven upon me, the fullness of the Spirit. I told him it would be folly and presumption for me to suppose that human education or any human talent or human industry had resulted in tens of thousands who had come to Christ under my ministry.

"I didn't mean that," he said. "I mean have you talked in tongues?"

I replied that I had talked in the English tongue, the tongue that people could understand, and that God had blessed it, and that I had not sought nor had I ever had any jabber in some language I did not know and which would do no one any good, nor did I understand that we were commanded to seek such.

"Oh, but you don't know how happy you would be if you just turned everything loose and said things you didn't understand or know anything about," he said.

And with deep emotion I answered him. "If God will just give me enough sinners coming down the aisles, turning to Christ, and if I can see enough drunkards made sober, enough harlots made pure, enough infidels made into believers, enough sinners made into saints of God, that is all the happiness and joy I ask for!"

There is a special promise of joy in answered prayer in John 16:24: "Hitherto have ye asked nothing in my name: ask, and ye shall receive, that your joy may be full." But to ask for a greater blessing and to receive it is to have the greater joy. And to have a soul kept out of Hell for billions of years of blessed gratitude is better than having a check for a hundred dollars, or having a new joy.

Here a woman bakes a beautiful cake and serves it. She has pleasure in it. There a woman makes a beautiful piece of needlework and displays it proudly. Another woman may paint a beautiful picture or write a book. But do you think any woman has really as great joy in these accomplishments as the woman who has gone down into the valley of the shadow of death and brought back a little life with her and nursed a baby at her bosom and has her whole life centered in the upbringing of the child who becomes a godly man? A woman's joy is more in her child than in some other work. And surely a Christian's joy is far more in soul winning than in other accomplishments of far less importance.

A soul-winning Christian then has joys beyond the joys of other people.

2. The Rewarding Gratitude of Souls Who Are Won Rewards the Soul Winner.

Paul was inspired to call the Philippian Christians whom he had won to Christ, ". . . My brethren dearly beloved and longed for, my joy and crown . . ." (Phil. 4:1). Those who are won to Christ are the soul winner's joy here and his crown hereafter. The love and gratitude of one we have led to the Saviour is one of the sweetest joys a Christian can have. Paul said he had approved himself as a good minister of Jesus Christ: "By honor and dishonour, by evil report and good report: as deceivers, and yet true; As unknown, and yet well known; as dying, and, behold, we live; as chastened, and not killed; As sorrowful, yet always rejoicing; as poor, yet making many rich; as having nothing, and yet possessing all things" (II Cor. 6:8-10).

Paul was often dishonored, beaten, put in jail, slandered and hated, but he was honored by thousands whom he had won to Christ and who loved him. Paul suffered evil report, but always there were some who would not believe any evil report; they knew him so well and loved him because he had won them to the Saviour. To many, Paul may have been unknown, but to those whom he won to Christ, he was the best preacher in the world. Paul might be sorrowful, hungry, or cold or mistreated, "yet always rejoicing." He was poor, but he made many rich. He had nothing. In a sense every soul winner may be persecuted for Christ's sake, but in the midst of his dishonor and evil report and his unknown state, he is honored and of good report and well known and makes many rich and is always rejoicing!

Once to Paul's children in the Gospel at Galatia he said: "For I bear you record, that, if it had been possible, ye would have plucked out your own eyes, and have given them to me" (Gal. 4:15). Oh, some of them were led into heresy and disaffected, and sometimes one's own children are ungrateful. But it is still true that that holy abandon of love which new converts so often have for those who led them to the Saviour is one of the sweetest joys a Christian can have.

I went back to my boyhood home in the ranch country of West Texas and a big strapping man came to hear me preach and said, "John, do you know me?" My mind went back to the time when I, a fifteen-year-old lad, had won a younger fellow to Christ in timidity and stumbling. I had urged him to trust the Saviour and he did! It was the first soul I ever won. And now, years later, he gripped my hand with both of his and told me I must come and meet his wife and children! He still loved the Lord and served Him, and my heart leaped for joy, as it has ten thousand times since I began to win souls over seeing the progress and joy and love of those I have helped to win to Christ.

Last week I was at a great university in a busy Commencement program. A young man stopped me and apologized for taking the time and then said, "But I was saved in your meeting at Dayton, Ohio, in Memorial Hall fifteen years ago. I want you to know I will never, never forget it. I thank God for you!"

We counted up the other day ten thousand and six hundred sixty-six letters from people who had written to tell us that they had found Christ through my printed literature in the English language. Many thousands more have written to tell how they found Christ through the same messages printed in thirty other languages. God is my witness, I had rather have the knowledge of those thousands of people who have trusted Christ as Saviour than to have a million dollars! Now many of them are preachers, missionaries, and soul winners themselves.

Several years ago I preached under a tent in a small Japanese city. A young evangelist interpreted for me, led the singing, and helped in the extended personal soul winning with inquirers afterwards. Then he was introduced to me, and he lifted his hands high and praised God aloud in Japanese. The only word I could understand was "Hallelujah," which sounds the same in all languages. Then he told me how he was my spiritual grandson. Through my message, *"What Must I Do to Be Saved?"* a life-term prisoner had been converted in Japan. That man was so changed that the warden besought the judge and the man was pardoned and released. He met in a park this same young man who talked to me, who was a confirmed drunkard. He had slashed his wrists trying to commit suicide. In the hospital he had gotten out of bed and tried to crush his head against the masonry wall. He could not quit drink. He did not wish to live. And that life-term prisoner now released, happy in the Lord, showed the young drunkard how to be saved, gave him my booklet *"What Must I Do to Be Saved?"* and then took him to a missionary to confirm it. Now he was a student in Japan Christian College and in the summer he went out holding evangelistic services winning souls. He shouted "Hallelujah" just to meet me and shake hands with the man who wrote the booklet through which eventually he had been won to Christ!

In Sherman, Texas, in a great open-air revival twenty-five years ago, hundreds found Christ as I preached the old Gospel. An old man was converted. A new church was organized; we built a baptistry, put up dressing tents, and had a public baptizing. This old man was baptized, along with others, and coming up out of the water he put his arms around my neck and kissed me on the cheek and went weeping to the dressing tent.

One evangelist, who himself has won thousands of souls, never sees me but that he reminds me it was through my book on *Prayer* that he found Christ.

I am poor in this world's goods. I preach so plainly against sin, modernism, and unbelief that some people hate me and many think it would be a blessing to the country if I were dead. I am slandered and abused, yet my heart is lifted up beyond measure by the love and confidence and gratitude of thousands who have come to Christ under my ministry. The soul winner's joy is above the other joys that men may have.

3. The Fellowship With Other Soul Winners Is About the Sweetest Possible Christian Fellowship.

When one has fellowship with soul winners, he has fellowship with people filled with the Spirit, for people do not win souls except by Holy Spirit power. To walk with soul winners means to walk with the people who suffer more for Jesus, who are abused and hated and who are thought to be fools because of their fervor and winning souls, their warnings of Hell and judgment, their persistent pleading.

How I treasure the touch I had with Billy Sunday, and Ma Sunday, with Gipsy Smith, and with Paul Rader. I knew well and loved greatly Dr. W. B. Riley, and he was one of my most faithful friends. I rejoice in the fellowship of Dr. Bob Jones, Sr., who has probably won more souls to

Christ than any man living. I have blessed, blessed fellowship with many, many soul-winning evangelists and pastors. All of us believe alike in the fundamentals of the faith from the verbal inspiration of the Bible, the virgin birth of Christ, the blood atonement, the bodily resurrection to the premillennial return of Christ. There is a oneness, a common bond of interest and aims. The fellowship of soul winners is surely more unanimous, and we rejoice together in the greatest blessings more than people can in other fellowships, not with soul winners.

Oh, it is wonderful to be a soul winner.

15. Heavenly Rewards for Winning to Christ

"His lord said unto him, Well done, thou good and faithful servant: thou hast been faithful over a few things, I will make thee ruler over many things: enter thou into the joy of thy Lord."—Matt. 25:21.

"For what is our hope, or joy, or crown of rejoicing? Are not even ye in the presence of our Lord Jesus Christ at his coming? For ye are our glory and joy."—I Thess. 2:19, 20.

"And many of them that sleep in the dust of the earth shall awake, some to everlasting life, and some to shame and everlasting contempt. And they that be wise shall shine as the brightness of the firmament; and they that turn many to righteousness as the stars for ever and ever."—Dan. 12:2, 3.

I T IS GREAT to be a soul winner, great in this life. It will be great and happy in all the grand hereafter. The soul winner has blessings after death such as others cannot have.

1. The Soul Winner Is to Have Happy Acceptance and Praise From the Lord Jesus Christ.

The Apostle Paul had a secret aim and ambition which controlled all his life. That is why he toiled day and night, "in labors more abundant" than any other apostle. That is doubtless why he had no wife nor child, no property. Paul looked forward to the time when he would come face to face with Jesus Christ, and he was inspired to explain, "Wherefore we labour, that, whether present or absent, we may be accepted of him. For we must all appear before the judgment seat of Christ . . ." (II Cor. 5:9, 10). Oh, to be acceptable to Jesus! To have the Lord Jesus smile and be pleased and greet Paul gladly!

It was that future approval which caused Paul to work day and night laboring in soul winning. For soul winning was the one thing on Paul's heart, the one end of all his labors throughout his ministry. He labored to win souls. He trained others to win souls. He said, "I am made all things to all men, that I might by all means save some" (I Cor. 9:22).

The Lord Jesus illustrated this truth, that the way Christians would be greeted upon Christ's return would be determined by how faithfully they brought forth increase to that which the Lord Jesus had given them. In the parable of the talents in Matthew 25:14-30, He illustrated His return by that of "a man travelling into a far country, who called his own servants, and delivered unto them his goods" (Matt. 25:14), and then eventually returned and demanded an accounting. The man who had received money to the value of five talents gained five more and the man who had received the value of two talents of money gained two more, and to each of them the Lord said, "Well done, thou good and faithful servant: thou hast been faithful over a few things, I will make thee ruler over many things: enter thou into the joy of thy lord" (Matt. 25:21). But the servant who had gained no increase on the money given him was rebuked, "Thou wicked and slothful servant . . . Thou oughtest therefore to have put my money to the exchangers, and then at my coming I should have received mine own with usury."

Now Jesus has deposited with us the Gospel and salvation.

That "well done, thou good and faithful servant" was what Paul was working for. And oh, what a triumphant entry Paul had when he went to Heaven and heard Jesus say to him, "Enter thou into the joy of thy lord."

The "joy of thy lord" which Jesus mentioned is the joy which He Himself will have when there come from all the earth the redeemed at the rapture. It was that joy referred to in Hebrews 12:2: "Looking unto Jesus the author and finisher of our faith; who for the joy that was set before him endured the cross, despising the shame, and is set down at the right hand of the throne of God." That joy is the soul winner's joy, too. For to the Thessalonians Paul wrote, "For what is our hope, or joy, or crown of rejoicing? Are not even ye in the presence of our Lord Jesus Christ at his coming? For ye are our glory and joy" (I Thess. 2:19, 20).

It is significant in the parable of a certain man that made a great supper and bade many in Luke 14:16-24 that the only servant the Lord Jesus pictures there is the soul winner, getting people ready for the great feast in Heaven. And the joy of the Lord Jesus and the joy of the soul winner will be to see them come in redeemed and now glorified at the heavenly wedding feast!

Oh, that happy day when he would look in the face of Jesus! Would the Lord Jesus be pleased? Would his labors be acceptable? Could he increase the joy of the Lord Jesus and have that joy for himself? That thought is under the surface in all Paul's epistles. It was in that sense that the Philippians were his joy and crown. It was in that sense that he feared he had bestowed labor in vain upon the Galatians. And in II Corinthians 11:2 he told the Christians at Corinth, "For I am jealous over you with godly jealousy: for I have espoused you to one husband, that I may present you as a chaste virgin to Christ." Paul looked forward to the soul winner's joy, the sweet approval of the Lord Jesus at the rapture and beyond!

2. The Greatest Rewards at the Judgment Seat of Christ Will Go to Soul Winners.

In I Corinthians 3:10-15 is a discussion of the judgment of Christians in Heaven, after the rapture, at the judgment seat of Christ. Christ Himself is the only foundation. "But let every man take heed how he buildeth thereupon," we are told.

"Now if any man build upon this foundation gold, silver, precious stones, wood, hay, stubble; Every man's work shall be made manifest: for the day shall declare it, because it shall be revealed by fire; and the fire shall try every man's work of what sort it is. If any man's work abide which he hath built thereupon, he shall receive a reward. If any man's work shall be burned, he shall suffer loss: but he himself shall be saved; yet so as by fire."—I Cor. 3:12-15.

The work will be tried. That which is permanent—gold, silver, and precious stones—will receive a reward. That which is temporary—wood, hay, and stubble—will be burned and destroyed. This does not refer to salvation, but to the rewards that some saved people will get and that other people will not get.

Some people helped build a church building, beautiful and expensive. But only in as far as it caused more souls to be saved will it have any eternal value. The money, the time, the energy spent on it, unless it increase the number of souls won beyond what would have been won otherwise, will have no value at the judgment seat of Christ. Burn it up!

Others built a school. They were for education, culture, music, the arts, and science. But except as the school trained people to win souls, it has no value at the judgment seat of Christ. Burn it up!

All the organization, all the administration work of

pastor and Sunday School workers and denominational secretaries, is only permanent in as far as it gets precious
souls saved. Otherwise it is wood, hay, and stubble. Burn
it up! A Sunday School, a church, a Christian magazine, the
writing of a book, the singing of a song, the work of a
denomination—all of it is temporary, fruitless and unre-
warded at the judgment seat of Christ except in that it resulted in souls being saved.

In my song, "The Price of Revival," are two verses and
the chorus that are pertinent here:

> "The treasures of earth, oh, how vain and how fleeting;
> They vanish like mist and they wither like leaves;
> But souls who are won by our tears and our pleading
> Will remain for our reaping up there.

> "To come to that reaping with wood, hay, and stubble,
> How sad to appear at the Lord's judgment seat,
> With no one we've won to trust Jesus our Saviour
> To present at the reaping up there.

> "Reaping, heavenly reaping!
> For souls won down here."

The same subject is brought up in II Corinthians 5:10:
"For we must all appear before the judgment seat of Christ;
that every one may receive the things done in his body,
according to that he hath done, whether it be good or bad."
Here again is the same truth. Christians will receive the
things done in the body according to whether it be good
or bad.

Go back again to I Corinthians 3:15: "If any man's work
shall be burned, he shall suffer loss: but he himself shall
be saved; yet so as by fire." If a man let his loved ones go
to Hell, they will still be in Hell. All the weeping will not
change that. Christ may have forgiven him, but that does
not change the fact that the loved ones are in Hell and not in
Heaven. So a man's happiness and his reward at the judg-

ment seat of Christ will depend principally upon soul winning. The one thing Jesus died for is to save souls. Those who helped Him do that one main thing will be rewarded more than those who did not.

3. The Soul Winner Is to Shine as the Stars Forever.
In the resurrection many of the first shall be last and the last first, as Jesus said. There will be a great shifting in human estimates of values then. And who will be first? Who are they who may be counted last now, but in the eternal glories of Heaven will be counted first? Daniel 12:2, 3 tells us in these words:

"And many of them that sleep in the dust of the earth shall awake, some to everlasting life, and some to shame and everlasting contempt. And they that be wise shall shine as the brightest of the firmament; and they that turn many to righteousness as the stars for ever and ever."

Oh, the wisdom of soul winning! The man who is willing to take the long look and do the main thing now for Jesus' sake will find that one day he will be famous. One day he will "rise and shine!" Many a mediocre and now unknown man or woman will in that day "shine as the brightness of the firmament." And those soul winners who turn many to righteousness shall shine "as the stars for ever and ever," says the holy Word of God!

We had better adjust our thinking to another economy besides that of earth! We had better set our heart on things that do not so easily pass away, and are of such moment in the next world.

What does it matter whether you had a sirloin steak or a hamburger for dinner? In an hour or two you will not know the difference! What will it matter whether you had a limousine or a jalopy five minutes after you are dead? What will it matter whether you had, on earth, a beautiful home with hardwood floors, tile bath, lovely drapes, rugs, and every convenience, with objects of art, and surroundings of culture, if you are a pauper in the next world? I would rather be a simple soul winner and shine as the stars forever and ever in the next world, than to be the richest man, or the most famous, or most honored one in this world today! The great men in the next world will not be the Roosevelts, the Eisenhowers, the Churchills, the Edisons. The great men in the next world will not be the scientists, nor educators, nor statesmen, however noble a man may be in these vocations. The great men of the next world will be the Moodys, the Billy Sundays, the Torreys and Spurgeons, the Chapmans, the Gipsy Smiths, the Sam Joneses, and the Bob Joneses, along with the rescue mission workers, the soul-winning pastors, and every compassionate, wholly surrendered soul winner.

I do not wonder that Proverbs 11:30 says, "He that winneth souls is wise." Yes, the soul winner is wise with the eternal wisdom of the long look! How foolish it is to waste our time and efforts and energies on things that are soon gone with no permanent reward. The profligate who spends his heritage on one wild drunken fling is a fool. But he is no more the fool than the rich plantation owner who says to his soul, "Soul, thou hast much goods laid up for many years; take thine ease, eat, drink, and be merry" (Luke 12:19). The man who seeks to populate Heaven and seeks to still the pain in the heart of Christ over lost sinners and seeks to empty Hell of its potential inhabitants is the man who will be great in the world to come!

In a southern city the other day a man telephoned and left me word. He must see me and hear me preach while in the city. He was sure I would know him. He came to one of the services. "Don't you remember me? I'm one of Mrs. McNeely's boys. You won me to Christ in Fort Worth!" Twenty years have gone by and he is living out and out for the Lord and talked the language of a well-taught and spiritual Christian. He brought his wife to meet me.

In the same town I was entertained in a lovely home. The husband said, "We feel so honored to have you in our home." The family had bought the finest milk-fed frying chickens. The dinner was better than in the finest hotel. The children were well-behaved, the house beautifully kept. All about were my books and other books which I recommended and which came to them through the Sword Book Club. They were proudly displayed to me. Into that home ill health had come, and worry and care and discension, but God had made my book on *Prayer—Asking and Receiving* a special benediction. Health and joy were restored. That wife had prayed that some day I might sit at her table and that she might tell me how she had been blessed.

After we had had our meal and our prayer together and I started to leave, the wife began to weep and said to her husband, "I would like to hug his neck, if it is all right." With a hint of tears he said, "Of course, it is all right!" And without saying yes or no, or having time to have much reaction about the matter, I had my neck hugged! It was chaste and delicate, and tears of gratitude fell on my shoulder in that brief instant.

And one day when there are no implications of evil, and when there can be no hint of sin, nor danger of it, I have no doubt that God's soul winners will have the joyful embrace and the holy greeting of many a soul kept out of Hell by their witness and prayers and tears! How could we have Heaven at its best hereafter without winning souls here?

I think this was in Paul's heart, by divine inspiration, when the Spirit led him to write in I Corinthians 3:10-15 about the judgment seat of Christ when every Christian's work will be made manifest. There the Word of God says, "If any man's work abide which he hath built thereupon, he shall receive a reward. If any man's work shall be burned, he shall suffer loss: but he himself shall be saved; yet so as by fire." The Christian who did not win souls will find his life reckoned nothing but trash, and he himself, though saved, "shall suffer loss" and not receive a reward.

And in II Corinthians 5:9-11 Paul tells, by divine inspiration, how he labored so hard in order to be acceptable to Christ at that "judgment seat of Christ," where every Christian "may receive the things done in his body, according to that he hath done, whether it be good or bad." Then Paul adds, "Knowing therefore the terror of the Lord, we persuade men . . . ." Paul says it will be a terror for a Christian to face Jesus Christ not having done his duty in this world! He is not talking about a Christian's losing his salvation, for salvation is of grace, not of works. Salvation is received in this life, not in the next. One who believes in Christ already has everlasting life, according to John 3:36, John 5:24, and many other Scriptures. But in Heaven, rewards will differ according to our works. Oh, that God will give us grace to win the eternal rewards which will go to the soul winners! "They that be wise shall shine as the brightness of the firmament; and they that turn to righteousness as the stars for ever and ever."

"They that be wise"—here are the soul winners, for Proverbs 11:30 says: "The fruit of the righteous is a tree of life; and he that winneth souls is wise." The proper fruit of a righteous man, represented as a tree, is to bring forth fruit that grows into another tree. And the Lord is talking about soul winning and says, "And he that winneth souls is wise."

Oh, then the soul winner, the man who played for eternal rewards and spent his time and energy and money and tears in keeping people out of Hell, how wise! And how blessed the reward! He will shine as the brightness of the firmament. And the Scripture continues, "They that turn many to righteousness [shall shine] as the stars for ever and ever."

There can be no doubt that here God makes a promise

to soul winners which is not made to other Christians who
do not win souls.

The Lord Jesus spoke of "a prophet's reward." And
there He tells us that all who receive a prophet in the name
of a prophet, those who support and advance the soul-
winning work, will join in the rewards of the prophet. "He
that receiveth a prophet in the name of a prophet shall receive a prophet's reward; and he that receiveth a righteous
man in the name of a righteous man shall receive a righteous
man's reward" (Matt. 10:41).

The term *prophet* in the Bible is used of those who are
filled with the Spirit, and prophesy or witness. That is
what happened at Pentecost. Peter stood up that day and
said, "But this is that which was spoken by the prophet
Joel; And it shall come to pass in the last days, saith God,
I will pour out of my Spirit upon all flesh: and your sons
and your daughters shall prophesy . . . And on my servants
and on my handmaidens I will pour out in those days of my
Spirit; and they shall prophesy . . . And it shall come to pass,
that whosoever shall call on the name of the Lord shall be
saved" (Acts 2:16-18, 21). Those who are filled with the
Spirit and witness for Jesus and win souls receive a prophet's reward. And all who advance the work of soul winners
will join in the soul winner's rewards.

Oh, how blessed are the soul winners and how eternal
are the rewards! How foolish that any of us should miss
those blessings which God specially gives His soul winners.

I hope you will prayerfully take to heart the message in
my song, "Remembering in Heaven."

> "Should I, up in Heaven, remember the heartache,
>   All the pain and the cross, all the shame and the loss,
>   The reproach of the Saviour I'd borne in earth's conflicts;
>   In Heaven I'd laugh at the cost!

> "Or if, on the gold streets I think of earth treasures,
>   Of the things I had bought, of the fame dearly sought;

I'd smile in my mansion, my gem-studded mansion,
In Heaven I'd smile, 'They are naught!'

"Should I, in the Glory, remember a loved one,
One who walked by my side, but is lost and outside;
If I never had begged him to trust in the Saviour,
In Heaven I'd sit down and cry.

"Oh, then, spread the message, the work He has given,
Never mind the world's praise, nor possessions men crave.
But oh! for the Saviour, bring souls in to Heaven,
And joy through Eternity's Day!

"Jesus' blood paid my ransom, and I'm bound for Heaven,
But what will I think when rememb'ring in Heaven?"

Personality Index

Illustrations

Scripture Index

Page

Page

For a complete list of books available from the Sword of the Lord, write to Sword of the Lord Publishers, P. O. Box 1099, Murfreesboro, Tennessee 37133.